The Locus of Meaning

Six Hyperdimensional Fictions

THEORY/CULTURE

Editors:
Linda Hutcheon, Gary Leonard
Janet Paterson, and Paul Perron

The Locus of Meaning

Six Hyperdimensional Fictions

HERBERT F. SMITH

UNIVERSITY OF TORONTO PRESS
Toronto Buffalo London

© University of Toronto Press Incorporated 1994
Toronto Buffalo London
Printed in Canada

ISBN 0-8020-5711-X

Printed on acid-free paper

Canadian Cataloguing in Publication Data

Smith, Herbert F. (Herbert Franklin), 1933–
    The locus of meaning : six hyper-
dimensional fictions

(Theory/culture)
Includes bibliographical references and index.
ISBN 0-8020-5711-X

1. Structuralism (Literary analysis). 2. American
fiction – 19th century – History and criticism.
3. American fiction – 20th century – History and
criticism. I. Title. II. Series.

PN98. S7S55 1994   801'.953   C93-095449-1

This book has been published with the help of a grant from the
Canadian Federation for the Humanities, using funds provided by the
Social Sciences and Humanities Research Council of Canada.

To my wife, Virginia,
my son Geoffrey,
and the memory
of our beloved Alyson

Contents

Acknowledgments

Any work that has been in progress for some ten years, like this one, leaves behind a trail of contributing suggestions, hints, ideas adopted, ideas considered then amended, even ideas so far out that they seem from a different species, yet have affected this text. I have been particularly fortunate in the many friends and colleagues who have aided and abetted me in the development of this text. Some come to mind easily: the readers for the two journals who published earlier versions of chapters 1 and 4: John Cassidy of *Language and Style* and Linda Hutcheon for *English Studies in Canada* (Linda, obviously, for many other reasons as well); conference organizers (like Mirko Jurak) and participants (like Ryan Bishop) who read or listened to versions of various chapters and commented constructively; John Barth for reading (with some amusement and some pleasure, I hope) the chapter on him and N. Katherine Hayles for much more than reading the chapter on Pynchon – but for that, too, certainly; colleagues with congruent interests who suffered obsessive conversations with me – Tom Cleary on quincunxes, Evelyn Cobley and Steve Scobie on theory, Mert Sealts on Melville, Alex Liddie on just about everything; the anonymous readers for University of Toronto Press and for SSHRC who were willing to take a chance on a work that deviates from the academic norm; the editors at University of Toronto Press, especially Laura Macleod and Ken Lewis, who bore the brunt of the typographic irregularities and interdisciplinary *bricolage* of all sorts contained herein; Lawrence Henderson, who did many of the graphics. All these people and many others contributed to what is good about this text; I of course take full responsibility for what is lacking in it.

I also wish to thank the Collection Haags Gemeentemuseum, The Hague, for permission to publish M.C. Escher's *Liberation*.

The sunflower design on the title and part-title pages of this volume originally appeared in H.E. Huntley's *The Divine Proportion: A Study in Mathematical Beauty* (New York: Dover 1970).

L'artiste, l'analyste refait le chemin du sens, il n'a pas à le désigner: sa fonction, pour reprendre l'exemple de Hegel, est une *mantéia*; comme le devin antique, il *dit* le lieu du sens mais ne le nomme pas.

Roland Barthes, 'L'Activité structuraliste'

[Every Schoolboy Knows ...]

THE DIVISION OF THE PERCEIVED UNIVERSE INTO PARTS AND WHOLES IS CONVENIENT AND MAY BE NECESSARY, BUT NO NECESSITY DETERMINES HOW IT SHALL BE DONE.

Gregory Bateson, Mind and Nature

Did we say that literature is entirely involved with language, is merely the permutation of a restricted number of elements and functions? But is the tension in literature not continually striving to escape from this finite number? Does it not continually attempt to say something it cannot say, something that it does not know, and that no one could ever know? A thing cannot be known when the words and concepts used to say it and think it have not yet been used in that position, not yet arranged in that order, with that meaning. The struggle of literature is in fact a struggle to escape from the confines of language; it stretches out from the utmost limits of what can be said; what stirs literature is the call and attraction of what is not in the dictionary.

Italo Calvino, 'Cybernetics and Ghosts'

'You don't see something until you have the right metaphor to let you perceive it.'

Robert Shaw to James Gleick

Hamlet: Do you see yonder cloud that's almost in shape of a camel?
Polonius: By the mass, and 'tis like a camel, indeed.
Hamlet: Methinks it is like a weasel.
Polonius: It is backed like a weasel.
Hamlet: Or like a whale?
Polonius: Very like a whale.

Axiomatic
(to take the place of a foreword)

In a sense, this book began when I was in grade ten and first encountered plane geometry. I had had some trouble in my first encounter with algebra the year before, partly because of the onset of puberty, partly because of a personality conflict with my math teacher, but when I discovered that the figures and constructions of plane geometry made pictures of the abstractions of algebra, it all began to come clear to me. That *number* and *relationship* can be illustrated by *quantity, area, volume,* and *shape* seemed to me then – and still does – a remarkable aid to understanding. Indeed, I began to believe, and have never given up the notion entirely, that a concept, no matter how abstract, is not really understood unless it can generate some sort of picture in the mind.

I made it through grade ten and went on to become a professor of English, but that one insight from plane geometry stayed with me. As time went on, it seemed to increase in importance. I found in my teaching that I was drawing more and more diagrams and that these diagrams were leading me to conclusions about the nature of literature and literary criticism that were often not generally shared by my colleagues. In particular, I found the idea that a literary work created a *locus* of meaning, rather than a specific meaning, was a most useful critical tool. *Locus* (Latin for 'place,' correspondent to the Greek *topos*), as used in geometry, describes *all* of the points that satisfy a given relationship (as the locus of points equidistant from a single point describes a circle). To look at literature that way seems to me more satisfying than to attempt to name all those points – or worse, to name *one* and try to convince the world it is the only one.

Then, in 1963, I took a Fulbright professorship at the Université d'Aix-Marseilles and, during the course of that year, but especially at a 'réunion des anglicistes' held in the spring of 1964 at Pau, discovered that a whole group of structuralist critics were creating a framework for what I had been doing on my own. Indeed, one of them, Roland Barthes, in his *Essais critiques*, had even made precisely the distinction I had long felt about the locus of meaning and had described it as the essential critical duty. I came back to North America feeling completely justified in continuing to play with my spatial isomorphisms.[1] (Yes, I had by then discovered that very useful word.)

I began reading the basic structuralist texts: Peirce, Saussure, Jakobson, Lévi-Strauss. As my structuralist thinking became more generalized, I read the other eclectics who were moving isomorphically among disparate disciplines: Gregory Bateson, Michael Thompson, Douglas Hofstadter, Dean MacCannell.[2] Then, about ten years ago, a whole series of loose ends of strings I had been pulling randomly for some time began to come together in a web of meaning. At the centre of things was the verb *to be* as = sign and the resultant confusion between metonymy and metaphor. Try as I might, I could not generate a satisfactory isomorphism that consistently worked as a 'picture' of Jakobson's distinction between the metaphoric and the metonymic. I was stuck on the neatness of the ratio *digital* : *analogue* :: *metonymy* : *metaphor*. Peirce was helpful with the notion of *abduction* (Bateson also uses that term), which started me thinking in terms of *three-dimensional* isomorphisms. But the notion of the participation of the receiver in the process of abduction is so much a matter of will, acceptance – in a word, so *political* – that I could not be satisfied with any of the theoretical treatments of it. Then I began to think in terms of analogues *beyond* three dimensions. The solution is given in detail in chapters 1 and 2. The conventional mapping of catastrophe theory provided one solution. Another was my discovery that aesthetic coding could be represented by isomorphisms involving closed curves and surfaces around the origin (which I associated with polar coordinates), while

---

1 'Isomorphism' (from Greek *isos* [equal] + -*morphous* [form]) derives from biology and chemistry, where it is used to describe similar organisms or crystalline structures which differ in their evolution (biology) or composition (chemistry). Thus the use of the term in mathematics/topology and criticism/semiotics *isomorphically* is already highly metaphorical. The reader should presume that my use of this word and other words like *paradigm*, *locus*, and *topology* itself carries primarily a critical and humanistic content.

2 For these and other theoretical texts, see the Bibliographical Notes, 177–9.

ideological coding required isomorphisms involving unbounded curves and surfaces extending indefinitely (which I associated with Cartesian coordinates). Tying the two concepts together was the figure of the *quincunx*, with its wonderful flexibility of detail combined with certainty of pattern, its simplicity of structure yet infinity of possible shapes (see the figure used as a decoration on the title and part-title pages and the discussion in the following chapters). *Abduction* marked the intersection between the two systems, but needed another correspondent term, which I would like to call *seduction*, to distinguish between Cartesian analogues, like Peirce's governor in the sedan chair, and polar analogues for texts like

> *The Lord is my shepherd; I shall not want.*

I did not discover chaos theory until much later, but it provided a fine topology for works that had puzzled me because of their *disintegrate* qualities, as may be seen in chapters 8 and 9.[3]

In this text I have tested a technique, not of resolution for the problem of metaphor, but for the examination of the problem in the light of many of the new metaphors which have sprung from recent developments in science. The underlying concept is *hyperdimensionality*. As chapter 1 develops this idea, texts which do no more than produce data are essentially two-dimensional. Texts which have interest as texts add a third dimension. *Almost all literary criticism takes place within these three dimensions.* But there are some texts which are not limited to this dimensionality of common sense. For me, and for many readers, such texts are among the most interesting just because they resist two- and three-dimensional analysis. This book is primarily devoted to an exploration of how six of these texts came to be written and what semiotic processes are involved in their creation and are therefore necessary for their decoding and further encoding in criticism. The first three chapters develop theories for use in such an exercise, and the six chapters that follow are applications of various techniques arising

---

3 One is tempted to discover some kind of a fortiori relationship between catastrophe theory and chaos theory. That is not the case. One looks for some sort of analogous relationship between structuralist and post-structuralist theory, but I believe that search is also meretricious. The great division, for me, is between pre-structuralism and everything afterwards, which I would compare to the difference between pre-lapsarian and post-lapsarian, B.C. and A.D., and the changes that marked that period of history that was 'the best of times and the worst of times.'

from hyperdimensional metaphors of modern science which seem to be appropriate aids in critical examination of the specific works chosen. Since my area of specialization is American literature, I have used six works by American writers as 'specimens' for analysis. It should not be surprising that each application is different, and that each generates new theoretical possibilities.

The test of any critical theory ought to be that it leads to new and interesting readings. I believe that is the case with all six of the *exempla* in this text, and I hope their number and the variety of critical applications I use to analyse them will encourage others to apply similar techniques to appropriate works of other periods. I also hope, as an ancillary result, a 'spin-off' from the main thrust of my theoretical examination, to demonstrate that what we call 'postmodernism' is just a contemporary blossoming of a literary style that has occurred infrequently but always interestingly in the past. Finally, I would like to disavow any appearance of attempting to produce a 'final' exegesis of any of these works, or a 'more correct' one than other critical investigations have produced. As my title suggests, I believe with Roland Barthes that the critic's duty is 'to *speak* the locus of meaning,' but not to name it.

PART ONE

A Theory of
Hyperdimensional Isomorphisms

1

Topological Isomorphisms
in Semiotic Analysis

If Barthes is correct and criticism, ever resembling more and more the literature it criticizes, is to '*speak* the locus of meaning, and not to name it,' the modern critic would be wise to recall some of the sign systems that have served in other disciplines, at other times. One of those is the ancient relationship between *quantities* and *shapes* best illustrated by the well-known isomorphisms between numbers and geometry. No system of signs comes closer to identity between signifier and signified than the familiar one of *numbers* as signifiers and their geometric representations as their signifieds. Take the signifiers *one*, *two*, and *three*. They can be completed as signs by taking a pencil and

Fig. 1.1

marking the space anywhere once, then again, and again (fig. 1.1). Or, more complexly, to imply the equality of value of the intervals between the three signifiers, take the pencil again and mark three equidistant points on the *x–x'* axis (fig. 1.2). Notice that the second

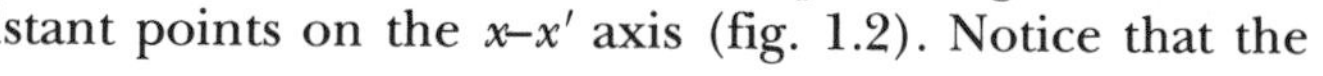

x – x'

Fig. 1.2

decoding encodes more information by assuming an equality of difference among the three signifiers. Now write the three signifiers next to the marks made on the two scales. In the first case the value of the three signs is *number*; in the second the value is *length*. Add another dimension and the process of encoding and decoding yields still more complex signs, but signs which still clarify the relationship between the signifier and the signified meaningfully. The familiar $a^2 + b^2 = h^2$ made a lot more sense to us as schoolchildren when it was given the new locus of meaning that the geometric representation produced

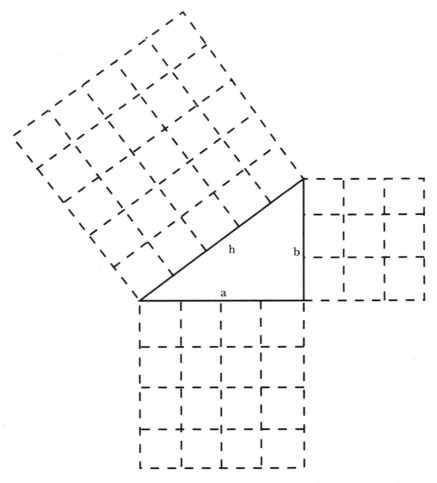

Fig. 1.3   Adding the squares

(fig. 1.3) – especially if the numbers corresponding to *a*, *b*, and *h* were 3, 4, and 5! We liked it even more when the quantities of the hypotenuse were clarified by the appearance of motion (fig. 1.4). These

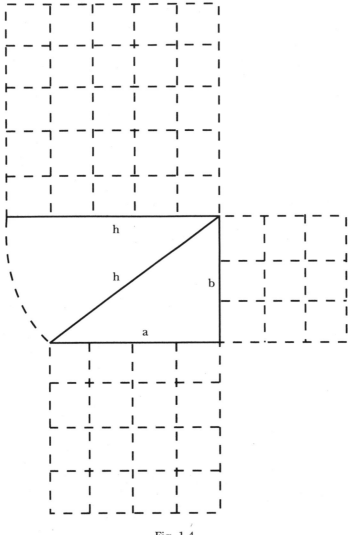

Fig. 1.4

isomorphic relations between numbers and geometry are useful re-
minders of the *topoi* of the sign for a variety of reasons. In some sense,
all these figures are both undercoded and overcoded, both *closed* and
open figures.[1] They are closed in the sense that the *topos* of this particu-

---

1 See Umberto Eco, *A Theory of Semiotics* (Bloomington: Indiana University Press
   1979), section 2.14. The figures are undercoded in the sense that they 'speak for

lar right-angle triangle of sides *abh* answers the formula perfectly; they
are open in the sense that to grasp the structural relationship between
a, *b*, and *h* and the equation is to be enabled to draw an endless series
of triangles exhibiting the same relationship, even though the angles
and lengths may be infinitely variant.

While these concepts are familiar to most schoolchildren and to
many adults engaged in some of the more arcane regions of data-
processing, like CAD-CAM technology and digital-analogue interfacing,
unfortunately they have not been disseminated very widely in the humanities, for reasons which are not hard to understand. Humanistic
communication is through the study of texts, and the very concept of
the text having a value greater than the data it transmits would seem
to complicate the use of topological isomorphisms beyond any value
their application might warrant. Nothing could be further from the
truth. It is precisely at the point where texts pass from data-transmit-
ters to Roman Jakobson's fifth and sixth categories, *metalinguistic* and
poetic texts,[2] that creating spatial isomorphisms becomes most exciting
and revealing.

Let us take as an example a text of assembly instructions for a
Japanese bicycle. The study of the text ordinarily proceeds by the
decoding of such linguistic structures as 'Insert bolt *A* through flange
B and thread washer *a* and nut *b*; tighten.' These signifiers might well

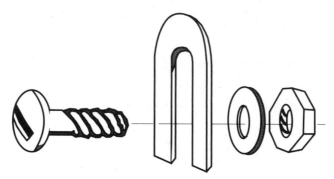

Fig. 1.5   An 'exploded view'

be accompanied by a descriptive isomorphism themselves, such as
figure 1.5. Notice that these are two isomorphic signifiers, not a com-

---

  themselves'; they are overcoded in that they also speak for all groups of three, all
  equidistant points on a line, all right-angle triangles.
2 Roman Jakobson, 'Linguistics and Poetics,' in *Selected Writings* (The Hague: Mouton
  1981), 3:25

pleted *sign*. The 'exploded' sketch is a restatement or translation into pictographs of the original statement in words. Either or both of the statements require the actual insertion and threading of the bolt, flange, washer, and nut to become complete as *signs*. Although, to be sure, that completion need not take place physically – a mental or theoretical insertion, thrust, and turn will perform the semiotic act without scarring the knuckles – it is usually true in the case of this kind of text that the completion of the sign corresponds to a measurable expenditure of centimetre-dynes of torque, foot-pounds of work, or the like. Suppose that act completed; is it possible to create a spatial or topological isomorphism for the *semiotic* act just concluded? We have examined a certain number of signifiers and decoded them by the manipulation of a certain number of signifieds, and as a direct result and dependent upon the relationship of those two acts, a certain amount of bicycle was built. Let us keep in mind that while the manipulation of the signifieds seems like a *constant*, it is not. Anyone who has ever assembled a bicycle on Christmas Eve knows how variable that performance can be. Similarly, the act of examination of the signifiers and its conversion into action can vary from the 'When all else fails, read the instructions' school to the disciplined assembler. Thus, if we think of the sign for this semiotic structure as a pair of x–y axes, any individual instance of assembly is likely to produce a different line of 'bicycle built.' As the instruction hawk reads, pausing now and then to turn a wrench, we have steep but orderly steps up the y-axis (fig. 1.6), his performance looking like the graph of the inflation rate for Brazil. Meanwhile, the mechanical genius proceeds, damn him, effortlessly, along an almost perfectly horizontal line (fig. 1.7), the odd step here and there showing as an occasional reference must be made. Whatever the character of the construction of the bicycle, it is important to note that this graphic representation of its assembly is two-dimensional and bound by the x and y axes.

Now, suppose that the text of the assembly instructions is prefaced by the statement 'Assembly of Japanese bicycle require great peace of mind.' Presto. Our text of data-producing signifiers has now become a *literary* text and our apprehension of it necessarily changes. What had been a problem of the representation of the conversion of signifiers read to wrenches turned now becomes occasion to inquire into the problem of the responses of a series of putative readers. The 'content' of the message has not changed: for the signifiers examined and the signifieds manipulated, a certain amount of bicycle will be built. But the reader's response to the prefatory statement will necessarily change her *attitude* to the following text, which will, in turn, have a certain

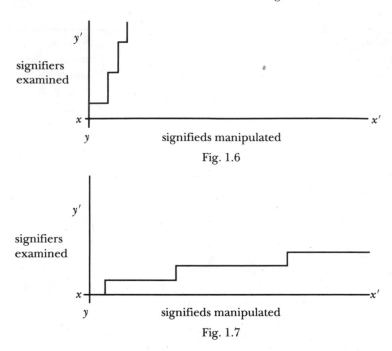

Fig. 1.6

Fig. 1.7

effect upon her performance of the assembly. This effect can only be represented by a change in the *number* of dimensions being plotted,

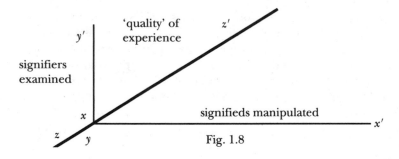

Fig. 1.8

since the contents of the initial two axes remain the same (see fig. 1.8). Notice that in this case the z-axis must have the potential for negatives. While a minus signifier or signified is unthinkable, a negative response to our literary-text-defining statement is quite likely in certain circumstances. Imagine, for example, a racist redneck, blind to the delights and paradoxes of language, reading that statement and responding to it as he reaches for his screwdriver and pliers. 'Damn,' he mutters. 'Japs can't even write English. Bet they've screwed up the instructions so it'll take me hours to get this thing together.' He then proceeds to examine the same number of signifiers and manipulate the same number of signifieds as anyone else, but he does so on a scale of 'life expended' which would compare negatively to the assembler who has not read the preface. The time spent, the foot-pounds of effort, and the amount of bicycle built may all be the same, but in this case the *quality* of the experience has suffered. This can best be seen through an isomorphism. The negative distortion of the *ground* or *plane* of the *x–y* signifiers-read, and signifieds-manipulated is the *only* way this difference in the experience can be described (fig. 1.9).

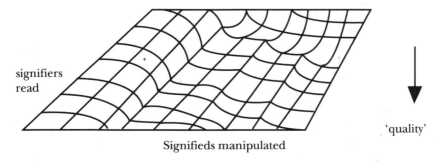

signifiers
read

'quality'

Signifieds manipulated

Fig. 1.9   Loss of quality

Imagine as our second reader a positivist who has no time for affective texts. She skips over the preface, ignoring whatever impact the comment on 'peace of mind' might have, and proceeds directly to the building of her bicycle. The figure of her experience would differ not at all from that of our first builder's; it must be totally dependent upon her skills at signifier-grasping and signified-manipulating. She escapes all of the negative qualities undergone by our redneck builder; on the other hand, she gets little more pleasure out of the experience than would a robot.

A third facultative reader is the only one we have a secure text for. He is the narrator of *Zen and the Art of Motorcycle Maintenance* by Robert Pirsig, and he has done an extensive semiotic analysis of just this text:

What I wanted to say ... is that I've a set of instructions at home which open up great realms for the improvement of technical writing. They begin, 'Assembly of Japanese bicycle require great peace of mind.' ... At first I laughed because of memories of bicycles I'd put together and, of course, the unintended slur on Japanese manufacture. But there's a lot of wisdom in that statement ...

Peace of mind isn't at all superficial, really ... It's the whole thing. That which produces it is good maintenance; that which disturbs it is poor maintenance. What we call workability of the machine is just an objectification of this peace of mind. The ultimate test's always your own serenity. If you don't have this when you start and maintain it while you're working, you're likely to build your personal problems right into the machine itself ...

It's an unconventional concept ... but conventional reason bears it out. The material object can't be right or wrong. Molecules are molecules ... The test of the machine is the satisfaction it gives you. There isn't any other test. If the machine produces tranquility it's right. If it disturbs you it's wrong until either the machine or your mind is changed. The test of the machine's always your own mind. There isn't any other test.[3]

For this reader the locus of meaning includes the positive quality rhapsodized in this passage. Its topology would have to reflect that positive response by a swelling along the z-axis (fig. 1.10), just the opposite of the negative response of our racist assembler.

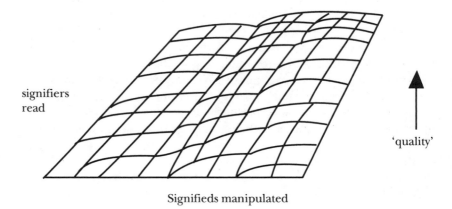

signifiers
read

'quality'

Signifieds manipulated

Fig. 1.10   Gain of quality

The first point to notice about these three topographies we have just created is that they make the Derridean *différance* a lot more

3 Robert Pirsig, *Zen and the Art of Motorcycle Maintenance* (New York: Bantam 1964), 158–9

comprehensible for even the most confused student of deconstruction. The third dimension along the *z*-axis and the *volume* it creates in the isomorphisms are necessary functions of the 'literary text' but not of data texts. *Différance* does more than simply *differ* and *defer*, as non-isomorphic definitions suggest;[4] it literally adds a new dimension. We may call this new dimension, following Pirsig, *quality*, or the Greek *aretê*. Our redneck racist suffers from the lack of it; our positivist data-processor is unaware of it; and our semiotic sophisticate is richly rewarded by a full appreciation of it. Notice as well that our extensional definition alone points out that *différance* has both positive and negative potentials. The writer may produce a text which has little volume of quality, or it may be puffed out of all due proportions by the purple of its prose. The mean-spirited reader will always be concerned primarily with his own presuppositions and prejudices; for him the literary quality of a text will always be an interference to his manipulation of the signifieds – always, of course, with the intention of getting the damned task done and returning to the couch and the TV. Our third reader reverses this process, enjoying the text and the reflections on quality that the 'unintended slur' provokes. As her bicycle is a-building, her experience of life swells outward with the pleasure of the text, both the signifiers examined and the signifieds manipulated.

But, of course, there is more to literature than the building of bicycles. When we move from texts in which signifiers have a 'real' correspondence to the world of 'things,' the locus of meaning shifts. When there are no signifieds to be manipulated, only imaginary toads in real or imagined gardens, the shape of any topological isomorphism must also be different, although the *structure* upon which the shape is built may be the same. When a text is specifically literary – that is, when it has no correlative performance function – decoding becomes almost narcissistic. The bicycle builder has bolt, flange, nut, and washer, appropriate threads, his good right arm, hands and fingers to aid in his decoding. The reader of a literary text has for an equivalent nothing material before her. Instead, she must make do with her previous experience of the syntax and what similarities she can remember from textual paradigms. At first the process seems familiar (see fig. 1.11).

But only the briefest consideration of the two isomorphisms reveals that the apparent similarities are meretricious. Examining signifiers and manipulating their correspondent signifieds is projective; as a

---

4 See, for example, Jonathan Culler, *On Deconstruction* (Ithaca, NY: Cornell University Press 1982), 97.

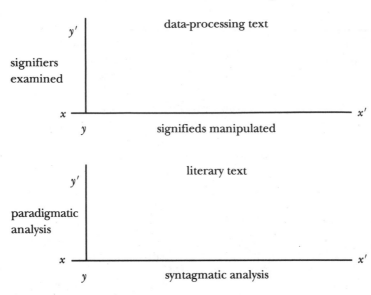

Fig. 1.11

result, a bicycle is built. In a literary text, syntagmatic and paradigmatic analysis, separately or in combination, is recursive. No matter how long and hard the reader works on a literary text, nothing material is created. The reader ends up right where he started. Therefore we should visualize paradigmatic and syntagmatic analyses, not as extending indefinitely along the Cartesian x and y axes, but as defining closed curves in three-dimensional space around the text at the origin (fig. 1.12). Such figurations around the origin are often most conveniently described in terms of polar and spherical coordinates.[5] Notice that the relative lengths of the intersecting radial axes will differ from reader to reader and from one literary text to another, depending

---

5 This change has philosophical implications. See Gregory Bateson and Mary Catharine Bateson, *Angels Fear: Towards an Epistemology of the Sacred* (New York: Bantam 1988), 59–60, where, among other comments, is this comparison between *quantity* and *pattern*: 'The world of Cartesian coordinates relies on continuously varying quantities, and while such analogic concepts have their place in descriptions of mental process, the emphasis on quantity distracted men's minds from the perception that contrast and ratio and shape are the base of mentality. Pythagoras and Plato knew that pattern was fundamental to all mind and ideation. But this wisdom was thrust away and lost in the mists of the supposedly indescribable mystery called "mind"' (60). Other implications of this shift are examined in chapter 2 and chapter 9 in relation to aesthetic and ideological coding.

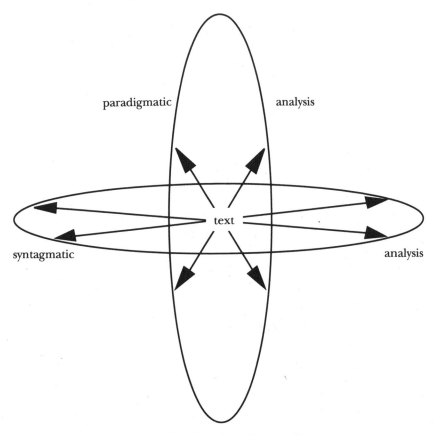

paradigmatic   analysis

text

syntagmatic   analysis

Fig. 1.12   Graphing in polar coordinates

upon the complexity of the text and the sophistication of the reader. The spherical shape is the ideal; in the world of real texts and real readers, one is far more likely to find odd combinations of ellipses, truncations of all sorts, bumps and pimples of various kinds, as may easily be imagined. 'Graphing' these shapes is possible because of the flexibility of the quincunxes which constitute the basic unit of the surfaces on their various axes; notice how they are contorted in the individual instances yet flow with the grander pattern. Figure 1.13, for example, is a fair representation of an encounter with *Hamlet* by a reader who had no knowledge of Oedipus – either the play or the complex. Notice that her 'paradigms lost' work directly against her 'paradigms regained.' Finally, and more interestingly, there are some texts which are infinitely referential. Blake's 'The Sick Rose' and

paradigms regained   paradigms lost

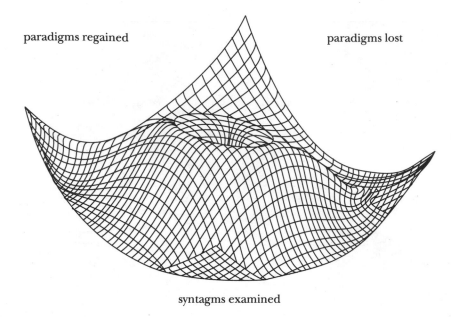

syntagms examined

Fig. 1.13   Hamlet without Oedipus

Whitman's 'Song of Myself,' different as they are in every other way, would not be *circumscribable* in Euclidean geometry. For them we would have to make use of a Lobachevskian pseudo-sphere, something like figure 1.14.

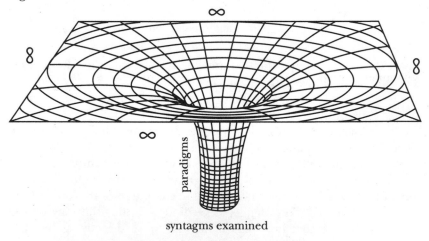

syntagms examined

Fig. 1.14   Infinite intertextuality in two poems

These isomorphisms are all useful in visualizing how the quality of syntagm and paradigm interact. There are, however, some decoding experiences which may not be either described or graphed quite so simply. These are texts in which the reader is thrown completely off the course by a sudden discontinuity and a *metamorphic* continuation. In these texts the signifiers which have been exhibiting data-producing syntagms and structurally comparative paradigms in the ordinary three-dimensional way that textual analysis requires suddenly – there is no other way to describe this – shift their centres and move them into a fourth (or more) dimension. It is not exactly a common phenomenon, but then neither is it excessively rare. It happens when the text begins to talk about itself – when it becomes *recursive* or *metatextual,* as the current jargon has it. A simple example – well, the simplest I can muster – of such a discontinuity occurs in John Donne's 'Elegy xix, To His Mistris Going to Bed.' The poem seems a fairly direct, if bawdy, lover's lyric in heroic couplets urging his mistress to hurry up and undress for bed as he waits, impatiently. The first verse paragraph importunes her to disrobe, praises her features, and compares her first to an angel and then to a ghost, remarking that ghostly spirits 'set our hairs' but she 'our flesh' upright. The next paragraph starts a new subject, which leads to a striking discontinuity:

> Licence my roaving hands, and let them go,
> Before, behind, between, above, below.
> O my America! my new-found-land,
> My kingdom, safeliest when with one man man'd ...

The first line merely continues the lover's plea for liberty-libertinage. The key word is 'roaving,' which has both a paradigmatic and syntagmatic function. Describing the hands, 'roaving' implies the active caressing of the mistress syntagmatically, but sets up the paradigm of the roving explorer, the two coming together at the line 'O my America! my new-found-land.' But the line between those two lines, consisting of five adverbs or prepositions of place, strikes the reader as a rather extraordinary performance. Syntactically, it recalls *Lear*'s 'Never, never, never, never, never.' But unlike that line, this one must serve both a syntagmatic and a paradigmatic purpose. It furthers the syntagm – rather peculiarly as we shall see – but it seems quite out of place in the paradigm of the explorer. Could it be that it is there only conventionally – or, even worse, for the rhyme? The semiotically aware reader struggles with this line because she wants to grant it more than adverbial or (excuse the pun) 'pre-positional' significance, but if she limits her investigation to syntagm and paradigm, she will get nowhere. The line makes sense only when the reader discovers that this line – uniquely[6] in iambic pentameter in English – has five 'hands' instead of the usual five 'feet.' That's right. A five-*handed* line instead of a five-foot line.

Now, that discovery shakes the reader up. He simply cannot continue to read the poem the same way he has been reading it, syntagmatically and paradigmatically, because this line is neither syntagm nor paradigm. Reflecting on the poem itself and its formal requirements, it is truly a *metadigm*, in that it moves the interaction between text and reader into a fourth dimension, beyond syntagm and paradigm. Like the effect of the Japanese preface to the bicycle instructions, the metadigm will have different effects upon different kinds of readers. The equivalent of the redneck, anti-Japanese racist reader would in this case be a slavering, lecherous, but literal pornographee. His response to the metadigm is to pause and provoke images outside the intellectual ones created by syntagm and paradigm of explorer and hands; he turns *tactile*; he quivers with sensual meaning ... he delectates ...

before

bninbd

/between\

above
below

Essentially his loss of quality is a waste of sensuality equivalent to the anger wasted by the bicycle builder. There is no doubt that he responds to the poem *more* than the reader who passes over the line, but

---

6 Well, not quite. There is a poem by the American Robert Francis that begins with these lines: 'Two boys are tossing a poem together, / Overhand, underhand, backhand, sleight of hand, every hand, / Teasing with attitudes, latitudes, interludes, altitudes ...' (Robert Francis, 'Catch,' in *The Orb Weaver* [Middletown, CT: Wesleyan University Press 1950]). Obviously line 2 is also a 'five-handed line,' demonstrating that Donne's witty invention is not quite unique.

if a value judgment is possible about such matters, it is equally obvious that he does not respond *better*.[7]

At the opposite extreme from this reader is our ideal semiotician. She too is stopped in her tracks by the peculiarities of the line, but she's no gross sensualist. She too turns away from the syntagmatic and paradigmatic readings into the fourth dimension of the metadigm, but instead of turning inward into her senses, she turns the poem inward and explores sensuously *the nature of the elegy itself.* Just as syntagm and paradigm come together triumphally in 'O my America! my new-found-land,' so the metadigm joins them in that triumphal line as the poem bends back upon itself recursively and celebrates the history of the elegy as an experimental form. Our semiotic reader recalls, with the aid of Donne's play on footedness and handedness, that the elegy in Greek and most often in Latin dealt with love and war and consisted of a specific verse form: couplets of six and five feet. Then the Alexandrian Greeks began to use the uneven distich for erotic poems only, and the Latin elegy began to be distinguished from other genres by the uneven distich, the tone of complaint, and the theme of love. Specifically, our semiotic reader will be led to recall Ovid's *Amores* 1.1, where he, like Donne, reflects recursively in the *form* of his verse the content of his rumination on his poem, when he writes that he would have written in double hexameters (a martial form) had Cupid not amputated one foot from the second line:

> Par erat inferior versus; risisse Cupido
> Dicitur atque unum surripuisse pedem.

But later he writes,

> Sex mihi surgat opus numeris, in quinque residat!
> Ferrea cum vestris bella valate modis!

which may be translated as 'Henceforth in six feet let my work commence, in five let it close. / Farewell ye ruthless wars, together with

---

7 An argument could be made here for the reader's *jouissance* based on Barthes's *The Pleasure of the Text.* The difficulty with such an argument about *this* line in *this* poem is in the erotic nature of so many of the lines. Nothing is more damaging to free play and arousal and the moment of bliss than surfeit. For an extensive examination of *The Pleasure of the Text*, see chapters 3 and 8.

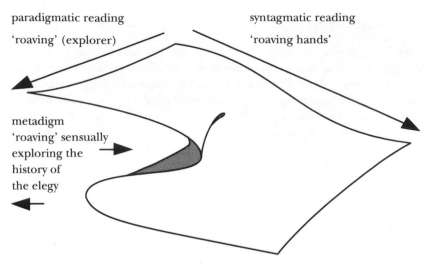

Fig. 1.15   The metadigm as catastrophe

your number!' Thus both Ovid and Donne comment on the forms of their poems within the poems by the forms themselves, metadigms to go with their paradigms and syntagms. Sexy as Donne's poem is, it is not a *love* poem; it is a love *poem*, as itself reminds us here.

Now in ordinary Euclidean geometry there is no convenient way to provide a topological isomorphism for this four-dimensional poetic effect. But Réné Thom's catastrophe theory has generated a system of conventional representation for multi-variable phenomena that is made to order for just such representations. Figure 1.15 shows how those four lines from Elegy XIX look on such a conventional diagram.[8] No-

---

8 Catastrophe theory, a mathematical discovery-invention by the French mathematician Réné Thom, is a technique of analysis of discontinuities in multi-variable relationships. Thom discovered that when from two to five variables are affecting each other in an apparently harmonious relationship, they sometimes break into discontinuities which seem at first inexplicable, but which nevertheless may be described topographically in eight basic forms. He gave these forms the colourful names 'simple minimum,' 'fold,' 'cusp,' 'swallow tail,' 'butterfly,' 'hyperbolic umbilic,' 'elliptic umbilic,' and 'parabolic umbilic.' The theory has always been controversial because, while the mathematics underlying it is unassailable, its application is not quantifiable, but descriptive. So far the most important applications have been in the biological and social sciences: accounting for changes in embryonic development (in evolutionary theory); explaining the pathology of anorexia nervosa; interpreting the biting behaviour of angry and frightened dogs. There have been at least four humanist applications of catastrophe theory that I know of, including two

tice that the action over the 'folded' region of figure 1.15, describing the motion of the metadigm or the poem as process, refers to both syntagm and paradigm bimodally and is bidirectional itself. It is hard to imagine how better to describe the brilliant complexity of the referentiality of that line of adverbs! This system of representation can be a powerful tool for literary analysis, and we shall have occasion to use it several times in the chapters that follow.

---

examples of graphing on a conventional representation of such topologies, as I do here. See Michael Thompson, *Rubbish Theory: The Creation and Destruction of Value* (Oxford: Oxford University Press 1979), 211; Dean MacCannell, *The Tourist* (New York: Schocken 1976), for the use of graphics; Evelyn Cobley, 'Catastrophe Theory in Tom Stoppard's *Professional Foul*,' *Contemporary Literature* 25, no. 1 (Spring 1984), 53–65; and Harold Bloom, 'Freud and the Sublime: A Catastrophe Theory of Creativity,' in *Agon: Towards a Theory of Revisionism*, (Oxford: Oxford University Press 1982), 91–118.

For the best explanation of catastrophe theory in layman's terms and a most perceptive series of examples showing how it can be of help in plotting various non-mathematical functional relationships, see Alexander Woodcock and Monte Davis, *Catastrophe Theory* (New York: E.P. Dutton 1978), *passim*. Here and elsewhere in this text I have added text and lines to a freehand version of what the authors call a 'cusp catastrophe graph' (46) suitable to serve as a conventional representation for more than three variables; these are not intended, of course, to be taken as literal topographies, but can function as a kind of shorthand for the representation of complex relationships like the ones I have been describing.

2

Metaphor and Metonymy Revisited

One of the most valuable tools that the alliance of formalism with structuralism has given the modern critic is the now famous dichotomy Roman Jakobson pointed out between metaphor and metonymy.[1] Working from the evidence of mutations and substitutions by aphasic patients, Jakobson brilliantly derived several general laws of language that may very well represent deep structures of human thought. First he noticed that two kinds of aphasia corresponded to the difference between the two basic semiotic acts, encoding and decoding: emissive or expressive aphasia with encoding, receptive or sensory aphasia with decoding (234).[2] These two kinds of aphasia, Jakobson then discovered, correspond with impairment in recognition of the two modes of relation, similarity and contiguity. The distinction arises because of the aphasic's ability to work with contexts. The patient who finds that the context provides suitable stimulus for word searching has difficulties with finding words at the start of a grammatical unit, and vice versa. The former may be said to have a deficit in similarity compensated by a surplus in contiguity, the latter the reverse (229). Further

---

1 See Roman Jakobson, *Selected Writings*, vol. 2 (The Hague: Mouton 1971). The theory is considered in various parts of a series of essays: 'Aphasia as a Linguistic Topic'; 'Two Aspects of Language and Two Types of Aphasic Disturbances'; 'Toward a Linguistic Classification of Aphasic Impairments'; and 'Linguistic Types of Aphasia.' All of these are in section B of this volume, 'Crucial Questions of Linguistic Theory,' 211–369. I will cite page references to these essays in parentheses in the text.

2 The distinction is useful in spite of what might be called the first law of semiotics, that every decoding is a new encoding. But that truth will exact a price, as we shall see.

consideration of the symptoms and structures of 'similarity disorder' and 'contiguity disorder' then led Jakobson to the conclusion that 'the development of discourse may take place along two different semantic lines ... similarity or ... contiguity. The metaphoric way would be the most appropriate term for the first case and the metonymic way for the second, since they find their most condensed expression in metaphor and metonymy respectively' (254).

The metaphoric and metonymic 'way' has just the right touch of the Tao about it to balance the careful progression of parallel dichotomies Jakobson used to arrive at this conclusion. But that is not to say that the dichotomy is either a scholastic exercise in a priori reasoning or a mystical leap of faith retroactively levered up a Platonic ladder. In 'Two Aspects of Language and Two Types of Aphasic Disturbances' Jakobson's conclusions are copiously supported by extensive inductive examinations of cases of aphasia based on neurological research done over the past eighty years by an impressive number of polymath linguists and neurologists.[3] Thus when this remarkable essay arrives at its conclusion in part five, which bears the title, 'The Metaphoric and Metonymic Poles,' what it concludes carries a lot of weight: neurological weight, linguistic weight, semiotic and structuralist weight. Indeed, one might predict, reading it for the first time, that it had the power to change the nature of the discipline of criticism – so important to that discipline is the mechanics of metaphor and metonymy. And that has indeed been the case.

One does not, therefore, lightly or casually object to the conclusion concerning the nature of the relationship between metaphor and metonymy that Jakobson makes in this section and elsewhere in his writings. International symposia have been held on the implications of the dichotomy. Critics have erected complex theories of genre and literary history upon it.[4] It is possible that the personal reputation of

---

3 If anything, his citations are weighted more heavily towards neurology than they are towards linguistics, although most of the workers cited published interdisciplinarily. Among the names cited in 'Two Aspects of Language and Two Types of Aphasic disturbances,' I would class Hughlings Jackson, A.R. Luria, F. Grewel, V.W.D. Schenck, Kurt Goldstein, André Ombredane, H. Myklebust, T. Alajouanine, F. Panse, A. Leischner, H. Head, S. Freud, F. Lotmar, R.E. Hemphil, E. Stengel, J. Ruesch, and Gregory Bateson as leaning more towards neurology than linguistics, while E. Sapir, N. Trubetzkoy, G. Kandler, D.M. MacKay, F. de Saussure, C.S. Peirce, R. Carnap, A. Kamegulov, J.G. Frazer, and C.F.P. Stutterheim amply represent a more linguistically based discipline.

4 See David Lodge, *The Modes of Modern Writing* (London: Edward Arnold 1977), and

one critic, Paul de Man, depends upon it. Nevertheless, I believe
Jakobson's theory concludes with a serious misapprehension and, as a
result, many of the critical superstructures based upon it have gone
awry.

   'Two Aspects of Language and Two Types of Aphasic Disturbances'
is the central and crucial essay in Jakobson's series on aphasia and
language. It is the last word of the title of its concluding section, 'The
Metaphoric and Metonymic Poles,' that has caused all the problems. I
believe that Jakobson did not mean to suggest that metaphor and
metonymy were polar opposites, as in the simplified isomorphism rep-

metonymy ————————————————————————— metaphor

Fig. 2.1

resented in figure 2.1, but they are better represented by a multiple-
axis catastrophe theory surface like the one used in the last chapter.
As we saw in chapter 1, distinctions in isomorphic decoding are anything but trivial. The differences between data-producing texts and
literary texts can best be defined *extensionally*, by means of a topological isomorphism. The same is true for such important concepts as this
one, the effect of which is to divide all language production into two
modes. If the dichotomy of metaphor and metonymy is seen as one-
or two-dimensional, as is implied by the word *polar*, there is not enough
room in the concept for all of the implications arising from the varie-
ties of textual distinctions that can be made. However, if the dichotomy
can be visualized as three- or more-dimensional, the concept can serve
brilliantly as a means of discovering where to 'speak the locus of
meaning.'

   To begin with, I do not believe that Jakobson himself really intended the word *poles* to imply a one- or two-dimensional relationship
between metaphor and metonymy. Although he uses the word in his
text as well as in the section title in ways that seem to support a linear
isomorphism ('the two polar types' [254], 'the bipolar structure of
language' [265]), elsewhere in this essay and in other essays on the

---

'Modernism, Antimodernism and Postmodernism,' in his *Working with Structuralism*
(Boston: Routledge and Kegan Paul 1981), especially 10–16; and Umberto Eco, *A
Theory of Semiotics* (Bloomington: Indiana University Press 1979), especially 3.3.9,
'Ideological Code Switching.' I will cite page references to these works in parenthe-
ses in the text.

same subject, he writes in such a way that at least the possibility of more than two dimensions is implied. Table 1 in 'Toward a Linguistic Classification of Aphasic Impairments' employs a switch-over image to describe the relationships among a set of six complex variables which combine to determine the patterns between encoding disorders and decoding disorders, implying the possibility of more than two dimensions (296):

$$
\begin{array}{cc}
\text{ENCODING} & \text{DECODING} \\
\textit{intact} - \text{constituents}^{-} & ^{-}\text{context} - \textit{antecedent} \\
\textit{impaired} - \text{context}_{-} \quad \mathbf{X} & _{-}\text{constituents} - \textit{consequent}
\end{array}
$$

This graphic representation is then further complicated by the addition of two more dichotomies, limitation/disintegration and successivity/simultaneity, which Jakobson illustrated with a multiform figure which is in two dimensions only because of the flatness of the page. Had the multidimensional conventional representation graph of the type I use in this chapter been available to him, I am sure Jakobson would have preferred it. Moreover, his text supports the assumption of the multidimensionality of the various dichotomies he presents: 'The two-dimensional (sequential and concurrent) contiguity of the distinctive features troubles the encoder suffering from an afferent aphasia, whereas the two-dimensional (paradigmatic and syntagmatic) similarity of paratactic words or clauses troubles the decoder suffering from an amnestic aphasia' (300). Two dimensions will serve for individual aphasic cases, but the text implies that an isomorphism for the general condition would need at least four dimensions.

The point is that the conditions, mental and physical, that go into the structures of relationships that have come to be called by the highly abstract signifiers *metonymy* and *metaphor* are extremely complex, and the apparent simplicity of the difference between the two signifiers masks this complexity. The problem almost certainly does not exist among linguists and neurologists when they use the two terms because they have a mental map that tracks relationships among the components of these portmanteau signifiers: content/constituent, limitation/disintegration, successivity/simultaneity, afferent/efferent/ amnestic/dynamic/semantic – all of these points of difference are available or present as *structures* upon which the sign *metaphor* or *metonymy* exists for these specialists. But for the humble critic of literature, long a victim of the division between the 'two cultures,' most, if not all, of the relationships inherent in the difference between *me-*

tonymy and *metaphor* are either lost completely or only vaguely perceived. After all, the critic is quite familiar with the old usage of the two terms and senses, correctly, that Jakobson chose them as signifiers for something very fundamental in their difference. Thus, even the best of critics and literary theorists may be excused for not quite grasping the multidimensional implications of this seemingly simple dichotomy. David Lodge is certainly among the best theorists who have written on this subject, but even he does not avoid shrinking the dimensionality of the dichotomy, even as he is proclaiming its value:

> Rhetoricians and critics from Aristotle to the present day have generally regarded metonymy and synecdoche as forms or subspecies of metaphor, and it is easy to see why. Superficially they seem to be the same sort of thing – figurative transformations of literal statements. Metonymy and synecdoche seem to involve, like metaphor, the substitution of one term for another, and indeed the definitions quoted above use the word 'substitution.' Jakobson, however (and there is no more striking example of the advantages a structuralist approach may have over a commonsense empirical approach) argues that that [*sic*] metaphor and metonymy are *opposed*, because generated according to opposite principles.[5]

It is easy to see why Lodge used the term *opposed* to describe the relationship between metaphor and metonymy here. He is arguing for a new distinction between the two terms in the sense that Jakobson had demonstrated. Metaphor and metonymy for the literary critic had always been seen as closely related terms, both involving the *substitution* of terms. Metonymy and synecdoche indeed are often classed as types of metaphor, under the general heading of substitution of different kinds: synecdoche, the part for the whole; metonymy, a closely related signifier for the intended signifier; metaphor, any substitution of vehicle for tenor, including those given for synecdoche and metonymy.[6] Lodge's purpose in this part of his work is to argue for the superiority of Jakobson's 'seminal distinction between the metaphoric

---

5 David Lodge, *Modes of Modern Writing*, 75–6. The definitions he refers to are from the *Shorter Oxford English Dictionary*, which defines metonymy as 'a figure in which the name of an attribute or adjunct is substituted for that of the thing meant'; and from Richard A. Lanham, *A Handlist of Rhetorical Terms*: 'Substitution of cause for effect or effect for cause' for metonymy and 'the substitution of part for whole, genus for species or vice versa' for synecdoche.

6 It is certainly true that critics and theorists have not been happy with these loose definitions and sloppily defined relationships. The very terms *tenor* and *vehicle* are

and metonymic poles' (73), and so it is not hard to understand why he emphasizes the 'polar' opposition of Jakobson's dichotomy compared to the fuzzy differences in all previous distinctions between the two terms.

In many ways, Lodge is like the biologists and philosophers who rushed to the support of Darwin during the last half of the nineteenth century. Having the intelligence to recognize an insight of great significance, the Darwinians fought bravely and honourably against the forces of ignorance and superstition for the recognition and acceptance of a new understanding of nature. They were defending the Great Fact of evolution against those who would suppress or deny it. In the process, some of the finer points of evolutionary theory were overlooked in the interest of winning the greater argument. Thus the problem of gradualism or catastrophism in evolution was finessed for over a century because catastrophism could easily be confused in the public mind with creationism. There can be no doubt that the greater good was served by stressing the seminal quality of evolutionary theory in general and *popularizing* it instead of confusing the issue with fine points that might seem to favour the older orthodoxy.

Clearly Lodge is following this pattern in his discussion of metaphor and metonymy in *Modes of Modern Writing*, if we grant the distinction that his audience is not the general public but the much smaller world of literary critics. From the beginning of his consideration of Jakobson's theory he stresses two aspects of it: its enormous significance as a possibly universal law of linguistics (the first to be discovered that may correspond to deep mental structures), and its possibilities as a natural 'cleavage point' for literary taxonomies of all sorts. Thus he emphasizes early in his discussion the linguistic background to the theory: the binary oppositions in semiotics like *langue/parole* and paradigm/syntagm, and the relative looseness and confusion in critical orthodoxy over synecdoche, metonymy, and metaphor (73–7). When he then arrives at the neurological basis for the theory in the 'two types of aphasia,' he avoids virtually all of the complexities that Jakobson was careful to assert that bridge the gap between neurologi-

only fifty years old and were coined by I.A. Richards as an improvement on the various rhe-torical terms in use before his *The Philosophy of Rhetoric* (New York: Oxford University Press 1936). These earlier terms included such vague distinctions as 'minor term' and 'major term,' 'thing meant' and 'thing said,' 'meaning' and 'picture,' and the like. Richards's coinage is a marked improvement and is essentially structuralist in that it calls attention to the *relationship* between the parts in the largest possible context instead of emphasizing their difference.

cal functions and linguistic expression of them. Essentially, he begins
with an introductory quotation from Jakobson asserting the basic neurological distinction between selection and combination (not at all
different from the one that began this chapter), and then proceeds
with a series of representative citations and quotations of aphasic confusions of the two types with representative 'selection deficiency'
metonymies and 'contexture deficiency' metaphors (77–8). He then
hints at some of the power of this dichotomy by concluding that in the
case of 'some modern writing, e.g. the work of Gertrude Stein and
Samuel Beckett, it is not an exaggeration to say that it aspires to the
condition of aphasia' (79).

It should then be no surprise that his next section is headed, like
Jakobson's, 'The Metaphoric and Metonymic Poles' and consists entirely of paired oppositions, concluding with a neat (and very useful)
summary in parallel columns:

METAPHOR	METONYMY
Paradigm	Syntagm
Similarity	Contiguity
Selection	Combination
Substitution	[Deletion] Contexture
Contiguity Disorder	Similarity Disorder
Contexture Deficiency	Selection Deficiency
Drama	Film
Montage	Close-up
Dream Symbolism	Dream Condensation & Displacement
Surrealism	Cubism
Imitative Magic	Contagious Magic
Poetry	Prose
Lyric	Epic
Romanticism & Symbolism	Realism

(81)

Lodge then goes on from this point to develop several interesting
applications of this valuable extension of the dichotomy, concluding
in the third part of his study with a generic interpretation of the
difference between 'Modernists, Antimodernists and Postmodernists.'[7]

---

7 Part 3 of *The Modes of Modern Writing*, 125–225, examines in detail the major
  representative genres and writers of the three categories as Lodge defines them,
  based on Jakobson's dichotomy.

The distinctions he makes in this section are essentially taxonomic, and they are based entirely on Jakobson's theory. As we shall see a little further on this chapter, they are remarkably insightful distinctions, but need a certain amount of modification to be fully useful and, indeed, not to be misleading.

Umberto Eco's dependence upon Jakobson's distinction between metonymy and metaphor in the most recent English manifestation of his ongoing theoretical pursuit of the semiotic basis of language, *A Theory of Semiotics*, is much less obvious than Lodge's.[8] Indeed, although the entries under Roman Jakobson's name cover a full page in the bibliography, not one of the essays on metaphor/metonymy and aphasia is listed (330–1). We should not find this surprising. Where Lodge intended to extend the value of the metaphor/metonymy duality to the classification of genres and styles with a very conscious awareness that he was 'preaching Jakobsonism' to an audience suspicious of semiotics and structuralism, Eco was writing primarily for an audience of semioticians.[9] Since that is so, we might look for two significant differences in his treatment of the metaphor/metonymy dichotomy: first, it will be accepted as a given without challenge to its essential truth – much as a modern biologist accepts the theory of evolution; second, its *complex* relationship to other linguistic structures and, ultimately, mental structures will be much more thoroughly understood (see above, page 23).

That is indeed the case. Nevertheless, when Eco arrives at the concluding sections of his 'Theory of Sign Production,' in which he considers first the creation of *aesthetic* texts and then the creation of *ideological* texts, he too vitiates otherwise valuable contributions to critical theory by oversimplifying Jakobson's insights into the metaphor/metonymy relationship.

In the case of aesthetic texts, Eco, like Lodge, bases his analysis on the advances in semiotic theory of the past century. After rejecting the tautologies of transcendent critics like Croce ('Every genuine artistic representation is in itself the universe' [262]),[10] Eco goes to Jakobson's

---

8 See his 'Foreword,' vii–viii, where he discusses the virtually organic growth of his theory in a polyglottal form from 1967 through 1974. Page viii includes a particularly important discussion of the two methods used to produce his *theory of codes* and his *theory of sign production.*

9 That this is so is borne out, for example, by the ongoing joke about seals and bachelors that makes sense only to readers who have read 'Katz, Fodor, and Postal (and in the circle that I [Eco] move in everybody has)' (282).

10 *Breviario di estetica* (Bari: Laterza 1913), 134

formulation of the six functions of language to rename Jakobson's *poetic* function as *aesthetic*, because he is dealing with every form of art, and to redefine it as language which is both 'ambiguous and self-focusing' (262). Both those words imply an isomorphism involving closed curves and surfaces around the origin, corresponding to syntagms and paradigms of the work at the centre. Eco treats this ambiguous and self-focusing language just as if it were a data-communicating text, but with several exceptional procedures that mark an effort

> to establish pragmatic relations between communicators, through a complex network of presuppositional acts. Inasmuch as the idiolect constitutes a sort of final (though never completely achieved) definition of the work, to read an artistic product means at once: (i) to *induce*, that is to infer a general rule from individual cases; (ii) to *abduce*, that is to test both old and new codes by way of a hypothesis; (iii) to *deduce*, that is to check whether what has been grasped on one level can determine artistic events on another, and so on. Thus all the codes of inference are at work. Like a large labyrinthine garden, a work of art permits one to take many different routes, whose number is increased by the criss-cross of its paths. (275)

Here is surely no effort to reduce the complex relationships between terms of linguistic dichotomies of all sorts; yet, as we shall see, the literary critic who follows Eco into this garden needs some very complex isomorphisms to find his path around the inductions, abductions, and deductions required of him.

When he goes on to a consideration of 'ideology as a semiotic category' (289), Eco makes clear by more than just position in the text[11] that he considers ideological semiosis a more complex version of aesthetic code manipulation. Where a mere mention of the 'Garden of Cyrus' of literature[12] sufficed for that part of his theory, Eco goes into a 'laboratory model' to illustrate how 'ideology is ... a message which starts with a factual description, and then tries to justify it theoretically, gradually being accepted by society through a process of overcoding' (290). His 'laboratory model' is an isomorphism mixing

---

11 Eco follows normal rhetorical procedure in leaving his most important and most com-plex arguments until the end; by placing ideology after aesthetic sign production, Eco is of course making an ideological statement.

12 I realize that I am being as elliptical as Eco in stressing the quincuncial nature of his 'labyrinthine garden' and 'the criss-cross of its paths.' For the significance of the quincunx to my argument and Eco's see footnote 25 – but don't skip to it until you have read the argument leading up to it!

metaphor and metonymy on Cartesian coordinates in a three-dimensional structure based on the interrelationship of heating, pressure, and productivity, derived, I believe, from the Nefastis machine imagined by Thomas Pynchon in *The Crying of Lot 49*.[13] It is, of course, a political statement itself – as is this comment on it.

All of which brings us to the case of Paul de Man. It would be hard to invent a more cogent case of the complexity of relationships between politics, morality, aesthetics, and the metaphoric and metonymic structures that are used to determine them than the controversy that has arisen over de Man's career-as-text. This brilliant theorist of post-Sartrean phenomenology and deconstruction had a reputation as the 'new world's Derrida' when it was made public that he had written a series of pro-Nazi, anti-Semitic articles for obscure Belgian magazines when he was young. One might reasonably respond to this criticism with a citation of St Augustine (among many others), but de Man's case is complicated by the critical theory he espoused. Deconstruction viewed from the outside looks (metaphorically) like 'a message' (political quietism) which has been justified theoretically and gradually accepted by society by a process of overcoding. Metonymically, deconstruction is a natural, if rather extreme, extension of formalism and structuralism.

This summary too is, of course, political.

Now, after this excursion into some of the significant areas of critical theory for which the Jakobson dichotomy between metaphor and metonymy may be seen as crucial, it is time to return critically to the dichotomy and observe what a few revisions in our isomorphic perceptions of it may make of the structures that have been built upon it. To begin with, let us do away once and for all with the simplistic polar model (fig. 2.1). We have seen that Jakobson himself set up isomorphisms of considerably greater complexity than this one. Even David Lodge, while attempting to transmit the main thrust of the Jakobsonian dichotomy as simply – one might even say simplistically – as possible, is forced over and over again to confront the paradoxes inherent in his application with this kind of modification:

---

13 I could very possibly be wrong about both of these obscure references, since Eco drops notes to neither Sir Thomas Browne nor to Pynchon, and there is no *specific* reference to any detail of either work that corresponds to the major points Eco makes on either literary or ideological overcoding. But Eco's interests and erudition are such that I cannot but believe that he has a quincuncial point to be absorbed in the first observation and a paranoiacal one in the second.

> We observed earlier that even Jakobson himself seemed somewhat baf-
> fled by the problem of how to deal, analytically, with the metonymic
> mode of writing; and we traced the difficulty to the fact that in his
> scheme the POETIC (i.e., the literary) is homologous with the metaphoric
> mode, which in turn is opposed to the metonymic mode. How, then, can
> the metonymic be assimilated to the POETIC?
>
> The solution would seem to lie in a recognition that, at the highest
> level of generality at which we can apply the metaphor/metonymy dis-
> tinction, literature itself is metaphoric and nonliterature metonymic. (109)

Wheels within wheels. One is reminded of the Ptolemaic system of
epicycles to explain the apparent motion of the planets. In a simple
linear polar system, every degree of 'metonymity' would have to correspond with an exact reduction in 'metaphoricity' to accommodate the
scale. Even shifting to a spherical model doesn't help much because it
remains *superficial* (see fig. 2.2). Perhaps it would be fun to describe
'Methinks it is like a weasel' as 50°N by 20°W, but the cause of literary
criticism is not much advanced by that kind of surface description.

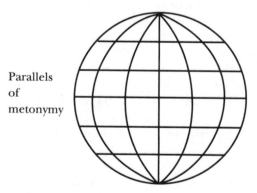

Parallels
of
metonymy

Fig. 2.2   Degrees of metaphor

As we saw in chapter 1, isomorphisms for literary texts must be
multidimensional and recursive to be of any use. The literary text,
unlike the data-producing text, creates nothing material – builds no
bicycle. Returning ever upon itself in the two dimensions we posited
of *paradigm* and *syntagm*, it can best be visualized, for most ordinary
cases, as the combination of a very large – perhaps infinite – number
of functions of these two dimensions; while, for some cases, the combination may be of numerous functions of four or more dimensions.
It is no accident that Jakobson suggests, and Lodge makes explicit in

his list of paired dichotomies from 'The Metaphoric and Metonymic
Poles,' these first four pairs:

METAPHOR	METONYMY
Paradigm	Syntagm
Similarity	Contiguity
Selection	Combination

If we can imagine these four pairs all present on a multidimensional catastrophe theory surface, reduced for our purposes to the
three dimensions practicable upon the plane of the page (fig. 2.3), we
will be ready to begin a serious examination of the powerful possibilities of the Jakobson dichotomy in all of the applications we have

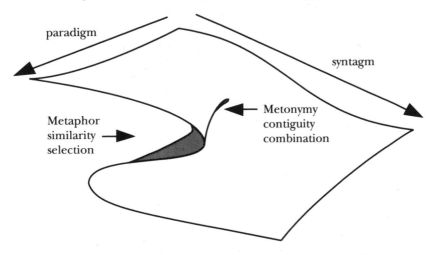

Fig. 2.3   Lodge's first four categories on a catastrophe theory diagram

presented in this chapter. It is hard to imagine a sixteen-fold multiple-
axis relationship, but if we are to do justice to the interesting and
powerful combinations described here, that is exactly what we must
do. The relationship can best be explained with a few fairly simply
examples, which two poems by Emily Dickinson will provide:

> I never lost as much but twice,
> And that was in the sod.
> Twice have I stood a beggar.
> Before the door of God!

> Angels – twice descending
> Reimbursed my store –
> Burglar! Banker – Father!
> I am poor once more! (J49)

This poem requires of the reader at first only a simple paradigmatic substitution of personal loss for material loss. The speaker syntagmatically has lost an unknown quantity (a coin? a purse?) in the sod, requiring him to resort to panhandling in a very select neighbourhood. The paradigms of losing something in the earth and begging God reflect grief for personal loss and prayer, respectively. Both of these substitutions are metaphoric primarily, being *selections* notable for their *similarity* to each other, once we grant the personal/monetary parallel for the loss and the prayer/beggar dichotomy resulting from it.

However, the neatness of the paradigmatic substitution begging/praying seems to be bought at the price of inexactness and confusion in the second stanza. When we beg, we require something material as evidence of the charity of the begged. Unrewarded begging is proof of the imperfection of the giver. Such a paradigm is, of course, a less-than-perfect metaphor for grief, but seems nevertheless to be the point here, since the *replacement* of the loss is emphasized in the first two lines. The last two lines resolve the problem in the act of the poem itself, as the beggar apostrophizes a most unorthodox Trinity, explaining the ironic nature of this prayer as well as the two which have preceded it.[14] A 'Father' who is both a burglar and a banker is a very complex mixture of metaphor and metonymy, similarity and contiguity, selection and combination, which saves this poem from being a mere collection of pious platitudes. A God-figure who 'giveth and taketh away' is one thing, but a *trinity* consisting of those qualities? And surely one does not have to be a Marxist or an atheist to find in the alliteration of *b*urglar and *b*anker a certain contiguity between those two professions? Suddenly, the reader is bewildered with a profusion of possibilities for interpretation, belying the greeting-card simplicity of the paired metaphors of the first stanza. In particular, the

---

14 A modern analogue of this sudden substitution of an unorthodoxy where it is most unexpected occurs in Georges Brassens's *chanson* 'Les amoreux qui se becottent sur les bancs publiques,' when he has the lovers necking on public park benches looked down upon by the Holy Family, 'Le père, la mère, la fille, le fils, le saint espirit,' a typical bourgeois family out for a stroll.

invocation of an unorthodox trinity calls into question the very simplicity of the begging/praying metaphor so confidently presented in
the first stanza, so ironically undercut here.

What has happened? Because of a confusion between metaphor
and metonymy (and any or all of the other paired qualities along our
multidimensional radial axes), speaker and reader share a moment of
enlightening confusion – and poetry is the result. Would the result
have been the same if the metaphor had not metamorphosed before
our very eyes in line seven? All we need do is imagine for a text of line
seven: 'Father! Son – Holy Ghost!' – and we are back in our simple
metaphor of begging/praying.[15] The reader's confusion about whether
she is reading a metaphor or a metonymy, straightforward syntax or
unorthodox paradigm, God as almsgiver or God as a second-story man
Daddy Gotbucks, the one or the many, *is* poetry. It is poetry because
for that moment, speaker and reader are one in a dense interpretive
confusion of values and meanings in a multidimensional garden.

There is, of course, more to it than that, as a second poem by Emily
Dickinson illustrates:

> If I shouldn't be alive
> When the Robins come,
> Give the one in Red Cravat,
> A Memorial crumb.
> If I couldn't thank you,
> Being fast asleep,
> You will know I'm trying
> With my granite lip! (J182)

The *granite lip* is the only part of the poem that need concern us. It is
a nearly pure metaphor, the granite of the tombstone replacing the
lively tissue of the lip as organ of speech, and being mute because it
lacks that organ's *quick*ness in both senses, being both slow and dead.
In an otherwise rather undistinguished poem, it does bring the simple
narrative to a strong conclusion – perhaps even justifying that excla-
mation point. The history of my own personal response to this metaphor, however, provides an illustration of the problem (and the power)
of the relationship between metaphor and metonymy. I had no difficulty with the poem until I took my first look at Emily Dickinson's

15 On the other hand, an alternative like 'Burglar! Banker – Indian Giver' is too light
and creates a false metonymy, like the next example.

tombstone. When I saw the shape of the stone, the image of the disk-distorted lip of the Ubangi popped into my mind, and the poem was ruined for me forever. Like the unfortunate art collector who suddenly discovers his Jackson Pollock has the image of an elephant standing on its head prominently displayed someplace in its abstract expressionist surface, I was the victim of an accidental metonymy.[16] The contiguity of disk-shape and grotesque lip will always interfere with my reading of that line; metonymy once again is mixed with metaphor, but this time to a negative purpose.

Thus we see that confusion between metaphor and metonymy resulting from the mixture of those two types of verbal/mental patterning can either create or destroy an aesthetic effect. If metaphor and metonymy were simply polar opposites, this would not be possible, since any increase or decrease in metonymity would necessarily result in a corresponding decrease or increase in metaphoricity. The results demonstrated here can only be caused by confusion raised by the simultaneous existence of the paired qualities. They are not polar opposites. The fact is that they do not even exist in the same *dimensions* when we look at them isomorphically. Figures 2.4 and 2.5 display isomorphisms of the two examples I have just cited as represented on a conventional catastrophe theory graph.

I am not competent to speculate – and I gladly leave doing so to the neurologists – concerning the question of whether the two-sidedness of the brain corresponds in any way to the multidimensional differences between the structures of metonymy and the structures of metaphor. I can only say that what I manage to understand from my readings in this area indicates that most competent neurologists are hesitant to locate such linguistic tendencies very specifically, but that the evidence cited in their case histories seems to support a right-brain metaphor and left-brain metonymy connection.[17] They are dealing, of

---

16 This sort of thing is universally known and certainly needs no proof; it is a source of good stories, however, and I can't resist telling at least two more. Look at Twain's 'Jim Blaine's Grandfather's Pet Ram' and Pound's *Hugh Selwyn Mauberly* for the references to Nixon running for office again. As we might expect, the effect of the anachronism on the Twain is comic, but I'm afraid it destroys the mood of *Mauberly.* I wonder who those Nixons were ...

17 See A.R. Luria, *The Man with a Shattered World* (New York: Basic Books 1972), and Oliver Sacks, *The Man Who Mistook His Wife for a Hat and Other Clinical Tales* (New York: Harper 1987).

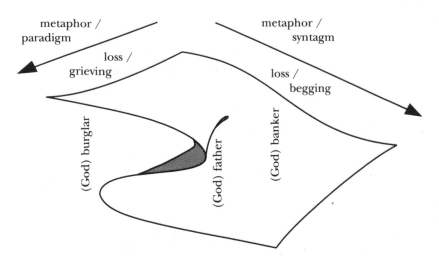

Figs. 2.4 and 2.5   Two 'catastrophes' from Emily Dickinson

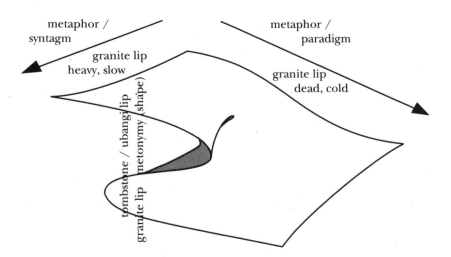

course, with pathologies, and literature or creativity of any kind is not pathological. But if one keeps in mind the multidimensionality of the two structures or processes, it is not too hard to imagine how the overlapping of the two functions produces in the pathological state confusion, incoherence, *noise*; while in the hands of an artist the same kind of overlapping generates textural complexity, depth and density, *delight.* Indeed, it is not impossible that the two situations may be interchangeable if we grant different contexts; thus Lodge's comment that the writings of Gertrude Stein and Samuel Beckett 'aspire to the condition of aphasia' (*Modes,* 79) might be reversed, as in the case of the dying words of Arthur Flegenheimer, a.k.a. Dutch Schultz, which could well have been written by either Stein or Beckett:

> ... All right look out look out. Oh my memory is all gone. A work relief. Police. Who gets it? I don't know and I don't want to know but look out. My fortunes have changed and come back and went back since that ... they dyed my shoe. Open those shoes ... Police mamma Helen mother please take me out. I will settle the indictment. Come on open the soap duckets. The chimney sweeps. Talk to the sword. Shut up you got a big mouth! Please help me get up. Henry Max come over here. French Canadian bean soup. I want to pay. Let them leave me alone.[18]

In its raw form, as the stenographic recording of a dying man, this is aphasic gibberish, but taken out of that context and placed in a book of parodies it acquires the resonance of art.

The problem is that for almost all of us both our brain hemispheres function perfectly well at the same time, thank God, and our receptivity for metaphor and for metonymy stands at 100 per cent of function all the time, independent of each other. As a result we are sometimes not aware which decoding process is engaged until it is too late to respond appropriately, and confusion is the result. Moreover, the confusion can be either purposeful and satisfying, as in the case of the first Dickinson example, or reductive and unsatisfying, as in the second. Perhaps an analogy might be helpful. If we think of words as an electrical current crossing a gap to create a spark, then the process of

---

18 From the dying words of Dutch Schultz, the 'Beer Baron of the Bronx,' taken down verbatim by a police stenographer after he was shot on 23 October 1935. They were published in Craig Thompson and Allen Raymond, *Gang Rule in New York* (New York: Dial Press 1940), and quoted in full by Dwight MacDonald in *Parodies* (New York: Random House 1960), 211, as an unconscious parody of Gertrude Stein. Remarkably, they are also incorporated into the text of E.L. Doctorow's *Billy Bathgate* (New York: Harper 1989), 461–4, and so have served three functions, two of them literary. See also Douglas R. Hofstadter, *Metamagical Themas* (New York: Bantam 1985), chapter 11 ('Stuff and Nonsense'), 213–31. When Hofstadter first published this chapter in the December 1982 issue of *Scientific American*, I passed on the Dutch Schultz passage to him as another example of what he was discussing. I'm a little disappointed that he didn't include it in his book.

metaphor is like a Van de Graaff generator which loads up static electrical current until it explodes across the gap violently. Metonymy, by contrast, is like those y-shaped spark-gaps in the Frankenstein movies that go up only so far and then pop and start over again. The forms are similar, the content identical ... but the results are totally different. Now imagine a machine that has both functions but conceals the results until the final moment: either a return to the bottom of the y-shape or a violent explosion, the one calmly satisfying, reassuring, the other nerve-racking, intense.[19]

One measure of the intensity of the effect of this irresolution is the greatness of the art that produced it. Another is the seriousness of the pathology.

Gregory Bateson describes the state of uncertainty that results from the need to discriminate between two modes of perception as 'Learning II.'[20] In 'Learning I' there are four necessary conditions:

(a) The notion of repeatable context ...

(b) This notion is not a mere tool of our description but contains the implicit hypothesis that ... the sequence of life experience, action, etc., is somehow segmented or punctuated into subsequences or 'contexts' which may be equated or differentiated by the organism.

(c) The distinction which is commonly drawn between perceptions and action, afferent and efferent, input and output, is for higher organisms in complex situations not valid ... perception is not by any means a process of mere passive receptivity but is at least partly determined by efferent control from higher centers. Perception, notoriously, can be changed by experience ... every item of action or output may create an item of input; and ... percepts may in some cases partake of the nature of output. It is no accident that almost all sense organs are used for the emission of signals between organisms. Ants communicate by their antennae; dogs by the pricking of their ears ...

(d) ... In Learning I, every item of perception or behavior may be stimulus or response or *reinforcement* according to how the total sequence of interaction is punctuated. (292; italics are Bateson's)

Bateson's four conditions for 'Learning I' are perfect analogues for

---

19 I am indebted to T.R. Henn, *The Apple and the Spectroscope* (New York: Norton 1966), 3, for the first half of this analogy.

20 Gregory Bateson. 'The Logical Categories of Learning and Communication,' in *Steps to an Ecology of Mind* (New York: Ballantine 1972), 279–308

our normal mental state of receptivity for the interpretation of metaphor and metonmy as they are normally perceived. When the organism shifts from Learning I to Learning II, which is defined as '*change in
the process of Learning I*, e.g., a corrective change in the set of alterna-
tives from which choice is made' (293), it is to move to a new level of
awareness. Just such a shift takes place when the critic becomes aware
that the *processes* of metaphor and metonymy are radically different
and that distinguishing between then cannot be simple application of
Learning I. But this new level of awareness does not come without
cost. As Bateson says, 'Learning II is a necessary preparation for ...
behavioral disturbance' (297). He cites the example of a laboratory
animal which has been taught by 'Pavlovian or instrumental learning
... to discriminate between some X and some Y; e.g., between an
ellipse and a circle. When this discrimination has been learned, the
task is made more difficult: the ellipse is made progressively fatter and
the circle is flattened. Finally a stage is reached at which discrimination is impossible. At this stage the animal starts to show symptoms of
severe disturbance' (296).

   Uncomfortable as that example is, it barely scratches the surface of
the deep pathologies of 'experimental neurosis.' Robert the Ram is
the pathetic hero of Howard S. Liddell's *Emotional Hazards in Animals
and Man*. First he is taught to respond to the clicking of a metronome
at 60 beats per minute by flexing his foreleg. He is taught this as a
conditioned response because the ticking is always followed by an
electric shock.[21] Then he is taught to discriminate between the metronome's ticking 60 times per minute, always followed by a shock, and
120 times per minute, which is never followed by a shock. At first both
stimuli create disturbances in his central nervous system: rapid heart
beat, shallow breathing, agitation. Eventually Robert learns that only
the slower clicking precedes the shock, and his CNS shows no response
to the faster clicking. Then gradually the two rates of clicking are
changed to make the discrimination more difficult. Poor Robert. He
is now ready for the demonstration Liddell begins his study with:

> The duration of each metronome signal will vary from 3 to 15 seconds and
> the signals will follow one another at irregular intervals of 2 to 5 minutes,
> thus preventing the sheep from reacting to any temporal cues other than
> the metronome rates themselves. This variability of signal duration and

---

21 The shock is not powerful enough to cause pain, only to surprise. Or so says
    Mr Liddell.

of interval between signals was maintained during training. Moreover, the positive and negative signals were always given in random order.

As Robert stands waiting our pleasure he no longer gives the impression of imperturbability which we noticed half an hour earlier [before the demonstration]. His respiratory rate has now increased from 40 to 90 per minute. Breathing movements are labored and audible. He occasionally sighs or yawns and there is much nose licking ... During the ensuing six tests, spaced two to five minutes apart, Robert reacts correctly to metronome 60 positive, metronome 92 negative, metronome 60 positive, metronome 78 negative, metronome 60 positive, and finally, metronome 72 negative. As the negative, or no-shock metronome signals approach more and more closely to the positive rate of 60 per minute our animal's discomfort at the negative signals rapidly mounts. At the sound of the metronome signalling no shock the body visibly tenses while the forelimbs are rigidly extended giving the appearance of the forefeet being glued to the platform. When the last negative metronome signal, metronome 72, is given, the respiratory rate abruptly rises from 94 to 139 per minute.[22]

The case of Robert the Ram holds two important lessons for the literary critic who wants to discriminate between metaphor and metonymy.[23] The first point to notice is that Robert's context is not self-determined but forced on him by the experimental process. Take Robert out of the laboratory, give him freedom to gambol in the fields, and he might never learn to distinguish between 60 and 72 clicks per minute, but he would certainly never suffer from experimental neurosis. Second, Robert suffers his most extreme pain when making a *negative* discrimination. Anyone who has ever waited for the second shoe to drop understands what that means. And, more to the point, being *correct* in his discrimination has no effect on the extent of the distress suffered. These two factors fit very well into the theories of discrimination between data-processing and literary texts discussed in chapter 1. Derrida's *différance* is aesthetically satisfying only to the 'gamboling lamb' of a reader freely playing with his text. And the reader who is not engaged in free play, but is hooked into a context

22 Howard S. Liddell, *Emotional Hazards in Animals and Man* (Springfield, IL: Thomas 1956), 8–9

23 I hesitate to add a third; Liddell indicates that mere submission to the experimental process and its consequent tensions made Robert permanently sexually disabled, even after deprogramming had ended his other neurotic symptoms (67).

which *requires* him to make discriminations – make the grade, publish or perish – is particularly liable to experimental neurosis.

It's almost enough to make one wish that Jakobson were mistaken. Alas, he was not.

The highest power of literature is the same force, positively present, as the tension which produces anxiety neurosis in the laboratory animal or the student in the classroom. It is only in those moments when confusion arises in the reader's mind about whether she is responding metaphorically or metonymically that she is at a Learning ii equivalent of either the most intense literary pleasure or experimental neurosis. As we have seen, the data-processing experience of a text may be visualized as two-dimensional; adding the uncertain quality of 'literary expression' – 'assembly of Japanese bicycle require great peace of mind' – adds another dimension and creates the possibility of *negative* response. Literary expression (which, of course, is not confined to 'literature') takes shape in either the metaphoric or the metonymic mode. As Jakobson, and after him, David Lodge, has pointed out, one or the other of these modes dominates in many divisible classes of genre, style, period, technique, etc., probably even in the periods of development of each individual artist. When Lodge uses this dichotomy as a taxonomic 'cleavage point' for all those genres and styles and specific writers in *Modes of Modern Writing*, he is not incorrect in doing so; he is merely using the least important aspect of the dichotomy for the least important task it might perform. For it is not in the difference between the act of metaphor and the act of metonymy that the greatest power of art lies, but in the ability of the artist to force the reader to rediscover their relationship. When that happens, when the reader is forced to discriminate between the appropriateness of two equally attractive (or even unattractive) responses, he moves from Learning i to Learning ii. And, as was the case of our bicycle builder, he risks a negative response. It is our Learning i familiarity that allows us to have preferences for one or the other of those choices on Lodge's list: you prefer drama, I like film; you like poetry, I like prose; you say tomahto, I say tomayto. All very civilized. But let the artist lure us into the belief that we are in the metaphoric mode and then suddenly spring metonymy on us, or vice versa, and, like Robert, we may begin to bleat.

Art at the level of Learning i, when we can rest secure in the knowledge that we are proceeding normally in the path of metaphor or metonymy, can be very good art indeed. Go down both columns of Lodge's list and you can cite innumerable artists and works corresponding neatly to each member of each dichotomy. But, I submit, you will find no great ones – or, if you do, perhaps you should take another look at how totally metaphoric or metonymic they are. The greatest literature, the greatest art of any kind, inevitably risks forcing its audience to Learning II by demanding that it discriminate *uncomfortably* between metaphoric and the metonymic modes. The effect is equivalent to the change in perception or dimensionality between data-processing texts and literary texts, except that in this case the dimensionality goes beyond our sensually reassuring limit of *three*. That takes us beyond the experience of our senses and beyond 'common sense,' which doubtless helps to explain why the ordinary man-in-the-street is so vehemently opposed to the avant-garde, while it is the avant-garde, and yet is quite content to accept its standards once it has become the orthodoxy.

As Lodge discovered, the *normal* pattern of literary modality is an *oscillation* between the metaphoric and metonymic.[24] As far as the recent history of literature is concerned, the most important dichotomy is the last one on his list (see page 26): Romanticism and Symbolism as representative of metaphor and realism as representative of metonymy. These two modes have dominated the history of literary taste, especially with regard to fiction, for almost two centuries, first one then the other representing the orthodoxy then the avant-garde again and again. As we shall see in chapter 3, superficial appearances of relative calm and mediocrity during each orthodoxy are accompanied by counter-cultural works which promise eventual change in the dominant mode, and which are often the best works of the period. But those triumphs of style and creativity do not come into being painlessly. The great works which arrive at the moments of transition between modes are usually the hardest to write, the least popular among readers of their day, and most thoroughly excoriated by the professional critics in charge of the then-reigning orthodoxy.

Lodge sees the one exception to this historical oscillation as occurring during our current period. Although he describes the major modal dichotomy of the first half of the twentieth century as a struggle between modernism and anti-modernism, in which, of course, modernism represents the metaphoric 'pole' and anti-modernism the metonymic, he asserts that the result of this confrontation has not

---

24 First pointed out and most succinctly described in the essay 'Modernism, Anti-modernism and Postmodernism' in the 1970s (see *Working with Structuralism*, 10), but developed thoroughly in *Modes of Modern Writing*, 220 and *passim.*

been another oscillation, as has always been the case in the past, but for the first time a new phenomenon, postmodernism, which is distinctly different from both of its predecessors. Postmodernism is neither metaphoric nor metonymic, but is totally concerned with distinguishing between the metaphoric and metonymic. Thus it is truly the first literary mode to confront the reader directly with a demand to discriminate at the level of Learning II *in the ordinary process of reading.* As such, of course, it makes *everybody* uncomfortable: writer, reader, and critic. What other literary movement provoked such a cautious *apologia* from one of its major practitioners – so cautious it has been misread by practically everyone – as John Barth's 'The Literature of Exhaustion'? How else explain the critical scandal that arose over the Pulitzer Prize committee's refusal to grant the prize to Thomas Pynchon for *Gravity's Rainbow?* Postmodernism asks more of the reader, the writer, and the critic than a simple quantitative increase in attention; it requires a qualitative change, a *dimensional* change in discriminatory ability.

David Lodge sensed the difference between postmodernism and the modes which were its predecessors, but he had no suitable isomorphism to grasp the multidimensionality of the difference. As a result, his final chapter in *Modes of Modern Writing* is his most disappointing. He admits his incapacity in the very first paragraph of that last chapter. After describing the 'history of modern English literature' as 'an oscillation ... between polarized clusters of attitudes and techniques,' he concludes that 'the metaphor/metonymy distinction explains why at the deepest level there is a cyclical rhythm to literary history, for *there is nowhere else for discourse to go* [italics mine] except between these two poles' (220). When he then considers postmodernism, he can only lamely work in those same dimensions: postmodernism 'tries to go beyond modernism, or around it, or underneath it, and is often as critical of modernism as it is of antimodernism' (220–1). Locked into his insufficiently dimensional isomorphism, he can only list a series of qualities which he suggests accounts for the difference. Unfortunately, these are so abstract that they prove nothing; only the last one he includes, the 'short circuit,' really moves towards the essential multidimensionality of postmodernism, and he does not pursue that aspect of it. Thus he vitiates his otherwise important work in developing the taxonomic significance of Jakobson's discovery, which, of course, did not require an understanding of the multidimensionality of the concept. In several of the following chapters we will first pursue his insight into the oscillation of the metaphoric and metonymic modes in recent literary history and then suggest some useful modifications for his overview of postmodernism.

When we turn to Umberto Eco's contributions to the development of
Jakobson's discovery, we must first make note of a procedural admis-
sion buried in the Foreword to *A Theory of Semiotics* (see above, footnote 8). There Eco confesses to the creation of 'a sort of "chiasmatic"
structure' (viii), because, while his development of a 'theory of codes'
for this book is based on 'Ockham's razor,' that is, on the principle
that the number of assumptions used to explain phenomena should
be minimal, the second part of the book, comprising his theory of
sign production, is based upon the opposite principle: that the number
of assumptions should be increased until it is adequate to explain the
phenomena. Such a distinction often marks a difference in dimensionality in isomorphic structures for decoding.

Yet, as we saw above, when he moves to an isomorphism to describe
the functioning of an aesthetic text, Eco is satisfied to call up the
image of a 'labyrinthine garden' with 'many different routes' available
in the 'criss-cross of its paths' (275). As I have noted, this is a charm-
ing image for the literary text and has much to recommend it as an
isomorphism for the literary act: the writer creates: the reader follows;
and the critic marks a mazy trail through a pleached garden of many
forking paths.[25] Surely that is sufficiently complex an image to describe the aesthetic act! But is it? In the logical description that accompanies this isomorphism of the garden, Eco notes three processes
which it is suggested are equivalent to the 'paths' of the Garden of
Aesthetics. These are inductions, abductions, and deductions. Inductions and deductions are familiar terms to logicians and describe logical operations which are safely two-dimensional; indeed, they are often decoded by Venn diagrams, just as algebraic statements may be
decoded by geometric diagrams. But *abduction* is a more amorphous
concept. Eco uses the term as it was coined by Charles Sanders Peirce,
who used it interchangeably with the term *hypothesis*. Eco quotes an
anecdote which Peirce used to describe the term:

I once landed at a seaport in a Turkish province; and, as I was walking up

---

25 In all of these the quincunx provides the dominant image. From the mystic hyper-
boles of Browne's *Garden of Cyrus*; through the elaboration of the image in such
works as Pope's 'Epistle IV' (to Richard Boyle, Earl of Burlington), where the three
qualities of the quincunx that are isomorphic to the 'garden of literature' are most
succinctly stated: 'He gains all points, who pleasingly confounds, / Surprises, varies,
and conceals the Bounds' (11. 55–6); to the 'nets and ladders' of Eco, the rookery
on Desolation Island in Poe's *Pym*, and the dominance of *phi* in Barth's *Chimera*;
the quincunx is omnipresent as the two-dimensional form stretching the mind
towards those other dimensions of art.

to the house which I was to visit, I met a man upon horseback, surrounded by four horsemen holding a canopy over his head. As the governor of the province was the only personage I could think of who would
be so greatly honored, I inferred that this was he.[26]

Eco analyses this passage at length and uses it to generate his most
mature theories of overcoding and undercoding, the foundations for
his conclusions about codes which lead to his theory of sign production (132–42). The emphasis he puts on it is certainly justified, considering how important it is to the theory developed in the second part
of the book. For abduction, unlike induction and deduction, has two
qualities which mark it especially for aesthetic and ideological use.
Again, Eco quotes Peirce, who this time goes to music for an analogy:

Hypothesis substitutes, for a complicated tangle of predicates attached to
one subject, a single conception. Now, there is a particular sensation
belonging to the act of thinking that each of these predicates inheres in
the subject. In hypothetic inference this complicated feeling so produced
is replaced by a single feeling of greater intensity, that belonging to the
act of thinking the hypothetic conclusion ... Thus the various sounds
made by the instruments of an orchestra strike upon the ear, and the
result is a peculiar musical emotion, quite distinct from the sounds themselves. (Peirce, 2: 643, quoted in Eco, 132)

If Peirce had not added the musical analogy, the reader might have
interpreted the first part of the description as simple metaphor, *discordia
concors*. But the analogy, indicates that abduction is at the deeper level
of *discrimination* between different kinds of interpretive responses, the
kind Robert the Ram makes uncomfortably, the kind we readers make
with delight. Remember, distinguishing between 'music' and 'noise' is
the hallmark of Learning II, since metaphor and metonymy inhabit
different dimensions. But, as Eco comments further, this 'very complex instance of aesthetic interpretation' in Peirce's analogy is a case
of logical overkill. The anecdote about the canopy and the Turkish
governor is much 'more transparent' because, as Eco writes, 'it would
be difficult to recognize as a sign the rule in the light of which the
hypothesis interprets the case, *unless the abduction once performed becomes*

26 Charles Sanders Peirce, *Collected Papers* (Cambridge: Harvard University Press
1931– 58), 2: 625; quoted in Eco, *Theory*, 131.

a customary social reflex' [italics Eco's]. In other words, with use, even metaphoric/metonymic discrimination can become habitual. For Eco, this is the seedbed for his garden of aesthetics:

> Peirce recognized that a comment of hypothetical tension arouses a feeling similar to that engendered by a piece of music. One can thus understand why and how the interpretative effort demanded by a work of art releases this kind of strong and complex feeling that aestheticians have named in various ways (pleasure, enjoyment, excitement, fulfillment, and so on), always believing that it was a form of 'intuition.' There is some degree of philosophical laziness in merely labelling as 'intuition' every experience that demands an excessively subtle analysis in order to be described. But common artistic experience also teaches us that art not only elicits feelings but also *produces further knowledge* [italics Eco's]. The moment that the game of intertwined interpretations gets under way, the text compels one to reconsider the usual codes and their possibilities. Every text threatens the codes but at the same time gives them strength; it reveals unsuspected possibilities in them, and thus changes the attitudes of the user toward them. (Eco, *Theory*, 274)

This is a brilliant insight into aesthetic theory, but, as we have seen, it is slightly too inclusive. Not 'every text' threatens the codes; only those that force the reader to discriminate between the metaphoric and the metonymic modes do. And art which 'produces further knowledge' is merely art serving also as data transmission, unless that 'further knowledge' is at the Learning II level of discrimination between the two modes. Otherwise it is merely furthering art as a '*customary social reflex*' (132). Thus Eco supports his image of the Garden of Aesthetics as a Bower of Bliss, with its many forking paths and its quincuncial patternings suggesting a two-dimensional escape from the data-processing cares of the day. There are no tiger traps in his garden and no peaks from which a 'higher' (more dimensional) view may be perceived. Art has *only* to do with aesthetics. And, by placing his consideration of aesthetics as his penultimate topic, Eco suggests that aesthetic creation is the second-most complex area of sign production.

This is, of course, a political statement. Eco separates aesthetic sign production from ideological sign production and considers them in this order to emphasize the differences between them, when actually, if we concentrate only on texts which require modal discrimination, we find more often than not that they are ideological – often fiercely ideological – at the same time they are aesthetically challenging. To return to Lodge's taxonomic insight based on Jakobson's dichotomy, the struggle between metonymic and metaphoric texts essentially defines the difference between the avant-garde and the orthodoxy. To separate ideology from aesthetics is not merely to espouse a kind of 'quietism,' as the proponents of ideology always argue; it is to deny the aesthetics of the finest art: that which forces the reader to metaphoric/metonymic discrimination. These matters are always bound together in complex multidimensional relationships.

Eco himself implies that in his consideration of ideological texts. Once again he returns to Peirce's concept of abduction as his starting point. 'Ideology,' he writes, 'is ... a message which starts with a factual description, and then tries to justify it theoretically, gradually being accepted by society through a process of overcoding.' Once we recognize that his 'factual description' is really an abduction under another name, we are led to the conclusion that its acceptance 'by society through ... overcoding' recalls his earlier comment that '*the abduction once performed becomes a customary social reflex*' (132; italics Eco's). He then argues this point with a complex abduction based on a necessarily three-dimensional model of a structural relationship between heating, pressure, and productivity (fig. 2.6), which makes a fine paradigm for a number of political situations and for which Eco himself suggests applications to 'culture, world vision, religion, "way of life," etc' (297; his Tables 58, 59, and 60, on 294–5).[27]

Eco does not conceal the fact that the question of validity of one or another of the modes displayed demands modal discrimination of exactly the metaphoric/metonymic type, but neither does he emphasize it. He comments only that the values in question are 'mutually exclusive *only if* taken as absolute ... whereas in fact they are all *fuzzy concepts*' (296; italics Eco's). Fuzzy concepts indeed they are, since only metaphoric/metonymic discrimination can reveal their ideological aptness and *therefore their aesthetic beauty*, or their mere 'noisiness.' Here is the centre of the critic's job of work; here is the true structuralist activity: discriminating between the metaphoric and the metonymic modes is not merely an aesthetic task, it may be ideological as well. Indeed, in many circumstances it is both at the same time, as we shall see in several of the following chapters.

I believe there are isomorphisms that can aid the critic in discovering the true relationship between aesthetic coding and ideological

---

27 This isomorphism with all its implications will be taken up again in detail in chapter 9 in the discussion of Thomas Pynchon's *The Crying of Lot 49*.

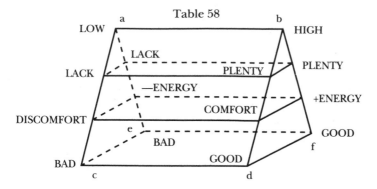

HEATING=PRODUCTIVITY (heating='abcd', productivity='abef')

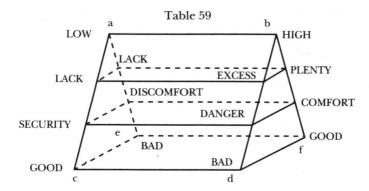

PRESSURE vs. HEATING (pressure='abcd', heating='abef')

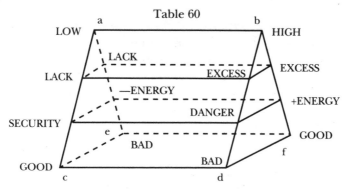

PRESSURE vs. PRODUCTIVITY (pressure= 'abcd', productivity='abef')

Fig. 2.6 Eco's 'three-dimensional' chart of ideological coding

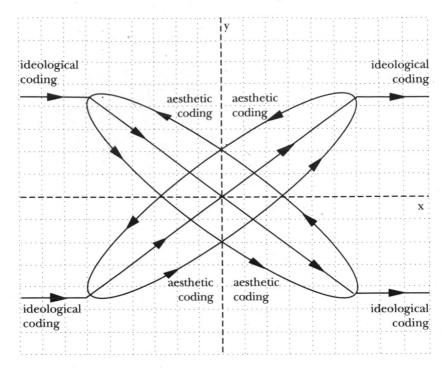

Fig. 2.7   Graphing aesthetic and ideological codes

coding in works (and there are many) in which both are present.
Aesthetic coding is always represented by isomorphisms involving closed
curves around the origin (often best expressed in polar coordinates)
because it is text-centred; ideological coding is always represented by
isomorphisms involving unbounded curves extending indefinitely (best
expressed in Cartesian coordinates) because it is action-centred. (To
return to our analogue of chapter 1, it builds or intends to build 'real
bicycles.') The two codes can correspond, but there will always be a
point at which, as figure 2.7 suggests, the locus of aesthetic meaning
swings back upon itself while the extensional meaning of the ideological coding goes on to build bicycles or change behaviour.

   Peirce unfortunately gives us only one term, *abduction*, to describe
the process in both cases; we need a second term to distinguish between aesthetic coding and ideological coding when confusion arises
as to whether they can be mapped on either polar or Cartesian coordinates. I would like to suggest the term *se*duction to describe the
latter. Working this distinction out in practice requires a real text to

examine. That will be done in chapters 6 and 9 in the discussion of *A Connecticut Yankee in King Arthur's Court* and *The Crying of Lot 49.*

And the case of Paul de Man? Fortunately for me, I am not competent to resolve that question any more than I have already sketched above. But I believe I have proven how the issue should be resolved. Is the Augustinian analogy metaphoric or metonymic? Is it to those orchard fruits or to the flirtation with Manichaeism? And, much more to the point, what is the nature of deconstruction, metaphoric or metonymic, in its own acceptance of the necessarily interlocking multidimensionality of aesthetics and ideology? And, perhaps most important of all, can any of these questions be answered on any discriminatory basis other than that of the metaphor of faith, the metonymy of reason?

Whatever conclusion you reach after pondering these variables, it will be isomorphic only to a figure in many more than three dimensions.

3

Towards an Integrated Theory of Style

Although there are bewildering numbers of theories about the cycles of literary styles, almost all fall into two broad categories. One is that styles in art represent natural or organic cycles because of the very nature of art, especially its dependence upon what has preceded it. The other category depends more strongly upon sociology. Theories of this type are all more or less Marxist, but are alike in finding changes in style only superstructural manifestations of social infrastructures. Northrop Frye's theories in his *Anatomy of Criticism* and David Lodge's, discussed in chapter 2, are prominent examples of the first type; Renato Poggioli's *The Theory of the Avant-Garde*, Peter Bürger's *Theory of the Avant-Garde*, and Matei Calinescu's *Faces of Modernity: Avant-Garde, Decadence, Kitsch* represent the second.[1] Theories in the first category tend to regard the cycles as universal and perpetual, while those of the second category concentrate on what we might as well call the 'Modern' in the largest sense. That is, they do not deny that earlier styles may exhibit cyclical qualities, but they presume that modern styles are distinctive, not just old wine in new bottles, that the avant-garde could only happen in a century with sensibilities unique to our times.

---

1 Northrop Frye, *Anatomy of Criticism: Four Essays* (New York: Athenaeum 1967); David Lodge, *The Modes of Modern Writing: Metaphor, Metonymy and the Typology of Modern Literature* (London: Arnold 1977); Renato Poggioli, *The Theory of the Avant-Garde*, trans. Gerald Fitzgerald (Cambridge: Harvard University Press 1968); Peter Bürger, *Theory of the Avant-Garde*, trans. Michael Shaw (Minneapolis: University of Minnesota Press 1984); Matei Calinescu, *Faces of Modernity: Avant-Garde, Decadence, Kitsch* (Bloomington: Indiana University Press 1977). I will cite page references to these works in parentheses in the text.

Once again, these circumstances seem to suggest that the problem is one of multiple variables. However, it is rarely seen that way. The usual response of critics to situations in which there is more than one controlling factor is to take sides and argue that my controlling factor is the correct one and yours is nonsense. But in this case there are very good arguments for *all* of the supporters of the sundry variables.

Probably the case for Frye is the strongest. Although *Anatomy of Criticism* (1957) is a generation-and-a-half old (in a period of literary criticism when last year's theories are about as popular as last year's hairstyles), its influence persists. Perhaps that is so because Frye, like Darwin and Freud and Jakobson, proposed a Great Truth, which, while it may need tinkering and modification and may promote annoyance because it breeds both disciples and heretics, stands unassailable after considerable testing by time. Critics have chipped away at the periphery of Frye's cyclical theories of modes, symbols, myths, and genres, but none has disturbed the fourfold relationship that stands at their core. The inadequacies of Frye's theories are personal and human; the parts which will stand forever are structuralist and systematic. To discover that 'literature is not a piled aggregate of "works," but an order of words' (17) is to begin the study of a *system* of literature, much as Euclid began the study of a system of forms. Indeed, the final 'tentative conclusion' of the *Anatomy* is to recall the analogy 'several times hinted at' in the text between literature and mathematics (350; see 350–4 and 364n).

The analogy is fruitful. Euclid is never wrong; he is only limited by the *contexts* in which he organizes his systems. He only had three dimensions to work with. Frye is never wrong; but he is limited by his subjective vision. Euclid failed to see the possibilities implicit in the parallel postulate for other geometries besides his; Frye failed to see the possibilities for multidimensionalities and recursive systems in art. Thus he rejects out of hand the concept of art for art's sake, which he. describes as 'a retreat from criticism which ends in an impoverishment of civilized life itself' (4). From that beginning, it is inevitable that he arrive at 'transcendental signifieds' at the core of art. Here is a representative example of his thinking:

Knowing that *The Two Gentlemen of Verona* is an early Shakespeare comedy and *The Winter's Tale* a late one, the student would expect the later play to be more subtle and complex [1]; he might not expect it to be more archaic and primitive, more suggestive of ancient myths and rituals [2]. The later play is also more popular, though not popular of course in the sense of giving a lower-middle class audience what it thinks it wants [3]. As a result of expressing the inner forms of drama with increasing force and intensity, Shakespeare arrived in his last period at the bedrock of drama [4], the romantic spectacle out of which all the more specialized forms of drama, such as tragedy and social comedy, have come, and to which they recurrently return. In the greatest moments of Dante and Shakespeare, in, say *The Tempest* or the climax of the *Purgatorio*, we have a feeling of converging significance, the feeling that here we are close to seeing what our whole literary experience has been about, the feeling that we have moved into the still center of the order of words [5]. Criticism as knowledge, the criticism which is compelled to keep on talking about the subject, recognizes the fact that there *is* a center of the order of words.

Unless there is such a center, there is nothing to prevent the analogies supplied by convention and genre from being an endless series of free associations, perhaps suggestive, perhaps even tantalizing, but never creating a real structure. The study of archetypes is the study of literary symbols as parts of a whole. If there are such things as archetypes at all, then, we have to take yet another step, and conceive the possibility of a self-contained literary universe. Either archetypal criticism is a will-o'-the-wisp, an endless labyrinth without an outlet, or we have to assume that literature is a total form, and not simply the name given to the aggregate of existing literary works. We spoke before of the mythical view of literature as leading to the conception of an order of nature as a whole being imitated by a corresponding order of words. (117–18; index numbers in square brackets added)

There is a remarkable combination of unsophisticated assumptions and brilliant insights in this passage. Frye begins with what we would now call an 'agist' assumption: early Shakespeare cannot be as 'subtle and complex' as late [1]. But his own insights in the *Anatomy* about the importance of myth make him qualify such a simple chronological assumption with perceptions about the 'archaic and the primitive' [2]. This is followed by a particularly painful elitist dig at middle-class values [3] and then another chronological 'agism' which rather discounts *Hamlet* and *Lear* [4]. Then follows the ultimate elitist value judgment, which we might as well call (on the analogy of sexism, racism, and elitism) *geometrism*: that there is a centre and that it is more important than the periphery [5]. The next paragraph spells out the results of this ill-judged conclusion. If it were true that without a centre there can be no structure, then archetypal criticism is indeed 'an endless labyrinth without an outlet.'[2] Euclid would agree. But imagine a literary 'geometry' like the post-Euclidean one that modern mathematicians now almost casually program into their computers; there is no limit of dimensionality, no hierarchical centre and periphery, no 'transcendental signified.' Thus Frye's imaginative awareness of 'the possibility of a self-contained literary universe' is undermined by his inability to see how extensive that universe is. As Michelson and Morley's discovery of the invariability of the speed of light broke down the primacy of Euclidean geometry in a Newtonian universe, so the recursiveness of postmodernism breaks down the Arnoldian assumptions of Frye's theory.

Underneath the shifting dunes of those assumptions, however, lies the Great Truth of the structural relationship among modes, symbols, myths, and genres.[3] When Frye discovered these relationships in 1957, he did so in the context of the New Criticism. In that limited context there is little or no need to examine the deep structures of literary works. In effect, while Frye despised the New Critics, his theory was co-opted by them; the study of myth and archetype was simply added to the rhetorical study that was the staple of New Critical analysis. In other words, the main effect of the *Anatomy* on the criticism of its time was to add myths and archetypes to the list of items, mostly rhetorical, that the critic would test a text for in hopes of finding subtleties and ambiguities which could then be trumpeted (muted, of course) to the greater glory of the discoverer. I know that is true because I was a graduate student when the book appeared and, along with my colleagues and peers, used it in just that mechanical way.

---

2 It is interesting that Frye here uses the same image of the 'rhizome maze' that is so important for Eco in *The Name of the Rose*, although, of course, it is used here to decry it. See below, note 9.

3 Just how much credit he deserves is sometimes disputed and indeed is made more uncertain, I believe, because of his own descriptions of what he intended. Frye himself conceded that he was influenced by Spengler, and the idea of the analogy of the seasons and its pertinence to human experience has long been a commonplace. Emerson, in *Nature*: 'The motion of the earth round its axis and round the sun makes the day and the year. These are certain amounts of brute light and heat. But is there no intent of an analogy between man's life and the seasons?' It is just that matter of *intent* that seems to separate Frye from Spengler and Emerson and the others. Frye builds his structures of modes without the excess baggage of a deterministic fate driving the cycles. But although he never specifically states that it is the human tendency to discover seasonal cycles in serial events, his theories proceed on that principle.

When viewed structurally, however, Frye's fourfold overlay discovery of the relationship between modes, symbols, myths, and genres takes on the kind of significance that Jakobson's insight into aphasia had. Just as the brain may have internal structures which then create linguistic patterns, metaphor and metonymy, different in kind, so a universally observed phenomenon like the seasons may virtually force the creation of archetypes, genres, modes, and myths in series, like patterns from a template. Just as we can only observe two-part relationships as a function of contiguity or similarity, so we are most likely to observe and therefore create *serial* relationships in the pattern the seasons force upon our perception. The major difference between the two cases is that confusion arises between metaphor and metonymy because we sometimes don't know which system is operating; but confusion arises among the serial states of mode, symbol, myth, and genre because each state yields to the next as a qualitative change pursuant upon many quantitative changes. In other words, each state, though demonstrably different from each other state in each series, has a *cusp* at either end. And, as we saw was the case in problems of oscillation between dominance of metaphor and metonymy, the texts arising from these cusps are often the most interesting and challenging of the period.

Moreover, these two discoveries – Jakobson/Lodge's that the cleavage between metaphor and metonymy represents a deep structural cleavage between parts of the brain (or at least the mind), and that this cleavage dominates the artist's choice of style; Frye's that the continual exposure to the process of the seasons influences all serial choices of genre, mode, symbol and myth – must necessarily interact. The simplest isomorphism for each is a wave motion: for Lodge/Jakobson's relationship, a simple sine wave (fig. 3.1) showing either metaphor or metonymy dominant at the expense of the other of the pair;[4] for Frye's relationship, another sine wave of equal period, with alternate maximums and minimums over two wavelengths corresponding to the seasons from spring to winter (fig. 3.2).

The question is how do these two relationships interact? If they are superimposed in phase (at the corresponding points in their periodic

---

4 As we saw in chapter 2, this is not an adequate representation since the true relationship between metaphor and metonymy is more than two-dimensional. However, this oversimplification is functional for our present purposes. Later we will examine both this isomorphism and the one for Frye's seasonal metaphor in their full dimensionality.

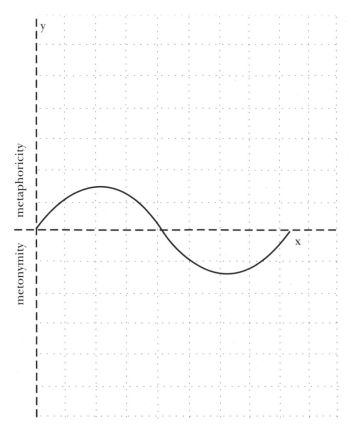

Fig. 3.1   Metaphor/metonymy sine wave – 2/4 time

variation), then the result will be simply another sine wave of the same
period, but greater amplitude, much as a 2/4 rhythm over a 4/4 will
be indistinguishable to all but the most critical musical ear. Is it possible that the two cycles could get out of phase somehow, and what
would be the result if they should? The immediate response to such a
question is negative, since both the tendency to observe serial change
on the analogy of the seasons and to contrast similarity with contiguity
would seem to be as invariable as they are 'natural' and 'structural.'
But are there any influences on style which go 'against nature' –

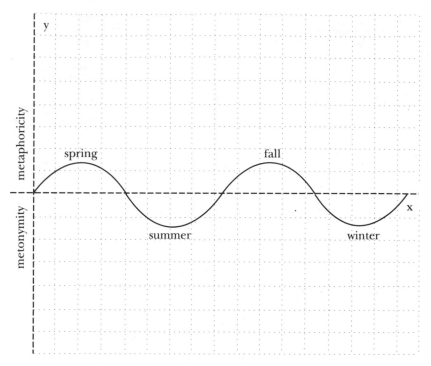

Fig. 3.2   Seasonal/modal/metaphor/metonymy sine wave – 4/4 time

which treat art *à rebours*,[5] as it were? To phrase the question that way is to go halfway to another answer, for it is the recurrence of the decadent and its association with the avant-garde that provides the most striking answer to that problem of phase. Here we must turn to the other theories of stylistic change and move from the stately periodicity of natural rhythms to the jazzier syncopations of the Marxist beat.

Just as Frye found the idea of art for art's sake 'is a retreat from criticism which ends in an impoverishment of civilized life itself,' so the Marxist critics, beginning with Marx himself, treat the phenomenon as a baleful and negative reflection of culture. But whereas Frye sees decadence as an absolute destroyer of art, Marxist critics see it as a symptom of the disorientation of the artist from his society. Plekhanov, one of the earliest and best of these critics, using the examples of Pushkin, Gautier, and the Parnassians, concludes that '*the tendency of*

---

5 The many possible translations into English of the title of Joris-Karl Huysmans's *A Rebours* reflect the extraordinary concatenation of the natural, material, structural, and aesthetic at the moment when an artist determines to 'go against nature,' or

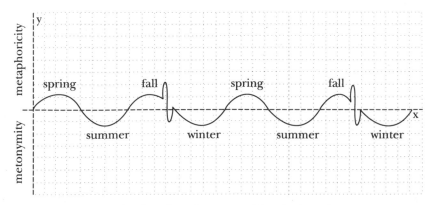

Fig. 3.3   The 'burp' on the seasonal/modal/etc. sine wave

artists and those concerned with art to adopt an attitude of art for art's sake arises when a hopeless contradiction exists between them and their social environment.[6] Moreover, he continues with the example of David and his school and the publication of *Le Salut Public* after the events of 1848 to arrive at the converse of his first conclusion: this time, that the '*utilitarian concept of art ... as a judgment on the phenomena of life and a readiness to participate in social struggles*' develops when the artist and his culture are not in discord (48; italics in original). In other words, Plekhanov, like Frye, sees a concordance between art and society when that society is just and 'natural,' but he also allows for a counter-wave, against the grain, as it were, when nature and culture are out of phase.

If we plot this counter-wave into our integrated sine waves of the natural seasonal cycle and the reciprocal domination of metaphor and metonymy,[7] it produces a little hiccup at the cusp of the fourth beat of Frye's period (fig. 3.3): the genre of parody, the mode of what we would now call the postmodern (but what Shklovsky called the 'strange'), the symbol as monad, the myth as Phoenix. That little hiccup has given birth to an extraordinary amount of theorizing because it changes shape as it is seen from different perspectives.

'against the grain,' to 'rub things the wrong way,' to 'kick against the pricks.' Some very deeply held notions are violated by the very idea of the phrase.

6 George V. Plekhanov, *Art and Society* (New York: Critics' Group 1937), 48 (italics in original)

7 Here the author cries 'help' to those of his readers who are aware of the physical laws governing the creation of waves from forces out of phase with each other. The result would *not* be as simple as the hiccup described in figure 3.3. Instead it would

Renato Poggioli was the first to deal with the problem using the ideas of Marx as well as other critical theorists of the left ranging from Ortega y Gasset to Georg Lukács. He recognizes that the avant-garde is really a *Kunstwollen* and traces it back to the eighteenth century. He defines it as consisting of four somewhat redundant tendencies: activism, antagonism, agonism, and nihilism, with the last two being 'transcendental' manifestations of the first two (26). All of these forms are produced by the alienation of the artist from his society, but because there are two variables – artist/society – the four-part division results, depending upon whether *internal* or *external* forces are emphasized as the more important causes. Among the critics who have followed Poggioli, the problem seems to have resolved itself into a consideration of which of these two (or four) forces are either dominant or more likely to become artistically productive. Bürger's emphasis is on the amount of alienation and the resultant 'strangeness' as a dominant aesthetic. His conclusion is the despairing one that shock and schlock must inevitably be the end of such a progression (18). Calinescu is more hopeful, as he emphasizes, from his title on, the variability of the avant-garde. But one tends to respond to his 'three faces' by adding others. I, for one, would want to add *camp*, *schlock*, and *postmodernism* to his avant-garde, decadence, and kitsch; and then, of course, continue with others – dada, surrealism, expressionism, *blau reiter* – until the *reductio ad absurdum* had been reached.

The reality of the matter is that the hiccup, the burp, at the fourth beat of the smooth oscillation between nature and culture, metaphor and metonymy, high and low mimetic, and all the other oppositions one might adduce, is the shock of the approach to what we called in the last chapter Learning ii. As orthodoxy hardens over the period of any one swing of the sine wave and the unorthodox artist correspondingly becomes more and more alienated, her awareness of the complex relationship between alternative forms, genres, and modes pushes her towards the uncomfortable choice of creation at the level of the confusion of these forms. Let me emphasize again that the choice is *un*comfortable. Everyone suffers like Robert the Ram when the experience of art challenges the complacent acceptance of the domination of one of these many forms over the other. Nevertheless, it is only this challenge to the thinking about the *structure* of art that is truly creative at the level of Learning ii.

---

more resemble a jump-rope doing double-dutch; please tolerate some artistic license at this point. Anyway, as I noted in note 4, this part of the argument is only *artificially* in two dimensions.

Among critical theorists only Roland Barthes and Umberto Eco seem to have fully realized this difference. Naturally, one finds the evidence of their awareness in their formally most postmodernist/ deconstructive works: for Barthes in *The Pleasure of the Text* and for Eco in *The Name of the Rose*.[8] Both of these works begin with a deconstruction of formal critical apparatus and are therefore rather hard to incorporate in a more orderly and straightforward work like this one.

The Pleasure of the Text is built upon the extended metaphor of the act of literature as the act of sex. With that isomorphism underlying his text, Barthes may then explore the nature of the literary act apparently randomly (the text consists of segments arranged alphabetically), and with assurance that his reader will be stretched to the equivalent of Learning II as she tries to discriminate between the metaphoric mode of literature as sex and the metonymic mode of literary criticism. Thus whenever Barthes seems most rational and Appolonian in his discourse, the reader must be equally aware of the passionate and Dionysian implications and must integrate *both* modes into the act of reading-*qua*-sex. This technique effectively destroys any possibility of complete analysis of the work as a data-producing text. *The Name of the Rose* somewhat less aggressively creates an equivalent effect. Read as an *exemplum* of an 'artefact' which creates its own metaphor, it invites the reader to interpret it as it gradually recedes into metaphoricity before him.

The action of *The Name of the Rose* takes place at a moment of historical and novelistic crisis: Christendom is divided between Rome and Avignon, between *auctoritas* and *libertas*; and a series of unexplained deaths has occurred at the abbey where a meeting of representatives of the two ecclesiastical parties is to take place. William of Baskerville attempts to decode both issues hermeneutically, thereby to resolve them. He is partially successful, partially defeated, but his 'Watson,' Adso of Melk, in his ignorance asks the implied question that itself contains the implied (and most unsatisfactory) answer. The two of them are disputing about what has happened as the abbey is burning down before them. William speaks first, confessing his failure:

---

8 Roland Barthes, *The Pleasure of the Text*, trans. Richard Miller (New York: Hill and Wang 1975); Umberto Eco, *The Name of the Rose*, trans. William Weaver (New York: Warner Books 1983). We are fortunate that in the case of Eco we have a more traditional critical expression of the point in the essay he wrote while wearing his non-postmodernist hat, *Reflections on 'The Name of the Rose,'* trans. William Weaver (London: Secker and Warburg 1985). I will cite page references to these works in parentheses in the text.

'Where is all my wisdom, then? I behaved stubbornly, pursuing a sem-
blance of order, when I should have known well that there is no order in
the universe.'

[Adso:] 'But in imagining an erroneous order you still found something ...'

... 'The order that our mind imagines is like a net or like a ladder,
built to attain something. But afterward you must throw the ladder away,
because you discover that, even if it was useful, it was meaningless ... The
only truths that are useful are instruments to be thrown away.'

'You have no reason to reproach yourself: you did your best.'

'A human best, which is very little. It's hard to accept the idea that
there cannot be an order in the universe because it would offend the
free will of God and his omnipotence. So the freedom of God is our
condemnation, or at least the condemnation of our pride.'

I dared, for the first and last time in my life, to express a theological
conclusion: 'But how can a necessary being exist totally polluted with the
possible? What difference is there, then, between God and primigenial
chaos? Isn't affirming God's absolute omnipotence and His absolute freedom with regard to His own choices tantamount to demonstrating that
God does not exist?'

William looked at me without betraying any feeling in his features, and
he said, 'How could a learned man go on communicating his learning if
he answered yes to your question?'

I did not understand the meaning of his words. (599–600)

This wonderful passage has an extraordinary effect upon the reader.
To this point he has been dividing his time as a novelistic reader,
interested in the solving of the murders; as a sociological reader,
looking for a solution to the dispute between the parties of the church
(through the power of empathy, he hopes for the defeat of Bernard
Gui, the triumph of William); as a historical reader, knowing that the
schism of Avignon is to be bridged, confidently attending the resolution of that matter; and as a semiotic reader, delighting in the sophisticated play with signs. Suddenly the reader discovers that all these
modes are but *nets* or *ladders*, useful truths, but ones which must be
'thrown away.' Nets and ladders are the quincuncial stuff of the garden of literature; they are the *hypotheses* or *abductions* (Peirce's terms)
which, as we saw in chapter 2, are the essentials for moving from the
three-dimensional world of metonymy or metaphor to the hyperdimensionality of Learning II. Adso's expression of a 'theological con-

clusion,' even couched as a question, brings William to the threshold of the kind of painful awareness that is the human equivalent of the suffering of Robert the Ram – and, in the time of this novel, unspeakable heresy.

The discourse is interrupted at this moment when a 'section of the dormitory roof collapsed with a huge din, blowing a cloud of sparks into the sky. Some of the sheep and goats wandering through the grounds went past us, bleating horribly [Robert the Ram among them?]. A group of servants also went by us, shouting, nearly knocking us down.' This almost too neat demonstration of the pathetic fallacy as catastrophe theory then leads William to cry out in the last words of the principal action of the novel, 'There is too much confusion here ... Non in commotione, non in commotione, Dominus' (609). These bleating words are as much the *conclusion* of the novel as the ones Eco chose to emphasize by alluding to them in his title: 'stat rosa pristina nomine, nomina nuda tenemus' (611).

In *Reflections on 'The Name of the Rose'* Eco chose to 'explain' his choice of title by giving its provenance (a poem by Bernard of Morlay) and citing Abelard's use of the hexameter 'to demonstrate how language can speak of both the nonexistent and the destroyed' (1). He immediately undercut those data by remarking that a *narrator* 'should not supply interpretations of his work' and that a novel 'is a machine for generating interpretations' (1–2). But some interpretations are more acceptable than others, so that the *author* (who Eco also says should die once he has finished writing, 'so as not to trouble the path of the text' [7]) chose to emphasize one *conclusion* over the other. The second conclusion, by Adso, not William, and many years later, is reflective and wise; William's is the cry of a laboratory animal in the harness. Eco preferred Adso's conclusion for the title because 'the rose is a symbolic figure so rich in meaning that by now it hardly has any meaning left' and 'a title must muddle the reader's ideas, not regiment them' (3).

Adso's conclusions about the events of the novel contradict the conclusions drawn by both Adso and William at the fire. The 'muddling' of the reader's ideas in this case is to retreat from the heretical and nihilistic conclusions William and Adso draw. William has employed his 'nets and ladders' for ordinary hermeneutic purposes, to solve the problem of a labyrinth; however, as Eco explains his use of that metaphor, 'the labyrinth of my library is still a mannerist labyrinth, but the world in which William realizes he is living already has a rhizome structure: that is, it can be structured but is never structured definitively' (57–8).[9] Thus the 'novel' metafictionally describes the manner by which fiction, as it approaches Learning II, forces the reader into those painful challenges to *authority*, divine or authorial, that those nets and ladders have been used to assault.

Roland Barthes's attack upon 'authority' is more paradoxical, risqué, and dependent upon double entendre than Eco's. Scattered throughout *The Pleasure of the Text* and peeping through the forests of discourse as paradox and equivocation, the 'argument,' if argument it can be considered, appears perhaps most coherently in two passages alphabetized as 'Modern' (39–44) and 'Recuperation' (54–5). The texts are, to say the least, far from self-explanatory; so I shall examine them in some detail, keeping always in mind that the need to 'muddle' the reader is no less important to Barthes than it is to Eco.

Barthes begins his consideration of the Modern with a semiotic truism, that his language is 'not of [his] time; it is prey, by nature, to ideological suspicion' (39–40). Our language is of course the sum of all language that has preceded it; and, as such, is subject to the corruption of ideologies of all sorts. So Barthes struggles against this truth and writes 'because [he does] not want the words [he finds]' even though he admits that the language of Zola, Proust, Verne, and others is the language of his 'pleasure.' But, in the central opposition of *The Pleasure of the Text*, unfortunately confused in translation, 'pleasure' is to be distinguished from 'bliss,' and his bliss, he writes, 'may come only with the *absolutely new*, for only the new disturbs (weakens) consciousness (easy? not at all: nine times out of ten, the new is only the stereotype of novelty)' (40).

If we think of 'pleasure' as domestic or monogamous lovemaking, this passage shows that Barthes does not intend 'bliss' to represent mere infidelity or sexual variation as an alternative. Rather, that one time out of ten that disturbs (or 'weakens' consciousness – notice that ambivalence) is of a new order of significance, a qualitative rather

---

9 By that he means that the library maze is solvable by a trial-and-error process for which one needs an 'Ariadne's thread' to avoid getting lost. Ariadne's thread is a perfect sign for metonymic reasoning: trial and error aided by the contiguity of memory. But William's view of the world as a rhizome structure implicitly compares the reasoning of Learning I with the painful awareness of Learning II. The rhizome structure is fundamentally unknowable because it is 'never structured definitively.' Therefore metonymy and hermeneutic produce 'wrong' readings, and, as Eco remarks, the most ingenuous readings are the most 'structural' (*Reflections*, 58). Here and elsewhere Eco cites Gilles Deleuze and Alan Guattari, *On the Line*, trans.

than quantitative change. The 'stereotype of novelty' is the ordinary oscillation of mode or style between metaphor and metonymy or, serially, using Frye's patterning, the romantic, tragic, comic, or ironic. The New that brings bliss, that 'disturbs/weakens consciousness,' challenges those very patterns.

Barthes continues to explain this relationship in a passage that, allowing for the inevitability of paradox in this text, is unusually transparent. It is also directly relevant to the problem of the avant-garde and bears direct quotation in full:

> The New is not a fashion, it is a value, the basis of all criticism: our evaluation of the world no longer depends, at least not directly, as in Nietzsche, on the opposition between *noble* and *base*, but on that between Old and New (the erotics of the New began in the eighteenth century: a long transformational process). There is only one way left to escape the alienation of present-day society: *to retreat ahead of it*: every old language is immediately compromised, and every language becomes old once it is repeated. Now encratic language (the language produced and spread under the protection of power) is statutorily a language of repetition; all official institutions of languages are repeating machines: school, sports, advertising, popular songs, news, all continually repeat the same structure, the same meaning, often the same words: the stereotype is a political fact, the major figure of ideology. Confronting it, the New is bliss (Freud: 'In the adult, novelty always constitutes the condition for orgasm'). Whence the present configuration of forces: on the one hand, a mass banalization (linked to the repetition of language) – a banalization outside bliss but not necessarily outside pleasure – and on the other, a (marginal, eccentric) impulse toward the New – a desperate impulse that can reach the point of destroying discourse: an attempt to reproduce in historical terms the bliss repressed beneath the stereotype.
>
> The opposition (the knife of value) is not necessarily between consecrated, named contraries (materialism and idealism, revolution and reform, etc.); but it is *always and throughout* between the *exception and the rule*. For example, at certain moments it is possible to support the *exception* of the Mystics. Anything, rather than the rule (generality, stereotype, ideolect: the consistent language). (40–1; italics in the original)

John Johnstone (New York: Semiotext[e] 1983) for the rhizome metaphor. See also Eco's *Semiotics and the Philosophy of Language* (Bloomington: Indiana University Press 1984), 26.

That seems simple enough; mass banality is so smothering and re-
pressive that any and all exceptions to it are justified. And, even though
Barthes allows the contradiction in the very next paragraph (that repetitions like 'obsessive rhythms, incantatory music, litanies, rites and
Buddhist nembutsu, etc' also create the desirable 'zero of the signified' [41]), he concludes this section with the very positive observation that 'the word can be erotic on two opposing conditions, both
excessive: if it is extravagantly repeated, or on the contrary if it is
unexpected, succulent in its newness' (42). That is to say that the
'newness' of the word must not be the newness of the stereotype of
novelty but *structurally* new. As Barthes summarizes the case, 'Nausea
occurs whenever the liaison of two important words *follows of itself*.
And when something follows of itself, I abandon it; that is bliss' (43;
italics his).

It is fallacious to assume that observations that follow other observations in *The Pleasure of the Text* need be consistent with each other, but
it is nevertheless true that Barthes's observations under 'Recuperation' extend the values of the 'Modern' segment. 'Recuperation' seems
at first to be deliberately outrageous, even facetious. 'Art seems compromised, historically, socially,' Barthes begins. 'Whence the effort on
the part of the artist himself to destroy it.' That seems a far cry from
the writer who took pleasure, if not bliss, from the language of such
predecessors as Zola, Proust, and Verne. Then Barthes describes the
artist's efforts to destroy art as consisting of changing his 'signifier':
the writer to become a painter, the painter to become a cinema critic,
etc.; or the writer can become a scientist or, finally, 'purely and simply
scuttle himself, stop writing, change trades, change desires' (54). Such
advice goes beyond dada. But, as Barthes quickly explains, the strategy
cannot work. The self-destructive machine either 'becomes imperti-
nent, or else it quickly exposes itself to recuperation (the avant-garde
is that restive language which is going to be recuperated)' (54). The
avant-gardist lashes out against, 'destroys,' the *doxa*, but in so doing
advances it. As Barthes explains, 'both sides of the paradigm [of convention and art] are glued together in an ultimately complicitous
fashion: there is a structural agreement between the contesting and
the contested forms' (55). In other words, the frustrated avant-gardist
finds himself at Learning II, advancing the larger cause of art while
attempting to destroy the old forms. To combine Eco's image with
Barthes's, the old 'nets and ladders' refuse to be discarded in the
artist's attempt to 'retreat ahead of' his alienation with contemporary
society; instead, they bind him to the system he is rejecting because, as

Barthes explains, 'destruction of discourse is not a dialectic term *but a semantic term* [italics his] ... within the great semiological "versus" myth' (54) that meaning derives from difference. Meaning does derive from difference, at Learning I; but both Robert the Ram (painfully) and the avant-gardist (to her discomfort, often, but to the advantage of art) discover that even the *destruction* of meaning evolves new meaning.

Now, keeping these observations in mind, let us return to the periodic cycle of styles as posited by Frye and Jakobson/Lodge. The artist who finds himself at the conclusion of a wave on the contiguity/metonymy side of a series (spring to summer, fall to winter // romantic to tragic, comic to ironic) will tend to see his art through 'utilitarian concepts,' to quote Plekhanov, because he is in tune with his culture and is '[ready] to participate in [its] social struggles.' Although he wants to *stretch* his art and his audience, even to the point of changing his mode, he believes in the utilitarian value of art to the point that he wants more to communicate than he wants to shock. Thus the romantic mode becomes the tragic as the artist turns a *mythos* towards higher seriousness, and the comic generates the ironic when the ridicule of folly serves a community purpose. Such modal change is never without critical contentiousness; all change is shocking to some extent. But because the basic structural mode is unchanged, the longer 'leap' of the artist, the higher intensity of the art, does not 'break the circuit' of semiosis: sender – message – receiver.

When the evolution is on the other side of the wave, ending the similarity/metaphor mode of the mind (moving from summer to fall, winter to spring // tragic to comic, ironic to romantic in Frye's modal progression), the results may be strikingly different. If the artist is ready 'to participate in social struggles' and retains a 'utilitarian concept of art,' he will curtail his desire to shock to the point that his writing remains within the limits of intelligibility for his culture. But if he is not, if he is completely at odds with his society for whatever reasons, then, to quote Plekhanov again, 'a hopeless contradiction exists between [artists and those concerned with art] and their social environment.' Chained to the conventions of the *doxa*, the artist kicks painfully at those chains and breaks the circuit of semiosis. The artist is exiled from her audience, who no longer want to hear or understand her. The mode of tragedy turns to black comedy as the artist rejects the assumptions about human dignity necessary for the tragic mode. Characters with no more control over their fate than Robert the Ram bleat *non in commotione*, while their authors seek to 'muddle' their messages. Domestic sexuality in the missionary position yields to whips and chains, the novelty of de Sade.[10] The world as we know it, with art docilely pulling society's dog cart through the muck of progress, is in total upheaval, and the screams are heard everywhere until it gets back to normal. We are approaching Learning II.

This is the world of the late Latin writing des Esseintes was so fond of in *A Rebours*; the world of Shakespeare's dark comedies, of Jacobean tragedy, of the *décadence* at the end of the nineteenth century, of the black comedy of the 1950s and the schools of 'fabulism' and 'metafiction' that evolved from it, now subsumed under the general description of the 'postmodern.' Certainly it is not a phenomenon unique to our time; nor is it even limited, as Barthes, Eco, and Poggioli all stipulate, to art since the eighteenth century. Rather, it is a condition that will arise quite naturally when the gap between the artist's awareness and that of his audience has grown to the point that the artist is no longer concerned with the need to be understood. It has its parallels in other human concerns, as one might imagine. In theology it results in mysticism in certain circumstances, belief in sorcery in others (as Michelet has explored in *La Sorcière*). In politics it gives birth to revolutions. But our concern is with art, and it is perhaps most shocking when it occurs in art just because of the universality of the semiotic circuit of art: sender – message – receiver. We are so used to experiencing our artists' either supporting or condemning our *doxa* that we are inordinately shocked when they no longer seem to give a damn even to communicate.

What the artist is doing in these circumstances is completely incomprehensible as long as our abduction of it is based on two- or three-dimensional forms. Our earlier isomorphisms of the sine wave of the alternating dominance of metonymy and metaphor, the integrated sine waves of Frye and Lodge, and the hiccupping integrated sine waves of Frye, Lodge, and Plekhanov break down because they lack the full dimensionality of the move from Learning I to Learning II. If we think of decadence, the avant-garde, and postmodernism as merely a burp in the orderly progress of society and art, we do not do justice to them. They are much more than that. They are true hyperdimensional *catastrophes*. They are breakdowns in the system. When we

---

10 David Lodge in *The Modes of Modern Writing* explores this aspect of modality particularly well, using three variations on the theme of death and sexuality; see 9–41 and appendices A, B, and C.

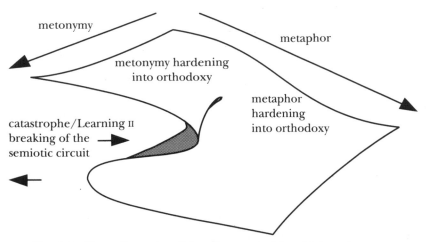

metonymy

metaphor

metonymy hardening
into orthodoxy

metaphor
hardening
into orthodoxy

catastrophe/Learning II
breaking of the
semiotic circuit

Fig. 3.4   Hyperdimensionalizing the seasonal/modal/etc. sine wave

try to rationalize them, treat them as ordinary artistic modes in two or
three dimensions, we only misread them and frustrate ourselves. However, when we accept their hyperdimensionality, we may come to recognize that their intent is *not* merely to add to orthodox thinking
about metonymy or metaphor, realism or tragedy, monad or archetype, but to proceed meaningfully through contraries and paradoxes
and meaninglessness to awareness of the relationship of *forms*. This
activity can be described on conventional hyperdimensional catastrophe theory graphs as in figure 3.4.

I believe this theory of modality may be usefully applied to all of the
works and writers mentioned above, and to several others as well.
Blake immediately comes to mind, as do Kafka and Bulgakov. The
image of nets and ladders recalls the quincunxes of Sir Thomas
Browne's *Garden of Cyrus*, even the descriptions of landscape architec-
ture in Pope, and their aptness to the case of his own poetry. In these
cases and others we find the same hallmarks: a disassociation from the
orthodoxy of the period almost to the extent of *exile*; metalinguistic
play that – to quote Lodge again on Gertrude Stein and Samuel Beckett
– 'aspires to the condition of aphasia' (*Modes*, 79); an effect upon the
supposed audience no less than catastrophic; yet, once understood for
what it is, an art which contributes meaningfully to the evolution of
forms of art – that is, art at the level of Learning II. When these circumstances pertain, it is critically useless to expect that normal exegesis
will do justice to any pertinent texts. The test of the theory ought to
be that finding hyperdimensional isomorphisms for such texts will

generate new and better readings – readings which will somehow
suggest an evolution of forms.[11] Moreover, this kind of criticism should
diminish the discomfort of the audience and re-establish the full
semiotic circuit, on a new basis of understanding, now dimensionally
complete.

One entire class of literature stands ready for this kind of analysis,
self-defined as *metafiction*. In the last three chapters of this book I will
attempt to demonstrate how the application of hyperdimensional isomorphisms can lead to new readings of three works, Nabokov's *Pale
Fire*, Barth's *Chimera*, and Pynchon's *The Crying of Lot 49*. These works
are typical of modern metafictions and illustrate the range of such
fictions in terms of chronology and style. They also illustrate the relationship, discussed in chapter 2, of aesthetic and ideological coding,
which is, of course, pertinent to the problem of succession of aesthetic
modes as well. Moreover, I believe that each of these texts drops hints
that the authors had specific hyperdimensional metaphors in mind
when they were being composed. If the technique works on these
texts, it follows that it should work on all texts which are generally
classed as 'metafictions.'

But the real test of this theory is its application to works which have
not been identified as metafictions and which have been misread or
misunderstood as a result. In the three chapters that follow I will
examine three such works from nineteenth-century American literature: Poe's *The Narrative of Arthur Gordon Pym*, Melville's *The Confidence-
Man*, and Twain's *A Connecticut Yankee in King Arthur's Court*. All three
of these works have been or are currently problematic texts with no
critical consensus concerning their interpretation or even their literary value. I will attempt to show in each case that the work proceeds
from 'discord ... between the artist and his social environment' at
different levels of intensity and that the response of each of the three
writers is indeed to move from the normal dimensionality of fiction to
a hyperdimensionality of *forms*. Furthermore, I hope to show that the
degree of hyperdimensionality corresponds to the degree of demonstra-
ble 'discord' between the three writers and their contemporary socie-
ties and is reflected in the degree of difficulty in making the semiotic
connection.

---

11 This means, of course, that specific applications will create new theory as well.

PART TWO

Three Nineteenth-Century Texts

4

Arthur Gordon Pym in
Five Barthesian Dimensions

Edgar Allan Poe is the ideal candidate for a writer who is prone to adopt an attitude of 'art for art's sake' because there is 'a hopeless contradiction ... between [him] and [his] social environment' (Plekhanov, 48). Always at odds with the crude and bourgeois artistic environment he found everywhere around him in America, Poe after his death became almost mythic in stature as a *poète maudit* among his French and decadent admirers.[1] And, among Poe's works, none is better suited than *The Narrative of Arthur Gordon Pym* as a test case of a work that has been misread for years because it is hyperdimensional in structure and is therefore painful to read when its true dimensionality is not recognized.[2] Moreover, Poe demonstrated equal capacities to

---

1 Admiring references to Poe among French writers from Baudelaire to Valéry and Gide are so common they hardly need to be cited, but perhaps special mention should be made of his importance to that arch-decadent, des Esseintes, in *A Rebours*. For contrast, see the many references to Poe in the Valéry-Gide correspondence, in which he becomes an embarrassment as both men discover as they grow older that their youthful enthusiasm for him was illusory. See *Self-Portraits: The Gide/Valéry Letters*, ed. Robert Mallet (Chicago: University of Chicago Press 1955), especially page 33 (16 Jan. 1891), where Gide says a 'supreme refrain' in a poem by Poe is 'an entire poem,' and page 234 [24 June 1901], where Valéry announces that he has 'no inclination' to write anything about Poe. Thus Poe's reputation and persistence in the *mythos* of *décadence* may serve as a barometer of literary styles.

2 I propose to substitute the term *hyperdimensional fiction* for the well-established generic term *metafiction* in the remainder of this text. Not that I favour the substitution of one faddish critical term for another as a matter of principle, but because in this case I wish to emphasize the isomorphic relationship between the metafictional and the hyperdimensional. As I believe I have demonstrated in the

write seriously about literature and art and to undercut his apparent seriousness with displays of irony and contempt for his readers. As a result, *The Narrative of Arthur Gordon Pym* has become *the* test case for the 'problem' of Poe and there is no agreement among critics about even so basic a question as whether it was intended as a serious work.[3]

Modern readers of Poe have evolved into two distinct and contradictory classes. In the first category are what we might call the 'hoaxers,' who take Poe at his word about his 'silly book' and solve all the cruxes of the text on the basis of a perceived intent to hoax the public with a pot-boiler adventure fiction. The hoaxers assume that *Pym* is a deliberate parody of fiction in violation of Poe's well-known critical opinions concerning the tale and its effect; for them it is a longer example of the genre of 'A Predicament.' In the second category we have the self-conscious symbolizers, who accept a parodic element in the narrative, but who see it as a superficial overlay, rather like the borrowings from '*Mellonta Tauta*' in *Eureka*. They prefer to emphasize the evidence for Poe's self-conscious symbolizing of the text – the shift of dates to achieve a nine-month voyage and the like – thereby underlining the archetypal structure of the narrative.[4] As a result, criticism

---

first two chapters of this text, when the isomorphism of *dimensionality* is applied to literature in general, hyperdimensionality best describes the postmodern. But *postmodern* is unfortunately diachronic, and *metafiction* emphasizes one genre unduly; the postmodern is not restricted to fiction. But if we think of the act of *fictio* as inclusive of poetry and drama and any other text that is not primarily data-producing, they are truly equivalents.

3 *Pym*'s importance as a problematic work is borne out by the calling of a conference of Poe scholars on it alone, '*Arthur Gordon Pym* and Contemporary Criticism,' sponsored by Pennsylvania State University and held at Nantucket, Massachusetts, 19–22 May 1988. No consensus was reached at this conference about the seriousness of the work.

4 So much has been written about *The Narrative of Arthur Gordon Pym* that it would be fatuous to attempt a listing of studies here. Frederick S. Frank, 'Polarized Gothic: An Annotated Bibliography of Poe's *Narrative of Arthur Gordon Pym*,' *Bulletin of Bibliography* 38 (1981), 117–27, gives all the important studies (and others, too) to that date in the third part. Burton R. Pollin's Introduction to the text of *Pym* in *The Imaginary Voyages* volume of *The Collected Writings of Edgar Allan Poe* (Twayne 1981) perhaps best illustrates the 'hoaxer' position (and some of the interpretive difficulties that follow from it), and Harold Beaver's Introduction to the Penguin edition of *The Narrative* (1975) gives about a page of lip-service to the possibility of a hoax and then goes on to a rather complete summary of the various psychological, sociological, and phenomenological readings that the text has generated. Structuralist and deconstructionist essays by Asselineau, Ricardou, Mourier, and Levy are listed in Frank; they are vastly different from the analysis in this chapter.

of *Pym* is deadlocked and unproductive. One side has all the bio-
graphical evidence in place but is forced to conclude that *Pym* is pretty
poor stuff; the other side struggles with what it perceives as the uneven and crude suggestions from the text to prop up the implications
that *Pym* is a masterpiece.

Exactly this kind of critical uncertainty and debate is the hallmark
of works approaching Learning II, works whose hyperdimensionality
has gone unrecognized. Let us instead proceed from the assumption
that *Pym* is neither a hoax upon its readers nor a masterpiece of
archetypal creation, but instead a work of many dimensions whose
readers have become confused by its paradoxical invocation of dimensions uncommon in the works of Poe and his contemporaries. In this
case I believe we can move towards an interesting uncoding of the
work[5] by assuming that it has no fewer than *five* dimensions.

Five as the number of dimensions is convenient because it corresponds to an existing example of decoding which can serve as a paradigm for our investigation. Roland Barthes decoded Balzac's short
story 'Sarrasine' by a technique which is essentially that of assuming a
five-dimensional narration and then proceeding to expose these dimensions through a lengthy exegesis. I propose to examine *Pym* in
something of the manner Barthes used in his *S/Z*.[6] I say 'something of
the manner' advisedly because Barthes's technique in *S/Z* was itself a
parodic example of exegetical overkill. The 'Tel Quel' edition is 278
pages long, of which 31 pages constitute a reproduction of the text of
'Sarrasine.' To keep those proportions with *Pym* would require, according to my calculator, no less than 1,354 pages of the size of *The
Collected Works* (Twayne 1981). Barthes's technique in *S/Z* may be
adapted to a longer work like *Pym* in other ways, however. Where
'Sarrasine' was, for Barthes, 'passing' as a 'straight,' realistic, hetero-
sexual fiction that needed exegetical undressing, *Pym* is a problematic
direct contradiction of the laws of verisimilitude and of Poe's own
strictures on the art of fiction.

For Barthes, the process of fiction consists of the manipulation of

---

5 Poe's interest in cryptanalysis is well known. For an exciting example of the kind of
   reading modern semiotic analysis can produce with Poe's 'ratiocinative' tales, see
   Daniel Kempton, 'The Gold/Goole/Ghoul Bug,' ESQ 33 (1987), 1–19.
6 (Editions du Seuil 1970). My quotations from Barthes are drawn from the translation of *S/Z* by Richard Miller (New York 1974). Quotations from *Pym* are drawn
   from Pollin's edition and are cited by the chapter and page numbers of the first
   edition given in Pollin's text.

five semiotic codes. The *proairetic* code includes all the *action* of the narration and is approximately equivalent to the less fancy notion known as *plot*. The *hermeneutic* code is the puzzle of the text that continues the reader's interest – approximately equivalent to the notion of *suspense*. The *cultural* code consists of the narrative's use of the reader's expectations concerning the relationship between cause and effect as they appear in the narrative – their *etiology*. The *connotative* code is the contribution to the narration of the *structure* of the work – its division into parts, breaks in chronology, place, perspective, point of view. Finally, the *symbolic* code is the code of the text itself insofar as it is a recursive generation of its own content.

It is not self-evident that these semiotic codes are representative isomorphically as dimensions of the text, but a brief examination suggests that is indeed the case. Proairesis is essentially data-production, the linear projection of event as sign: what happens. Hermeneutic adds the dimension of *uncertainty* of what precisely will happen to the certainty that the proairesis will continue. Cultural coding provides a framework for both proairetic direction and the reader's hermeneutic conclusions, only *as long as both author and reader agree on the correctness of the etiology.* When the author seems to violate ordinary expectations of cultural coding, he is really asking the reader to join him in the fourth and fifth dimensions of the work, the connotative and symbolic coding, which make no sense proairetically, hermeneutically, or culturally. We can show this relationship on a conventional catastrophe theory surface (see fig. 4.1).

Now, once we have in mind this multidimensional isomorphism of the text, it is quite simple to proceed with an orderly exegesis. If we think of each code as a dimension, we may proceed as if we are in an ordinary fiction as long as the first three codes/dimensions are operative. We may think of them as programming codes in a computer, adequate to the task of decoding the narrative as long as there is no conflict. In this we are merely following Barthes's example, for he wrote that the proairetic code 'is never more than the artifice of reading: whoever reads the text amasses certain data under some generic titles for actions ... and ... it unfolds as this process of naming takes place' (*S/Z*, 19). When the 'process of naming' includes a suspension of certainty until a question can be answered, the hermeneutic code is called up and may remain resident until determined; when the 'artifice of reading' contradicts our normal expectations of cause and effect, we may call up the cultural code with the same privileges. And when the cultural code cannot explain self-contradiction or para-

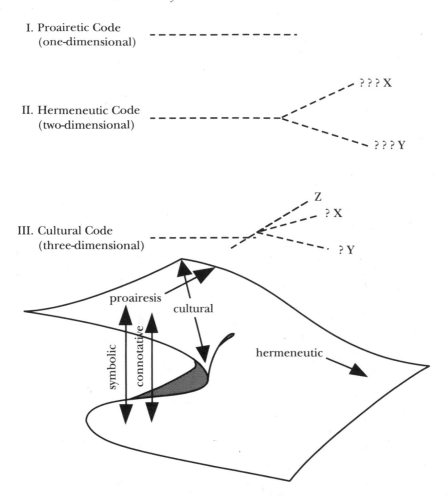

I. Proairetic Code
   (one-dimensional)

II. Hermeneutic Code
    (two-dimensional)

III. Cultural Code
     (three-dimensional)

Fig. 4.1   The five dimensions of Barthesian coding

dox in the text, we may – indeed, we *must* – call up the other two codes/dimensions as needed. Thus our 'dimensions' are treated like the 'stacks' in a computer, each summonable on a GOTO–RETURN or IF–THEN basis. In this way we should be able to proceed through the text in an orderly, manageable way, even though we are treating its multidimensionality directly.

The Narrative *of Arthur Gordon Pym:* we are instructed by the title to consider the work not as a novel or a story but *linearly,* and, at that, to

concentrate on the act of narration as well as the events being narrated. Thus the title calls for proairetic and symbolic decoding simul-
taneously. Moreover, we have barely passed that title and begun to
read the Preface when we discover that our narrator, Mr Pym, is at
odds with his 'editor,' Mr Poe, and that the opening section had been
first presented as fiction but is here restored to its original narrativity.
The Preface concludes with several assertions about the inescapability
of the conclusion that it is indeed Mr Pym's narrative, not Mr Poe's,
that the latter's contributions are not pertinent to matters of fact, and
that the least tutored of readers will be able to distinguish between the
styles of the two putative authors. Then the entire text is concluded
with a 'Note' by an unnamed third person whose voice is quite distinct
from the deceased Pym and the sceptical Poe, and who attempts a
striking exegesis on a hieroglyphic basis and concludes with a pseudo-
biblical injunction:

> I have graven it within the hills, and my vengeance upon the dust within
> the rock.

This tripling of voices has a curious effect upon the narrative. By
making the editorial function exclusively that of the character of Mr
Poe, and the exegetical function that of the author of the 'Note,'
'Pym' preserves a proairetic self which keeps his narrative exclusively
eventful and (apparently) *direct*. Such a division, of course, is suitable
only for the *hoaxable* reader, in which class no modern reader would
place himself except for the temporary delectation of the event, with
full critical faculties available to step out of the hoaxing mode whenever necessary. Hence, the modern reader is, like the tripartite narrators of *Pym*, *in tres partes divisa* from, if not the word *go*, the second
word of the title. Moreover, the reader is 'stacked,' in the modern
cybernetic sense, like our computerized filing system, and must 'push'
or 'pop' himself from one stack to another as the situation of the text
requires. The 'lowest' level of reader activity is utterly naïve proairetic,
and few texts deliver quite so much action in so little space. However,
we are not very far into the narrative before our proairetic reader is
challenged over the very possibility of *event*. When the *Ariel* is dismasted,
the sloop is described as 'boom[ing] along before the wind ... under
its jib only.' No reader who can define the words *sloop* and *jib* can
pass that comment by without moving from the level of event to the
other decoding levels. A sloop has a single mast; when it is dismasted,
the jib as well as the mainsail must fall; the narrative is therefore

impossible.[7] Even a proairetic reader cannot read an impossible event without moving out of that decoding mode into the *cultural* code.

The first conclusion one wants to draw is that 'Homer nodded,' that Poe simply forgot that a sloop is single-masted; the merely proairetic reader is probably happy enough to leave it at that. A more likely response invokes the hermeneutic code: obviously Poe knew that both jib and mainsail are attached to the mast of a sloop; this 'error' is to be treated like all the other errors and improbabilities of the text as a puzzle which requires a solution. Perhaps, indeed, the solution is in the connotative coding; Pym in the Preface complains that Poe, by presenting his narrative as fiction, has misrepresented him. Perhaps this incident is exactly what he had in mind. Alas, he also comments that 'no fact is misrepresented in the first few pages which were written by Mr. Poe' (56). Perhaps, then, the solution lies in the other two codes. Perhaps the patent impossibility of the dismasting of the *Ariel* is intended to undercut the straightfowardness of the narrative structure self-referentially, creating a *lucus a non lucendo*, a self-destroying dada narrative – in other words, a hoax. Perhaps. Perhaps not. At this stage all the reader can do is keep her decoding stacks ready.

As the proairetic reading continues, the number of gross improbabilities and even grosser absurdities increases. They are of various kinds. There are what we might call *pedantic* irregularities of narrative, like the extended disquisition on stowage, which seem to fulfil some sort of verisimilitudinous purpose but do so to our limit of tolerance. Even a naïve reader must conclude that perhaps his leg is being pulled. Then the events of the narrative themselves do not become any less unlikely after the extreme improbability of the *Ariel* episode, in spite of the deadpan delivery. Pym's entombment, the struggle with the mutineers, Peters's appearance and character, the shipwrecked mariners lashing themselves to the wreck so tightly they are almost cut in two: the cumulative effect of the proairesis is to build suspense of a most unusual kind. One begins to anticipate something like a *punchline* – 'and then he awoke and found it was all a dream ... ' – to cite the most common of such conclusions. But instead the reader goes on and on, it seems, southward with the *Jane Guy*, to the island of Tsalal, to the south pole of J.N. Reynolds and John Cleves Symmes.

Again we must pause in our narrative reading, the accumulation of

---

7 See Pollin, 221, note to 1.56, for a detailed analysis of the physical impossibility of the event and references to some early attempts at an explanation.

hermeneutic clues being too great to allow us to bypass the stack. It is true that every writer of *fictions* in the largest sense has what we might call 'freedom of cosmology' – the possibility of placing his fiction in a galaxy long ago and far away. Milton with his Ptolemaic solar system, Lucas in his Star Wars, Reagan in his: each has the right to make of his universe what he wills. But Poe's choice of Symmes's configuration of an earth with 'holes at the poles' is so important to the action of *Pym* by its appearance, unresolved, at the conclusion of the narrative that it becomes a central hermeneutic problem. That position is reinforced by the ancillary clues that accompany the problem. The congruence of names, Poe + Symmes = Pym, the increasing disassociation with the laws of nature as the narrative moves southward, the regression in historical time to biblical suggestions in the names Tsalal-Solomon and the Hebrew 'roots' in the hieroglyphic byplay, and especially in the ubiquitous quincunxes:[8] all tend to emphasize the *super-nature* that surrounds Poe's use of Symmes's cosmology. They *emphasize* it. They do not explain it. The effect is to hold back the conclusion of the proairesis and turn it into a hermeneutic problem. *Pym* becomes a narrative without a conclusion, a fictional rhizome maze that forces the reader out of the proairetic code into the other decoding modes willy-nilly just to make sense out of the narrative.

One other proairetic quality of the text is also germane to this consideration of the non-conclusive conclusion. Much of the action that Pym engages in has existential as well as proairetic purpose. Like Sartre's Oreste and Barth's Tod Andrews and Jacob Horner, Pym is

---

8 See John T. Irwin, *American Hieroglyphics: The Symbol of the Egyptian Hieroglyphics in the American Renaissance* (New Haven: Yale University Press 1980), who gives a plethora of detail about the use of hieroglyphics in *Pym* but hardly even attempts to explain it. He does the same thing for quincunxes in 'The Quincuncial Network in Poe's *Pym*,' *Arizona Quarterly* 44 (Autumn 1988), 1–14. A much more important work on this subject is G.R. Thompson, 'Romantic Arabesque, Contemporary Theory, and Postmodernism: The Example of Poe's *Narrative*,' *ESQ* 35 (1989), 163–271. Thompson brilliantly discourses on the relationship between the quincunx and the structure of *Pym* as an *arabesque*, concluding with a study of the 'icons of indeterminacy' of the narrative as a 'self-reflexive Figure in the Carpet' (241). He displays how Poe created a formal, two-dimensional version of Eco's rhizome maze, visible in the repetition of the number five and its square, in the nesting habits of the penguins and albatrosses on Desolation Island, and the many other references to lozenges, diamonds, v's and x's in the text. All of these riddles and clues encourage the indefinite postponement of a hermeneutic solution to the text in analogous ways.

sometimes *cursed* with freedom of choice, suffers from the postmodern disease of *cosmopsis*, the inability to choose to act and therefore to choose, perforce, inaction. Choice and non-choice, action and inaction, interweave contrapuntally through the episodes of the proairesis until they become themselves a structure of the work. From the dismasting of the *Ariel* (when Pym can do nothing to save himself) to his fall from the cliff into the arms of Dirk Peters, Pym explores the limits of action upon event existentially. One effect is to merge the proairetic with the hermeneutic. With the appearance of each new event Pym's response begins rationally, and then, with each turn of the screw, becomes more and more adroitly rational. His comfortable hiding place aboard the *Grampus* turned into an entombment, he deduces from the persistence of the larboard tack that the *Grampus* has proceeded normally from port; the dream-monster licking his face and hands, he concludes, must be his dog, Tiger; then, when taxed to his limit to read Augustus's message, he manages a climactic synthesis of ratiocination: he has Tiger retrieve the pieces of the torn paper; he fits them together like a jigsaw, trusts his sense of touch to determine which side has been written on, and uses the last of his phosphorus efficiently to read the seven concluding words of the vital message.

But each of these triumphs of reason is accomplished to a counterpoint of inaction brought about by a *failure* of reason. Pondering Augustus's absence in spite of the evidence of the *Grampus*'s progress, Pym falls into a deep sleep 'in spite of every exertion to the contrary' (2.12). Waking from his monstrous dream to a 'huge and real monster' pressing against him, he can do nothing to save himself 'had a thousand lives hung upon the movement of a limb or the utterance of a syllable.' He feels his 'powers of body and mind' desert him, believes himself to be 'perishing of sheer fright.' 'Making a last strong effort [he] at length breathed a faint ejaculation to God, and resigned [himself] to die – at which point Tiger begins licking his face and hands (2.13). And then, of course, he has to have Tiger 'go fetch' the torn note from Augustus for reassembling because he had 'childishly torn it to pieces and thrown it away' when he failed in his first reading and spent 'many miserable hours of despondency ... before the thought suggested itself that [he] had examined only one side of the paper' (3.3).

These are but a few examples of what seems to be the dominant structural mode of the proairesis. Perhaps it is not possible for even the most literal-minded proairetic reader not to become conditioned to this problem-solving system as part of the connotative coding of the text. The very thematic repetitiveness of the proairesis might well be intended to create a meta-structure to serve as an interpretive window into the text. Certainly the repetition of event *a* producing puzzle *b* solved by reason, but only to yield other puzzles *n* until reason fails and inaction *!i!* then brings about a final resolution *!r!* serves as a meta-proairesis of the narrative in a nutshell. One is tempted to reason to a conclusion from this evidence. The process of reason *can* control events to a limited extent, one might conclude about a text, but when logic yields only more deeply complex puzzles, a fall or retreat into inaction will arrest the process and bring about an end to the sequence with a final (and fortunate) result.[9]

Just such conclusions are borne out by involving the cultural coding of the narrative as well. Just as the *events* of the narrative present a meretricious proairesis, so the conclusions that the character Pym draws from events are equally snares and delusions. Once again, the coding is so common that the cultural and connotative codes merge. Augustus's vivacity aboard the *Ariel* is really a sign that he is falling-down drunk and totally incapable of action. Dirk Peters – he of the blood-thirsty behaviour and horrendous appearance – becomes the most nurturing and supportive of soul-brothers to Pym. The natives of Tsalal, friendly and innocent to all appearances, turn into blood-thirsty assassins. And so on. Just when the evidence becomes overwhelming in favour of the acceptance of appearances, the results are reversed. The proairetic reader who fails to invoke cultural and connotative coding for an explanation becomes like the Charlie Brown who believes Lucy when she tells him that *this* time she will not pull the football away as he attempts to boot it. Yet, what is the poor reader to do? When the 'shrouded human figure' with a skin 'of the perfect whiteness of snow' appears to Pym at the vernal equinox on the edge of the cataract spilling through the 'hole in the [South] Pole' leading to the centre of the Symmesian earth ..., does the signifier *believe* have any relevant signified left? Pym is ready to *fall* one more time – into the arms of the figure, down the cataract, into the earth's centre – and the concluding 'Note' affirms that on this occasion as on so many past occasions, his fall was fortunate.

The cultural coding of the work seems to present a progressively complex and intense critical examination into the heart of that

---

9 Notice how similar this process is to the throwing away of the 'nets and ladders' of hermeneutic that William describes to Adso in *The Name of the Rose*.

'proairetic sequence [which] is never more than the result of an artifice of reading.' If we cannot be certain of the very meaning of such
simple signifiers as *jib* and *sloop*, if our trust in the good faith of our
narrator concerning the likelihood of *event* makes us suspect that we
are reading about a dream, if our very faith in existential action is
shaken, what system of belief, what 'transcendental signified' can we
put our faith in? Even the great imperative, the need for self-preservation, is challenged directly by the cultural coding of the narrative. But,
again, although the proairesis suggests the paradoxical need to 'fall'
into life, the puzzle of what indeed Pym is falling into at the conclusion remains unresolved hermeneutically. Since the puzzle is unresolved, the reader necessarily calls up the next level of decoding and
attacks the etiology. But this time he does not limit himself to problems of the significance of simple event, like the definition of *sloop*
and *jib*, or of puzzles like the meta-structure behind the contrapuntal
rational-irrational behaviour of Pym. No, this time the reader must
question her own assumptions about life and death.

Is the need for self-preservation the 'categorical imperative'? The
use of the term itself suggests that it is not. Yet Poe was unlikely to go
to Kant for his cultural coding, considering the unusual spelling he
gives the name of that philosopher in '*Mellonta Tauta.*'[10] For Poe,
values beyond the mechanical and the rational were not likely to be
generated by an epistemological 'Copernican revolution.' Poe was far
more likely to look to science for inspiration in such matters, as
Coleridge, we are told, attended the lectures of Sir Humphry Davy
when he 'ran short of metaphors.' One of the 'scientists' Poe knew
was John Cleves Symmes and his theory of a hollow earth; another was
William Watson, whose essay 'On the Subjects of Chemistry, and Their
General Division' Poe read and even cited (ambiguously) in 'The Fall
of the House of Usher.'[11]

Watson's influence on Poe is pertinent to any consideration of *The
Narrative of Arthur Gordon Pym* because Watson presented an alternative to the empirical and mechanical view of nature. The essay on the
'Subjects of Chemistry' is a denial of the meaningfulness of distinguishing among the so-called 'kingdoms' of nature – the animal, vegetable, and mineral. Arguing from the example of coral, first thought

10 Cant
11 See my 'Usher's Madness and Poe's Organicism: A Source,' *American Literature* 29
   (1967), 379–89; the edition of Watson cited in that article and here is *Chemical
   Essays* (London 1787), 5:126–71.

to be mineral, then vegetable, then recognized as animal; from the
observed sensibility of plants; from reports that 'in the *Cretan* labyrinth it hath been observed, that the names of travellers, which have
been cut in the rock in former ages, are now in *alto relievo*, and that
the older the dates are, the greater in protuberance, resembling the
callus formed by incisions in trees,' Watson arrives at this remarkable
conclusion:

> ... supposing, however, that we pay no attention to any of these circum-
> stances, yet cannot we form any judgment concerning the internal state
> of the earth. The greatest depths to which Miners have penetrated even
> in mountainous countries, which may be considered as excrescencies
> from the true surface of the earth, or the level of the sea, have scarcely
> ever equalled one sixteenth thousandth part of its diameter; a distance
> altogether insufficient for the forming any probable conjecture about
> the inward constitution of the globe. The *strata* of stones, and veins of
> minerals, which are met with upon the surface, can give us as little
> information concerning the internal structure of the earth from which
> these are probably derived, as the contemplation of the scales of a fish,
> the feathers of a bird, or the *Epidermis* of a man, would concerning the
> bones and muscles, the veins and arteries, the circulation of the blood,
> and the several secretions of an animal body ... All the *strata* of lime-
> stones, chalks, marbles, all gypsums, spars, alabasters, & c. are confess-
> edly of animal origin. The *strata* of pit-coal, and of all bituminous fossils,
> and some species of slates, whatever may be thought of argillaceous
> strata in general, the mould everywhere covering the surface of the earth,
> and other substances, are supposed, probably enough, to have arisen
> from the destruction of vegetables; so that I know not whether it would
> be a very extravagant conjecture which should suppose that all matter is,
> or hath been organized, enlivened, animated.[12]

That the unresolved proairetic and hermeneutic problems of the
text of *Pym* are at least partially resolved by the suggestion that its
cultural coding derives more from Symmes and Watson than from
Aristotle and Newton is also borne out by a consideration of some of
the connotative coding of the narrative. The cycles we have already
considered – reason to inanition to more intense reason to despair
and total loss of control to a 'fortunate fall' – are paralleled by many

---

12 *American Literature* 29 (1967), 384–5; Watson, 167–9

other cycles: of burial-rebirth, belief-disbelief-new belief, repeated many times. These cycles are parts of larger cycles observable in the connotative coding, remarked by many critics. Pym's voyage takes nine months and ends on the vernal equinox; the longer voyage of Pym aboard the *Grampus* and the *Jane Guy* is a lengthened cycle of the voyage of the first chapter aboard the *Ariel.* Cycle generates cycle, wheel turns within wheel, inviting, almost demanding that the reader abandon simple proairesis and hermeneutic for the metatext. 'The key to the treasure is the treasure,' Barth's Scheherazade, inspired by her author, remarks. Well, perhaps. Let us at least consider something of that sort with regard to the cycles of Pym's 'falls.'

In the organic universe of Watson the avoidance of death is not nearly as important as the continuation of creation. Those coral atoll 'excrescencies' he cited in the beginning of his essay are but the death-induced evidence of the continuance of organic life. Watson is not, of course, the only one to notice that the cycle is of birth, *procreation*, death. Writers have always paid rather more attention to the middle third of that particular cycle than they have to the other two. Not so Pym, the author of this narrative. Aside from the suggestive comments about the aphrodisiac quality of the *biche de mère* found on Tsalal, sex is not present at all in *The Narrative of Arthur Gordon Pym.* There are no female characters in the narrative except for the three ships upon which Pym sails. Both the *Ariel* and the *Grampus* are referred to by the feminine pronoun, as is, of course, the *Jane Guy*, with its feminine (albeit ambiguous) name. Poe's granting femininity to the three ships is conventional, but the natives of Tsalal come closer to the organicism of Watson in their belief that the *Jane Guy* is a 'living creature.' The chief goes as far as to indicate his sympathy 'in what he considered the sufferings of the schooner, patting and smoothing' a gash where the cook had struck the deck with an axe (18.6). Pym makes the doubly ironic comment concerning this anecdote (doubly ironic, considering the final fate of the ship) that their behaviour showed 'a degree of ignorance for which we were not prepared, and for my part I could not help thinking some of it affected.'

One might argue that all the aspects of femininity are present in the various kinds of ships Pym sails in or encounters. The *Ariel* is woman as sister-companion of youth, promising the freedom of the imagination that its name alludes to. The *Grampus* ('she was an old hulk') holds Pym in her maternal womb to term and beyond, but nurtures the shipwrecked mariners with her stores when their need is great. The two ships which approach the shipwrecked group, by con-

trast, behave meretriciously indeed, luring with false hope and pros-
pects, and then disappointing utterly: the Dutch '*hermaphrodite* brig'
evidently being the vessel for some horrid disease; the second ship
metaphorically 'turning its tail' to the temporarily enlivened group.
Finally, the *Jane Guy* is wife and helpmeet to Pym's southerly quest
but, as its double and ambiguous name suggests, is only a 'plain Jane'
and 'guys' him as well as it directs him like a 'guy' wire or cable. The
final episode's canoe is too obviously reminiscent of the many surro-
gate-mother embarkations undergone by questing heroes of myth to
need further description. So if we are to conclude that the female sex
is absent from *The Narrative of Arthur Gordon Pym*, we must essentially
close down our connotative decoding stack.

Something of the same is true about the sex *act* in the narrative.
Again, there are no females and no untoward suggestions of those
activities which often, it is said, accompany 'the life of a seaman' even
in 'his more terrible moments of suffering and despair' (2.1) – that is,
buggery in the fo'c'sle. Indeed, the all-male cast of characters represents a wondrous variety of sexually ambiguous *yin* and *yang* and possibilities for all sorts of s & m activities without ever crossing even a
modern line of decorum, let alone violating nineteenth-century standards. Yet it is not hard to understand its appeal to the French Decadents,
to name just one ambiguously epicene group which assured the transmission of *The Narrative* to postmodern readers. Pym's original quest,
for 'shipwreck and famine; of death or captivity among barbarian
hordes; of a lifetime dragged out in sorrow and tears, upon some grey
and desolate rock, in an ocean unapproachable and unknown' (2.1),
is one that would cheer the cold hearts of de Sade and Sacher-Masoch,
and speak, in opposite ways, to both Jean Genet and J.K. Huysmans.

Pym's frequent *falls* in his narrative seem no more like orgasmic
ejaculations than they do falls from grace, but to the connotative code
stack their repetition requires decoding as both. Pym falls from the
'grace' of his control over his environment by reason into rescue at
the hands of a benevolent providence under such various names as
Tiger, Augustus, and Dirk Peters. In the same way, each of his 'falls' is
a 'little death,' an orgasmic escape of the self by bestowing itself,
giving itself up, to the Great Nonself. That these 'falls' are always
felicitous suggests a sexual decoding no less than a theological one. In
the organic universe described by Richard Watson, although the *mechanics* of sexuality might persist in mystery despite scientific probing,
the nature of the act is universal, metaphoric. Watson comments that
the disputes among biologists 'whether every animal be produced *ad
ovo femellae*, or *a vermiculo in semine maris*, are exactly similar to those

among botanists concerning the manner in which the *farina foecundans* contributes to the rendering the seed prolific.'[13] Doubly, trebly fortunate may be Pym's falls — into life, into grace, into ... a new encoding.

Indeed, the connotative coding of *The Narrative* is no more conclusive as a sub-program of investigation than any of the others, but the questions it raises *do* aid in some aspects of the proairetic and hermeneutic decoding. To see *The Narrative* as a cycle of cycles is to understand the conclusion as a 'rescue' analogous to the one performed on Pym and Augustus by the *Penguin* in chapter 1 and all of the other 'fortunate falls' intervening between the two, but this time into a new and somehow 'higher' state. The recursiveness of the multiplication of the cycles produces the paradox of the generation of a new *dimension* of meaning.[14]

That new dimension has something to do with the relationship between reason and faith, on the one hand, and sexuality and the organic creation, on the other. The 'death' of Pym is followed by the literary 'birth' of the author of the 'Note,' whose literally hermeneutic analysis of the hieroglyphics of the final episodes is obviously intended to mediate between the coding of the text and the further encoding by the reader. That encoding must be multidimensional since the 'new voice' of the author of the 'Note,' is specifically exegetic about the 'text' of Tsalal – the island, the text. The reader is forced by the 'Note' to an overview of the text as text-world. The interpretation of the hieroglyphics forces the reader to merge the creation of Pym with the larger creation of the (Symmesian and Watsonian) earth. The text is the world. It is / is not Pym/Poe, who has 'graven it within the hills ... [and] upon the dust within the rock.' The final act of falling is the merging of the author with the reader in hermeneutic copulation as the creative maleness of Pym merges with the reader and with mother earth to close the cycle of the text. Like the solitary spermatozoon uniting with the egg after its long night swim, Pym rushes into the self-immolating embrace of the shrouded figure and completes one cycle – the cycle of text – with the creation of the next – a cycle of meaning.[15]

---

13 *American Literature* 29 (1967), 383; Watson 146

14 For a consideration of the paradoxes involved in this kind of event, I can hardly improve on the general discussion (interpreted analogically) in Douglas R. Hofstader, *Gödel, Escher, Bach: An Eternal Golden Braid* (New York: Vintage 1980), *passim.*

15 See, among many other possible intertexts, Plutarch, *Moralia* (Loeb Classical Library), 5: 351, where an alternative to the island of Tsalal is offered as a location for the earth's omphalos; P.H. Gosse, *Omphalos* (London 1857), and Edmund

Our tour through the text of *The Narrative of Arthur Gordon Pym* completed, we are now ready to consider the question that opened this exercise. The dispute between the 'hoaxers' and the 'symbolizers' dissolves into nothing once the text has been decoded in its full hyperdimensionality. More than any other of the great writers of the nineteenth century,[16] Poe was capable of engaging in *freeplay* with serious content, hoaxing his readers at the same time that he was encoding culturally, connotatively, and symbolically ideas about which he could be deadly serious in other contexts. Pym's universe is the organic universe of *Eureka*, but Pym himself is only a blind and comical seeker probing the crannies of some of the private parts of that world. Indeed, the greatness of *Pym* resides in that very lightness and playfulness of the text, compared to which the profundity of *Eureka*, admired as it was by its author, sinks into bathos of its own specific gravity. Poe recognized the problem, trying to lighten the omelette with the soufflé excerpts from '*Mellonta Tauta*' and asking that *Eureka* be read as a poem, but no sensitive reader of Poe prefers *Eureka* to *Pym*. The continuing appeal of *Pym* through unsympathetic periods of Victorian repression and unsmiling realism argues for its success as a work of art. Now that we have reached an age which values writers like Borges, Barth and Nabokov, *Pym* must be appreciated for what it is, a classical hyperdimensional fiction.

Gosse, *Father and Son* (New York 1907), for the evidence linking the etiology of the belly button and the nature of creation, on the one hand, and the trouble that etiology can cause, on the other; Lewis Thomas, *The Lives of a Cell* (New York: Bantam 1979), 4, for a modern comparison perhaps even more shocking than Plutarch-Poe-Gosse's.

16 As we shall see in the next chapter, Melville also had this capacity, although he expressed it in a very different form in *The Confidence-Man*.

5

The Confidence-Man:
An Epimenidean View

Melville ranks right behind Poe as the American artist who felt the most discord between his art and his social environment. Unlike Poe, Melville had no interest in the concept of 'art for art's sake,' but in virtually every other matter of possible conflict he was at odds with American customs and manners. Most of these areas of conflict show up in *The Confidence-Man*, and for a long time critical study of the novel was content to identify these areas (the text of *The Confidence-Man* is sufficiently dense that identification of theme is not always simple) and comment on what was taken as Melville's satiric purpose. But for some time now *The Confidence-Man* has been recognized as a work which has much more in common with postmodernist fiction than it has with the fiction of Melville's contemporaries. As early as 1949 Richard Chase, in an influential article, affirmed its position in the Melville canon as Melville's 'second best book.'[1] This recognition was not immediately transformed into perceptive critical essays on the postmodernist qualities of the work, but it established the work's seriousness and called it to the attention of critics who inevitably, over a period of time, showed how various of its qualities were not the botches and abortions previous critics had called them but technical and structural gems of intellectuation. By the 1960s it had overtaken *Moby-Dick* as the hottest subject for critical treatment, and most of the best work on it was in one way or another very much *à la dernière mode* of whatever school of criticism was being invoked. In 1964 R.W.B. Lewis, in

---

1 Richard Chase, 'Melville's Confidence Man,' *Kenyon Review* 11 (1949), 122–40

the Afterword to the cheapest and best text available at the time, proclaimed it as the 'recognizable and awe-inspiring ancestor' of such postmodernist works as 'Nathanael West's *The Day of the Locust* ... Ralph Ellison's *Invisible Man*, William Gaddis's *The Recognitions*, John Barth's *The Sot-Weed Factor*, [and] Thomas Pynchon's *V.*' Moreover, Lewis also identified one of the qualities that places it so prominently in this line of works, which, in his words, 'comprise the continuing anti-face of the American dream': 'Melville bequeathed to those works – in very differing proportions – the vision of an apocalypse that is no less terrible for being enormously comic, the self-extinction of a world characterized by deceit and thronging with imposters and masquerad-ers, and the image of the supreme tempter (the 'super promiser,' as West called him) on the prowl through that world, assisting it towards its promised end.'[2]

Most good modern criticism of *The Confidence-Man* begins with the recognition that postmodernist ways of looking at the world are best suited for examination of the book, but there is still a wide divergence of critical opinion about *which* critical insights are most helpful. Most critics of the work can be divided into four quite distinctive groups. One group concentrates on the oxymoronic notion that the book is an ironic allegory. Irony, of course, is used to conceal truth, allegory to reveal it. Critics who stress this particular paradox of the narrative have problems determining which, if either, of the two opposed modes is dominant. As a result, critical determination of Melville's intent in such an important area of text as Indian-hating, for example, can lead to diametrically opposed readings. John W. Shroeder concludes that only morally incisive characters like the Indian-hater can effectively deal with the diabolic forces of this world. Edwin Fussell and Roy Harvey Pearce conclude the opposite, that Indian-hating serves only as a mask for unreason and/or venality.[3] Elizabeth S. Foster and Edward

---

2 R.W.B. Lewis, 'Afterword' to the Signet Classic edition of *The Confidence-Man* (New York: NAL 1964), 263. This edition cost seventy-five cents then and was based on the Hendricks House text. Probably the best recent treatment of the 'comic apocalyp-tic' in American literature is Douglas Robinson, *American Apocalypses* (Baltimore: Johns Hopkins University Press 1985). References to *The Confidence-Man* in this text will be to the Northwestern-Newberry Text, Evanston and Chicago, 1984.

3 John W. Shroeder, 'Sources and Symbols for Melville's *The Confidence-Man*,' in the Norton Critical edition of *The Confidence-Man* (New York: W.W. Norton 1971), 298–316; Edwin Fussell, *Frontier: American Literature and the American West* (Princeton: Princeton University Press 1965), 319; Roy Harvey Pearce, 'Melville's Indian-Hater: A Note on the Meaning of *The Confidence-Man*, PMLA 67 (1952), 942–8

Mitchell attempt to resolve the conflict by pointing out that the allegorical structure is fugal, while irony is a dominant mode for the many repetitions of the theme of confidence and charity. That reading is supported by Hershel Parker's conclusion about the 'metaphysics of Indian-hating': that it represents the moral norm of Christian thinking and therefore reveals the 'darker side' of Christianity.[4]

A second group of critics concentrates on the work's inimitable combination of Melvillean erudition in classical Eastern and Western myths and the potpourri of folk wisdom and humour he blended with it. H. Bruce Franklin's *The Wake of the Gods: Melville's Mythology* (1963) is the most interesting and successful work of this type, but to suggest that Melville is a kind of *bricoleur* predecessor of Lévi-Strauss is to reduce the work to a didactic allegory, however successful it may have turned out to be. Just the opposite tack is taken by the proponents of a third way of looking at the text. These are the critics who see it as a 'black comedy' with no didactic and only incidental satiric intent. For Stanley Trachtenberg and Lawrence Buell *The Confidence-Man* is an early avatar of that postmodern condition known as *Catch-22.* Elizabeth Keyser would agree and add that Frank Goodman and Yossarian conclude their fictions with equivalent epiphanies. Leon F. Seltzer finds Melville's insights more comparable to the absurd as observed by Camus, and Richard Boyd Hauck sees affinities between the actions of Melville's con men and such Barthian opinions as Joe Morgan's comment: 'Only in America can you have a cheerful nihilism, for Christ's sake.'[5]

Finally there are the critics who zero in on the most unsolvable puzzle of all: the voice of the narration. This aspect of the novel has been a focus of criticism from the beginning, and we should not be

---

4 Elizabeth S. Foster, Introduction to the Hendricks House edition of *The Confidence-Man* (New York: 1954), xci; Edward Mitchell, 'From Action to Essence: Some Notes on the Structure of Melville's *The Confidence-Man,' American Literature* 40 (1968), 27–37; Hershel Parker, 'The Metaphysics of Indian-Hating' in the Norton Critical edition, 323–31
5 Stanley Trachtenberg, '"A Sensible Way to Play the Fool": Melville's *The Confidence-Man,' Georgia Review* 26 (1972), 38–52; Lawrence Buell. 'The Last Word on *The Confidence-Man?' Illinois Quarterly* 35 (1972), 15–29; Elizabeth Keyser, '"Quite an Original": The Cosmopolitan in *The Confidence-Man,' Texas Studies in Literature and Language* 15 (1973), 279–300; Leon F. Seltzer, *The Vision of Melville and Conrad* (Athens: Ohio University Press 1970); Richard Boyd Hauck, *A Cheerful Nihilism: Confidence and 'The Absurd' in American Humorous Fiction* (Bloomington, Indiana University Press 1971), especially 112–29

surprised to find a considerable latitude of sophistication in the interpretation of this one labyrinthine problem. Generally speaking, the earlier
comments tend to be more naïve than the later ones. Thus Lawrance
Thompson sees little difference between Hawthorne's 'spiritual Paul Pry'
narrators and the unthinking orthodoxies of the 'stupid narrator' of *The
Confidence-Man* Edgar Dryden's view of the narration is much more perceptive. He sees it as the means to a kind of dada creation, self-destruct-
ing, as all 'wordy' narratives must be. Warwick Wadlington seems to
think he disagrees with Dryden in concluding that the narrative voice
'makes strange' purposefully to force the reader into 'fresh vision.'
And Henry Sussman identifies the con man as writer and the victim as
reader in a deconstruction of 'transcendental signifiers' of all sorts.[6]

Now this wonderful richness and variety of interpretation of *The
Confidence-Man* raises several interesting questions. In the first place, it
is not hard to understand why there should be such a difference in
the appreciation of Melville's closest approach to Learning II compared to that of Poe's equivalent work, *Pym*. Although the reputations
of both writers went into a decline from the middle of the nineteenth
century onward, their 'resurrections' differed considerably. Poe's de-
fenders emphasized the aesthetic; he was the poet's poet, the literary
theorist's literary theorist. Few defended his intellectual accomplish-
ments,[7] and those who defended his moral position were almost by
definition perverse. Melville, however, won respect as an intellectual
and as a moralist from the earliest revisionist criticism. Normative
morality had shifted so far by the time of Herman Weaver's *Herman
Melville, Mariner and Mystic* (1921), that Melville's earnestness found
an appreciative audience from the (modern) beginning of critical
awareness of his writing. Thus, even though the earliest criticisms of
Melville dismissed *The Confidence-Man* as a failure,[8] it did not take long

---

6 Lawrance Thompson, *Melville's Quarrel with God* (Princeton: Princeton University
  Press 1952), 300; Edgar A. Dryden, *Melville's Thematics of Form: The Great Art of
  Telling the Truth* (Baltimore: John Hopkins University Press 1968), 124; Warwick
  Wadlington, *The Confidence-Game in American Literature* (Princeton: Princeton
  University Press 1975), 140; Henry Sussman, 'The Deconstructor as Politician:
  Melville's *Confidence-Man*,' *Glyph* 4 (1978), 32–56

7 And those were sometimes curiously wrong-headed. See, for example, Clayton
  Hoagland, 'The Universe of Eureka: A Comparison of the Theories of Eddington
  and Poe,' *Southern Literary Messenger*, 1 (1939), 307–13, which credits Poe with
  hypothesizing the 'Big Bang' theory of the creation of the universe.

8 Weaver was so contemptuous of its intellectual content that he called it a 'posthu-
  mous work,' implying that Melville was at least brain-dead when he wrote it. See
  Herman Weaver, *Herman Melville, Mariner and Mystic* (New York: Doran 1921), 348.

for criticism to discover the rich possibilities of a work which had a Melvillean pedigree for intellectual content. In the years that followed, and especially in the 1960s, critical technique also caught up with Melville's peculiar genius and, more importantly perhaps, gave an academic cachet to the many ingenious readings the work supported. Richard Chase and R.W.B. Lewis were *éminences* of American literature; with their approval registered, what young graduate student could resist trying to cut his critical teeth on Melville's most ontologically interesting text? *Pym* during these same years continued to be suspect, at least partly because many of its supporters were either aesthetes, like Huysmans, or poets, like W.H. Auden and Richard Eberhart. Poe might be laughing up his sleeve at critics who took his 'silly book' seriously; Melville was known to conceal rich and often shocking truth beneath the surface of his narrative, as in 'The Tartarus of Maids.' True, Melville seemed to be 'playing' with the reader in *The Confidence-Man* as Poe was in *Pym*, but as he pointed out in *Moby-Dick*, even the gambols of great whales have a kind of dignity and beauty.

Most importantly, Melville was known to be at odds with 'serious' issues of American morality, while Poe seemed unconcerned about all the social issues except Philistinism and aestheticism. Melville wrote interestingly and enigmatically about problems of race in 'Benito Cereno' and *Moby-Dick*; Poe seemed able only to create minstrel-show negroes like Jupiter in 'The Gold-Bug,' and racist nightmares, as in his depiction of the natives of Tsalal. Melville probed deeply into the 'heart of darkness' appeal of the primitive from *Typee* on; Poe's characters all seem to suffer from hypersensitivity derived from too much culture. Melville attacked American materialism, Victorian sexual repression, and religious and philosophical hypocrisy throughout his career; Poe seemed content to write poems and stories to rival Israfel's noumenal perfection. Both men were involved in a 'hopeless contradiction' between their art and their social environment; both men were therefore led to the extremity of deliberately writing works which they knew risked breaking the 'galvanic circuit' that Melville described as the 'shock of recognition' that connects genius to genius. But the modern critic, armed with sophisticated tools for analysis, will always find Melville's problematic masterpiece the more enticing subject, if only because she is more sure it is worth the probing.

Yet *Pym* and *The Confidence-Man* have many points in common. Both are works based on voyages of 'discovery' not of 'new-found-lands' but of the symbolic self. Both deny they are novels or romances, *Pym* insisting it is a *narrative*, *The Confidence-Man* declaring itself a 'Masquerade.' Both have extremely unusual protagonists and narrative

voices. Both, it is fair to say, present problems of isomorphic representation which would have to be done in more dimensions than the
customary three.[9] It is tempting of course, to imagine that the same
kind of Barthesian decoding that worked so well for *Pym* might also
apply to *The Confidence-Man*. Alas, such is not the case – at least to the
best of my efforts. The problem is that *The Confidence-Man* has virtually
no proairetic and/or hermeneutic content. All the rules of proairesis
are broken from the first sentence, 'At sunrise on a first of April, there
appeared, suddenly as Manco Capac at the lake Titicaca, a man in
cream-colors, at the water-side in the city of St. Louis.' The only data
from that sentence which continue to be of value as the 'process of
naming' which is proairesis proceeds are the date[10] and place. Cultural, connotative, and symbolic coding are all immediately invoked.
Sunrise starts the diurnal cycle; April 1 invokes the possibility of hoax;
sudden appearance suggests the supernatural; the comparison to
Manco Capac invokes myth and religion; all suggest the exoteric inextricably mixed with the esoteric.

We may well be at the level of Learning II from those very first
words. Melville, unlike Poe, eschews the necessity to *abduce* the reader
into the questioning of *forms* and *structures* of semiosis. He *attacks*
those forms from the very beginning. It is instructive to compare the
opening chapter with the *Ariel* sequence in *Pym*. Both segments are
cycles which are to be repeated constantly in the works they introduce. But the *Ariel* episode in *Pym* draws the reader into the narrative
with wild action (proairesis), strange behaviour on the part of Augustus
not to be explained until the end of the incident (hermeneutic),
inexplicable violation of semiosis with the words *sloop* and *jib* (cultural), ambiguous shift of voice from Pym to Poe to Pym (connotative), and voyage-as-text cycle (symbolic): all these codes in nearly
equal measure.

Compare the opening chapter of *The Confidence-Man*. Here the *story*

---

9 One critic has recognized at least the mathematical equivalent of that observation.
John Bryant in '*The Confidence-Man*: Melville's Problem Novel,' in his *A Companion
to Melville Studies* (Westport, CT: Greenwood Press 1986), 316, comments, 'From its
sunrise opening to its midnight end, *The Confidence-Man* is an algebraic equation
with too many variables in plot, character, and narrative voice to allow for a definitive solution.' The statement is mathematically correct but ignores the possibility of
a 'non-solution' of the type this text only contemplates: that is the 'speaking' of the
'locus of meaning' as being preferable to a 'definitive solution.'

10 Is a hoax that calls attention to its being a hoax in its very first sentence a
metahoax?

told is of the simplest of confrontations: a mute abjures the members of a crowd who are reading a placard about an imposter by chalking lines from 1 Corinthians 13 on a slate. The crowd becomes ugly with him until his inability to hear the shouts of two porters carrying a trunk leads to the crowd's (and the reader's?) discovery that he is both deaf and mute, this peripeteia explaining the only *suspense* generated by the incident.

The crowd's suspicion of the mute, it seems, is partly a result of the juxtaposition of his appeal for charity with the poster about the mysterious imposter, suggesting that the mute may actually *be* this imposter. This cultural assumption is furthered by the extraordinary rhetoric of the chapter, for which this one-sentence-paragraph example will suffice:

> As if it had been a theater-bill, crowds were gathered about the announcement, and among them certain chevaliers, whose eyes, it was plain were on the capitals, or, at least, earnestly seeking sight of them from behind intervening coats; but as for their fingers, they were enveloped in some myth; though, during a chance interval, one of these chevaliers somewhat showed his hand in purchasing from another chevalier, ex-officio a peddler of money-belts, one of his popular safeguards, while another peddler, who was still another versatile chevalier, hawked, in the thick of the throng, the lives of Measan, the bandit of Ohio, Murrel, the pirate of the Mississippi, and the brothers Harpe, the Thugs of the Green River country in Kentucky – creatures, with others of the sort, one and all exterminated at the time, and for the most part, like the hunted generations of wolves in the same regions, leaving comparatively few successors; which would seem cause for unalloyed gratulation, and is such to all except those who think that in new countries, where the wolves are killed off, the foxes increase. (3–4)

Notice also that the entire chapter includes not one word of dialogue. All of the text-within-the-text consists of quotation from 1 Corinthians 13 and the sign the barber puts up:

No Trust

That is in contrast to the beginning of chapter 2, which consists of nineteen extremely various 'epitaphic comments, conflictingly spoken *or thought*' on the mute by a 'miscellaneous company, who ... had *not* witnessed preceding occurrences' (11; italics added). Thus we begin the work with a dialogue of chalked quotations on a slate contrasting with an ambiguously epigrammatic poster and arrive at a summation of critical comment about its content which is indeterminately spoken or thought by a company which had *not* witnessed what took place!

Then there is the content of the chalked quotations to consider. The mute adapts Paul's predicative comments about charity from verses five, seven (two), and eight to his own circumstances as he is jostled by the crowd. All of these commendations of charity are part of the first admonition of the apostle: that charity is the 'greatest' of the triumvirate of virtues and that faith and hope are only 'also rans' if the bet is to win. The second part of 1 Corinthians 13 admits that *now* we know 'in part' and only 'when that which is perfect is come' will we see not 'through a glass, darkly; but then face to face.' In place of this apostolic apology for uncertainty we have the barber's:

No Trust

Perhaps we have engaged in a wild-goose chase in attempting to discover the proairesis and hermeneutic of this first episode; perhaps Melville is really engaged here (and elsewhere in the work) in an attack upon the very possibility of proairesis (telling something straightforwardly) and hermeneutic (drawing conclusions, finding meaning, discovering truth). Perhaps the purpose of this introduction to the text by the cream-coloured and woolly man (who disappears from the text immediately after this chapter)[11] is to teach us the lesson that the lesson is unknowable. This 'strange loop' of meaning suggests that the 'true' interpretation of *The Confidence-Man* is analogous to Gödel's famous theorem in its best known (and most accessible) paraphrase: 'All consistent axiomatic formulations ... include undecidable propositions.'[12]

Now, obviously Melville was not a mathematical theorist or a logician, and it would be no less silly to suggest that Melville scooped

---

11 It's hard to make a definitive statement about any aspect of *The Confidence-Man*. Black Guinea is equally woolly-headed and may be intended as a photographic negative of the mute in his colour and his 'wordiness': the barber's name is William Cream.

12 Douglas R. Hofstadter, *Gödel, Escher, Bach: An Eternal Golden Braid* (New York: Vintage 1980), 17. The words 'of number theory' are represented by the ellipsis. Since much of what Hofstadter argues in this work concerns the extension of Gödel's Theorem to other disciplines, I do not think my ellipsis distorts his position.

Gödel in the formulation of his famous theorem than it is to believe that Poe had a universe like Eddington's in mind when he wrote *Eureka*, but one of the principles we are testing is that at certain levels of creative intensity brought on by a desire to go 'against the grain,' the artist transcends the ordinary limits of semiosis and approaches the incomprehensible even at the risk of leaving his best and brightest audience muttering *non in commotione, Dominus*. Certainly *The Confidence-Man*, in its universality of denial of common cultural coding and its dependence on connotative and especially symbolic coding, seems to be more concerned with the revelation of the undecidability of a whole series of otherwise helpful axiomatic formulations than it is with the usual concerns of fiction. We do not always think of epistemology, theology, economics, ethics, and, perhaps especially, semiosis itself as axiomatic formulations, but of course they are. They are no more than the 'nets and ladders' that may help us to seek the truth but that must be thrown away when *jouissance* rises.

Nor are they the 'real' subject of *The Confidence-Man*. That subject is undecidability itself. Its central metaphor is the river as Heraclitean flux[13] arbitrarily divided into such axiomatic formulations as April 1, the steamboat *Fidèle*, and St Louis. These apparently solid data and the many propositions that grow from them (the presence of a $mute_1$, the division of night and day_2 ... the extinction of the 'solar $lamp'_n$) may all be undecidable propositions. When they are bound up in axiomatic formulations (like theology or economics) that further simplify their general interconnectedness, their indeterminacy only increases. Now normally fictive works with a very considerable symbolic and connotative content are held together by plot, character, and narrative consistency, as in *Pym*. In place of normal proairesis and hermeneutic *The Confidence-Man* proceeds directly by means of its structure, a structure which can perhaps *only* be described by analogy. Three analogies, I believe, are especially fruitful.

In the first place, that arbitrary division of the movement of the river functions *spatially* as a moiré overlay of patterns of opposites.[14] The largest division of the work is between night and day, but that pattern is repeated in the contrast between the mute and Black Guinea

---

13 It is possible that Melville chose not to include 'The River' passage because it made this point too obvious.

14 Is it stretching to note that moiré patterns are one of the principal defences against counterfeit money (see chapter 45)?

Fig. 5.1 *Liberation* by M.C. Escher (lithograph, 1955): figure/ground,
con-man/victim. © 1955 M.C. Escher Foundation – Baarn – Holland.

and multiplied endlessly by the series of confrontations between confidence men and victims. As the pattern grows in complexity, it then becomes a problem in the indeterminacy of *figure* and *ground*, like an Escher print (see fig. 5.1). By the time the reader gets to the encounter between Frank Goodman and Charlie Noble, he should be thoroughly confused about which of those two seemingly inviolate categories (confidence man / victim) is which.[15] The same confusion is spread through the other 'nets and ladders' of the text: religion (the mute, the two clergymen), philanthropy (the Seminole Widow and Orphans Society and the World's Charity), economics (the Black Rapids Coal Company), etc. But here again, the 'day' half of the book is essentially introductory and preparatory for the 'night' half, in which the 'increase in seriousness' dominates over the 'polite spirit' of discussion.[16]

That apparent movement is two-dimensional.[17] Accompanying it is a development which is hyperdimensional and which causes most of the problems of interpretation. Because this is a fiction of forms and not character or plot, epistemology itself becomes an issue, and the problem of fictional semiosis is the most important means by which it is examined. Melville introduces the motif in chapter 14, which is entitled 'Worth the consideration of those to whom it may prove worth considering.' Now this rather peculiar sounding title has a considerable similarity to a curious logical phenomenon known as Epimenides's paradox, which, in its simplest form, reads, 'This sentence is false.' That is, it is self-referential and therefore *cannot be interpreted except as a formal statement about self-referential sentences (or chapters ... or whatever)*. The major difference between Epimenides's paradox and Melville's is that Epimenides's, because it uses the verb *to be* as an equal sign (=), creates a secure and definitive 'strange loop.' The reader is caught between accepting the correctness of the sentence, that it is false, and

---

15 One of the curious effects of moiré patterns is the appearance of colour where there are only shifting patterns of black and white. The multicoloured Cosmopolitan is there prefigured.

16 As always, beware my generalizations no less than Melville's (or anyone else's). The chapter which is entitled 'The Cosmopolitan Increases in Seriousness' includes the grossest joke of the work, in which a chamber-pot is mooted to be a life-saver (251).

17 Another possible useful analogy to the work is theme and variation in music. Much of what I suggest is comprehensible as moiré pattern and figure and ground may be more accessible to some as resembling a very complicated fugue, perhaps an 'eternally-rising' one (see Hofstadter, *Gödel, Escher, Bach,* chapters 5 and 6). The point really is that all these isomorphisms, fully represented – that is, with all their paradoxes intact – may serve as aids to reflection.

the conclusion that must be logically drawn from it, that it is true.[18] But Melville's title is less secure in its 'strange loopiness' in that it is copulative and subjunctive. The implication is that the reader *may* be caught up in the formal rhizome maze implied by it if he wishes, or he may not.

There is, of course, something deceptive about that statement. As a chapter title, it describes the contents of chapter 14 as 'true' (worth considering) if 'true' (worth considering). But to read something – to complete the semiotic circuit (writer – text – reader) – is to consider it. And to consider it implies a new encoding of it by the reader. But the reader, as we have seen, can only encode it meaningfully as a statement about form, not content. The 'content' of the chapter concerns consistency in characterization in fiction and in life. But the *form* of the chapter, as a strange loop, implies that the reader ought to be looking for a *formal* truth in it, a truth about epistemology and semiosis, fiction and the reality it is supposed to represent. This shifting of content to form-as-content may, if the reader finds it worth considering, shift the dimensionality to what Barthes called 'the zero of the signified' (*Pleasure*, 41) and bring on the 'bliss' of Learning II. Alternatively, if the reader is *forced* to contemplate the 'meaning' of chapter 14, she is like those naturalists cited in the middle of the chapter who, when the duck-billed beaver [platypus] of Australia was first brought stuffed to England ... appealing to their classifications, maintained that there was, in reality, no such creature; the bill in the specimen must needs be, in some way, artificially stuck on' (70).

Thus Melville is careful in this chapter and in the following chapters that consider the same issue to allow *free play* to his reader, not wanting any of us to suffer the problems of Robert the Ram. He therefore limits his specifically epistemological chapters to three and warns the reader each time to expect a 'strange loop' in contents. Chapter 33 is entitled 'Which may pass for whatever it may prove to be worth,' and chapter 44, 'In which the last three words of the last chapter [*quite an original*] are made the text of discourse, which will be sure of receiving more or less attention from those readers who do not skip it.' Epimenides would be proud.

The content of these chapters is no less 'strange loopy' than their

---

18 There is no substitute for reading *all* of *Gödel, Escher, Bach* for understanding self-reference and strange loops. But the reader who needs a quick fix should look at chapter 16, especially 495–500. For a wonderful example of the paradox in action, see 403.

titles. Chapter 33 is 'about' the strain that fiction produces in the reader when it moves away from the 'real' to the fictional. The narrator's comment on this loop is itself a loop: 'Strange, that in a work of amusement, this severe fidelity[19] to real life should be exacted by any one, who, by taking up such a work sufficiently shows that he is not unwilling to drop real life, and turn, for a time, to something different' (182). Fair enough, we are tempted to respond, and our narrator responds with us, or seems to, that

> there is another class, and with this class we side, who sit down to a work of amusement tolerantly as they sit at a play, and with much the same expectations and feelings. They look that fancy shall evoke scenes different from those of the same old crowd round the custom-house counter, and same old dishes on the boarding-house table, with characters unlike those of the same old acquaintances they meet in the same old way every day in the same old street. And as, in real life, the proprieties will not allow people to act out themselves with that unreserve permitted to the stage; so, in books of fiction, they look not only for more entertainment, but, at bottom, even for more reality, than real life itself can show. Thus, though they want novelty, they want nature, too; but nature unfettered, exhilarated, in effect transformed. In this way of thinking, the people in a fiction, like the people in a play, must dress as nobody exactly dresses, talk as nobody exactly talks, act as nobody exactly acts. It is with fiction as with religion; it should present another world, and yet one to which we feel the tie. (182–3)

More reasonable talk, albeit there may be a concealed hook in that last comment, particularly if we keep in mind the implied contrast between the mute's chalked borrowings from one part of 1 Corinthians 13 and the barber's terse summary of the other part.

But all this apparent reasonableness and *content* about fictionality is looped around with the final paragraph of the chapter:

> One word more. Though everyone knows how bootless it is to be in all cases vindicating one's self, never mind how convinced one may be that he is never in the wrong; yet so precious to man is the approbation of his

---

19 In the Bobbs-Merrill edition of *The Confidence-Man* (New York 1967), 259, the editor, H. Bruce Franklin, drops a footnote here that shows he was aware of the recursiveness of this chapter: 'In this word *The Confidence-Man* as a fiction merges with the characters aboard the Fidèle.'

kind, that to rest, though but under an imaginary censure applied to but a work of imagination, is no easy thing. The mention of this weakness will explain why all such readers as may think they perceive something inharmonious between the boisterous hilarity of the cosmopolitan with the bristling cynic, and his restrained good nature with the boon-companion, are now referred to that chapter where some similar apparent inconsistency in another character is, on general principles, modestly endeavored to be apologized for. (183)

I count no less than three recursive statements in that paragraph and sharper eyes can probably find others. 'Bootless' self-vindication persists anyway though one is '*never* [!] in the wrong'; the creator of a 'work of imagination' suffers 'under an *imaginary* censure,' here imagined, and sends his imagined readers off to read yet another of the three recursive chapters, where the same imagined conflict is no less well resolved than it is here. Thus do we the readers board the *Fidèle* and proceed either nineteen chapters backward or eleven forward to discover ourselves exactly where we were before.

Chapter 44 continues the same theme but seems to develop it more specifically if no less enigmatically. The barber's friends' comment that Frank Goodman is 'quite an original' is taken as a phrase to be considered and finally denied as a description of the Cosmopolitan. In the process, the narrative voice is 'led into a dissertation bordering upon the prosy, perhaps upon the smoky' (239), about the appearance of original characters in fiction. Of course, while denying the epithet to all but the rarest of fictional creations – Hamlet is mentioned twice, Don Quixote and Milton's Satan once – the case is made for the Cosmopolitan [?!] for the reader of content, while another case is made for *The Confidence-Man* for the reader of forms. This remarkable *tour de force* of recursion takes place in three very deceptive paragraphs. The first is the best known, in which the 'original' character is compared to a Drummond light 'raying away from itself all round it – everything is lit by it, everything starts up to it (mark how it is with Hamlet).' This is an extraordinary ontological claim, and it is bolstered by the one that follows, that 'in certain minds' who adequately conceive such a character, the effect is 'akin to that which in Genesis attends upon the beginning of things.' The second paragraph denies the supposition that more than one such original can exist in any 'one work of invention,' but that a good fiction may be full of 'new, singular, striking, odd, eccentric, and all sorts of entertaining and instructive characters.' 'To produce such characters,' the paragraph concludes, 'an author, beside other things, must have seen much, and seen through much: to produce but one original character, he must have had much luck.' Then follows the 'smokiest' paragraph of all:

> There would seem but one point in common between this sort of phenomenon in fiction and all other sorts: it cannot be born in the author's imagination – it being as true in literature as in zoology, that all life is from the egg. (239)

I don't know what the reader of content can make of this: that originality in fiction is rare indeed, perhaps. A more subtle reader, though still of content, might conclude that a case is being made ironically for Frank Goodman as 'quite an original' character by seeming to deny it. But the reader who is forewarned by the recursiveness of the title and his experience of chapters 14 and 33 will have no problem identifying the very act of semiosis as the essential quality of this description. The 'certain minds' who have an 'adequate conception' of the 'original character,' who 'is like a revolving Drummond light,' are 'akin to that which in Genesis attends upon the beginning of things.' They need only the Word to create. While only 'authors' who 'must have had much luck' may produce their one original character, that original character 'cannot be born in the *author's* imagination.' It must be, like all life, from the (*fertilized*) egg.[20] Author and reader must join to create the zygote text. Yet this conjunction is the one point that this 'sort of phenomenon' has in common with all other sorts of semiotic connections of writer with reader. Those are couplings of the most domestic kind. These, by contrast, are the couplings of *bliss*. Intercourse takes place in either case, but, ah, what a difference.

These epistemological chapters do not appear, of course, in a vacuum. Each is thematically connected with essential aspects of semiosis 'increasing in seriousness' as the text proceeds. Chapter 14 follows upon the story of Goneril and the 'unfortunate man' and the 'practical criticism' it engenders. The story of Goneril is well known as a marvel of indeterminacy from the very first comments leading to it

---

20 Notice how neatly this comment coincides with Pym's immolation with the shrouded figure, as well as with Barthes's and Barth's metaphors of semiotic juncture, discussed below.

to the last 'critical' conclusions drawn from it by both its teller and audience.[21] Chapter 14, in appearing to answer to the criticism of inconsistency in all these matters, of course merely adds its own Epimenidean level of indeterminacy to the others.

Chapter 33 is set in the middle of a series of narrative puzzles which together create perhaps the most striking example of dramatic indeterminacy before Pirandello. Preceding it is the scene in which, after Charlie Noble is upset by Frank Goodman's sudden request for money, Frank performs a 'magic act' before him by laying ten gold pieces in a circle around Charlie, 'who stood ... rapt ... spellbound, not more by the waving wand than by the ten invincible talismans on the floor.' Frank's incantation follows: 'Reappear, reappear, reappear, oh my former friend! Replace this hideous apparition with thy blest shape, and be the token of thy return the words, "My dear Frank"' (180). When Charlie steps out of the magic circle saying, 'My dear Frank,' the reader is at a loss to determine if a supernatural act has indeed taken place or if two sophisticates have joined in *play* with each other amusingly or competitively. This scene is followed by the story of Charlemont (after the apparent digression of chapter 33) and then the confrontation between the Cosmopolitan, Mark Winsome, and Egbert, and especially the scene played between Frank and Egbert as Frank and Charlie, in which is embedded the story of China Aster. This second play-within-the-play concludes with the Cosmopolitan scornfully handing Egbert a shilling and suggesting that he use it to buy a few woodchips to 'warm the frozen natures of you and your philosopher [Mark Winsome] by' (223). The juxaposition of the two plays-within-the-narrative is surely no accident,[22] and the abrupt shifting by Frank from his dramatic character (Frank) to his 'real' character (Frank) provides a climax to the formal byplay of this aspect of the text. It also immediately precedes the final two 'scenes' of the text: the confrontation with the barber (whom we have not seen since the first, mute chapter) and the *nunc dimittis* concluding scene with the old man.

---

21 These last two are perhaps the least *determined* of all, since we are told that the story is told to us 'in other words than' (59) those used by the merchant, and both teller (merchant) and audience (the man with the travelling-cap) draw every possible conclusion (and some hardly possible at all) from the same(?) text.

22 In 1968 I wrote an adaptation of the novel for the stage, which was produced in Madison, Wisconsin, in Bascom Hall, on April 1st. One of the licences I took with the text was to condense these two dramatic moments into one scene, in which Frank first exposes 'Charlie' with his incantations and then moves out of his acting character to his 'real' character as he dismisses him. Charlie is left wondering what happened and even who he is.

Inserted between these two scenes is chapter 44, and the conjuncture of figure-and-ground and recursiveness is then complete. Which is central in those last chapters, the recursive Epimenidean lesson or the playful dramatic representation of it in the confrontations of the confidence man and his victims? Lesser questions (How many confidence men there are? Is there but one? Is he Christ or Satan?) are forgotten as the formal problem (How can we know truth in a contingent world?) forces itself upon us. If we have paid attention to what Melville was up to, we have followed his clues to the awareness that the work is neither an allegory of ... whatever, nor a comedy ... *humaine* or otherwise; nor theme and variation nor moiré pattern nor Epimenides's paradox, for that matter, but a seamless hyperdimensional structure – indeed, a tesseract – of all these, *playfully* allowing the reader to arrive at the conclusion, so artfully hidden in the structure of the work as a whole, that it is 'as true in literature as in zoology, that all life is from the egg' (239).

Thus *The Confidence-Man*, like *Pym*, leads us to the contemplation of the paradoxical threshold of Learning II. Not the data we process from either text, nor the plums of morality we may pull out from them on our thumbs, but the free exercise of our incomplete selves makes 'the galvanic circuit' complete *through* the full dimensionality of the text. But whereas Poe's strategy is to outrage us with the enormity of Pym's quest to fertilize the universe, Melville's is to *in*rage us with the fertility of the simplest act of reading. He is content, as we must be, to arrive at the locus of meaning and sense the magic of its presence. In the next chapter we will consider a third text with this quality, but in a wholly different form.

6

Raising the Consciousness of
A Connecticut Yankee

Mark Twain's *A Connecticut Yankee in King Arthur's Court* has several
points in common with Poe's *Narrative of Arthur Gordon Pym* and
Melville's *The Confidence-Man* Like *Pym*, its interpretation remains problematic, and its interpreters generally fall into two distinct camps; like
The Confidence-Man, the central problem of interpretation seems to be
what the satire is directed at and how profound that satire is. Yet it also
differs from both those earlier works. No critic, as far as I know, has ever
suggested it is a hoax upon the reader à la *Pym*, and few, if any, would
claim for it the kind of ontological complexity routinely accepted for
The Confidence-Man. However, like Poe and Melville, Twain fulfils our
Plekhanovian criterion of experiencing discord between his art and
his social environment, even though Twain is a long way from being
either a practitioner of 'art for art's sake' or a profound social critic in
A Connecticut Yankee in King Arthur's Court. Still, the fact that the interpretation of the novel remains problematic suggests that the 'semiotic
circuit' has somehow been broken. Perhaps with this work, as with the
others, conventional three-dimensional analysis cannot do it justice.

The two critical camps formed with the very first reviews of the
novel, although at first there was some *nationalist* confusion about the
disagreement. While American critics for the most part simply did not
take the work seriously, those who did read it as a direct satiric attack
against social injustice. 'Who could have suspected Mark Twain of
being a political and social reformer?' asks the anonymous reviewer of
the novel in Henry George's New York *Standard*.[1] 'Yet that is the char-

---

1 7 (1 Jan. 1890), 8; Henry Nash Smith hypothesized the anonymous reviewer 'was
   quite possibly Henry George himself.' See his 'Introduction,' in *A Connecticut*

acter he assumes in [*A Connecticut Yankee in King Arthur's Court*].' This
interpretation is complicated by the problem of the book's illustrations, which were done by Daniel Beard, of whose character as a
'political and social reformer' there can be no doubt whatsoever. Beard
was a socialist and a 'single taxer' and makes specific and direct reference to these causes in his illustrations to the text, however anachro-
nistic they may appear – if it is possible to use the term *anachronism*
about a book like this one. Twain is on record as approving Beard's
illustrations. In one letter written shortly after the book appeared he
wrote that he thought 'the illustrations ... better than the book'; in
another, to Beard himself, he wrote, 'Hold me under permanent obli-
gations. What luck it was to find you! There are a hundred artists who
could illustrate any other book of mine, but there was only one who
could illustrate this one.'[2]

Such unequivocal praise for the specific political interpretation generated by Beard's illustrations would seem to clarify the author's intentions for the work beyond any doubt. But in this case there is some
question as to whether Twain really understood his own intentions.
While he was writing *A Connecticut Yankee in King Arthur's Court*, Twain
was busily engaged in two archetypally capitalist schemes, the publishing of Grant's *Memoirs* and the launching of the Paige typesetting
machine. Moreover, he seems to have associated the latter project
specifically with the novel, wanting to 'finish [the novel] the day the
machine finishes' with the intention of achieving such wealth that he
would never have to write again.[3] Even more bizarre was his interrupt-
ing his work on the novel to attempt to create a board game based on
the linearity of history; he spent several days marking out chronolo-
gies to be followed by the players, hoping, doubtless, to create a money-
maker of the type that moderns associate with *Monopoly*.[4] Indeed, let
us not forget that Twain numbered among his friends many of
the most successful capitalists in America and, although he was indisputably capable of writing forceful and unequivocal works in opposition to rampant capitalism and American and foreign imperialism,

---

Yankee in King Arthur's Court, ed. Bernard L. Stein, in *The Works of Mark Twain*
    (Berkeley: University of California Press 1979), 25; all subsequent references in the
    text are to this edition.
2 Clemens to L.E. Parkhurst, 20 Dec. 1889, Yale; to Beard, 11 Nov. 1889, Mark Twain
    Home Museum, Hannibal, Mo.; both quoted in Smith, 'Introduction,' 15
3 Letter to Theodore Crane, 5 Oct. 1888; cited in Smith, 'Introduction,' 11
4 Justin Kaplan, *Mister Clemens and Mark Twain* (New York: Simon and Schuster
    1966), 252

he was also socially gutless enough to withdraw his welcome to Maxim Gorky when criticisms arose over Gorky's travelling with his alleged mistress.[5]

This two-sidedness of Twain is reflected in Twain criticism in a singularly forceful way. One of the great critics of Twain, named literary executor of his estate in the tradition of Albert Bigelow Paine and Bernard DeVoto, Henry Nash Smith must be considered the foremost Twain expert alive. Yet Smith is on the published record of Twain criticism on both sides of the controversy over *A Connecticut Yankee in King Arthur's Court*. In *Mark Twain: The Development of a Writer* (1962) he argues that 'the novel is a kind of inverse utopia; it implies an endorsement of the political and economic structure of the United States in the 1880's without basic changes' (150). Supporting that assertion are a series of positive judgments about Hank Morgan's behaviour in the novel. He is a self-made man, like Twain himself (151); his autodidactic 'erudition may be ... merely an inadvertent consequence of the author's failure to keep his protagonist distinct from himself' (152). 'He is a Prometheus who undertakes to bring the light of freedom to the common people by first giving them control over the forces of nature' (153). And so on. Smith unequivocally supports a reading of the novel in which Mark Twain virtually identifies with Hank Morgan, The Boss, even at the Battle of the Sand Belt, when he and his fifty-three supporters annihilate the 'chivalry of England' to the tune of the death of twenty-five thousand men.

Of course, Smith is too sensitive a critic to accept the implications of that reading without concluding that such an inhuman result marks an artistic failure. His last two paragraphs on the novel are an attempt to explain its failure. 'Twain had staked all his hopes on history ... But when he put his belief to the test ... some force other than his con-

---

5 See, among others, 'The Czar's Soliloquy,' 'King Leopold's Soliloquy,' 'To the Person Sitting in Darkness,' 'The United States of Lyncherdom,' and much of *Letters from the Earth*. For the most complete analysis of this side of Twain, see Maxwell Geismar, *Mark Twain: An American Prophet* (New York: McGraw-Hill 1970). A propos of his loss of courage over the Gorky visit, when Geismar's book was excerpted by the old *Ramparts* magazine, I published a letter to the editor pointing out the exquisite irony of Twain's going to Stanford White for advice about how to deal with Gorky's apparent *faux pas* with his mistress. White took time out from his contemplation of Evelyn Nesbit on her red velvet swing to advise Twain to have nothing more to do with Gorky. As a result of that letter I was for years the target of fund-raising letters by every right-wing organization in America from the Heritage Foundation to the Minute Men.

scious intention convinced him that his belief in progress and human perfectibility was groundless' (170). Unfortunately, that conclusion leads Smith further to conclude that never again would Mark Twain 'regain contact with the vernacular affirmations that had sustained his development toward the climax of his achievement in *Huckleberry Finn*' (170).

Naturally enough, Smith could not long be satisfied with that conclusion either. A year later he used the opportunity to deliver the Brown and Haley Lectures at the University of Puget Sound to reconsider his reading of *A Connecticut Yankee in King Arthur's Court*.[6] As he explained his rethinking of the problem of the novel, his first reading was based upon considering Hank Morgan as a vernacular character in the style of Huck Finn. Although he still found that approach valid, he had 'become aware of another aspect of Mark Twain's thought which led [him] to place Hank Morgan in a different context, to see him as a member also of the numerous company of businessmen in nineteenth-century American fiction. He is a vernacular hero but also a capitalist hero' (4). This dual vision of Hank, then, almost inevitably leads him to a *rapprochement* with the text at the cost of concluding that the book is a failure as a work of art:

> My analysis has led me to dwell upon the inconsistencies in thought and technique that mar a potential masterpiece. My vision of what it might have become has perhaps made me unduly severe in dealing with the story that Mark Twain actually wrote. If I seem to regard it as on the whole a failure, I hope I have demonstrated that it is the failure of a great writer, and therefore both interesting and important. (5)

Smith was true to his word. His conclusion is that Twain's split vision of Hank Morgan as 'American Adam and American Prometheus' is a 'failure' comparable to Henry Adams's failure to 'interpret [the modern world] by means of scientific concepts' (104–5).[7] And, as he had done in his first consideration of the novel, Smith carried that conclusion further to its logical implication that Twain's later works are also failures:

---

6 Published as *Mark Twain's Fable of Progress: Political and Economic Ideas in 'A Connecticut Yankee'* (New Brunswick, NJ: Rutgers University Press 1964)

7 It's perhaps interesting to note the difference between this attitude concerning Henry Adams's historicism and that expressed in some of the critical comments about Thomas Pynchon's use of Adams. See chapter 9.

> ... at some point in the composition of this fable he had passed the great divide in his career as a writer ... When he found it impossible to show how the values presented by his vernacular protagonist could survive in an industrial society, he lost his faith in the value system of that society. Henceforth he worked as a writer in a kind of spiritual vacuum. His imagination was virtually paralyzed. He was never again able to reach the level of his achievement in *Adventures of Huckleberry Finn.* (107)

When the foremost critic of a great writer analyses the same work twice and comes to diametrically opposed conclusions about it, but both conclusions agree that the work is a failure, it seems likely that we are once again confronting a work that approaches Learning II, the confusion of metaphor and metonymy, and hyperdimensionality: some or all the problems we have seen in *Pym* and *The Confidence-Man.*

From the very first references to the topic that was to become *A Connecticut Yankee in King Arthur's Court*, Mark Twain projects an ambivalent attitude about the subject matter and the manner of dealing with it. A telegram to Charles Webster signed by 'Sir Mark Twain' and 'Sir George W. Cable' is written in a respectful parody of Maloryan English.[8] A journal entry from about the same time sketches some ideas for a tasteless burlesque of modern sensibility in medieval circumstances:

> Dream of being a knight errant in armor in the middle ages. Have the notions & habits of the present day mixed with the necessities of that. No pockets in the armor. No way to manage certain requirements of nature. Can't scratch. Cold in the head – can't blow – can't get at handkerchief, can't use iron sleeves ...[9]

This schism of both style and content continues through the writing of the book, its reception, and down to the present day in Henry Nash

---

8 Arlin Turner, *Mark Twain and George W. Cable: The Record of a Literary Friendship* (East Lansing: Michigan State University Press 1960), 96, gives the text, which is clever and suggestive of a writer's respect for Malory's language. For other examples of Twain's philology, see his essay 'The Awful German Language' and his retranslation from the French (of the *Revue des deux mondes*) back into English [?!] of 'The Celebrated Jumping Frog of Calaveras County.'

9 *Mark Twain's Notebooks and Journals, Volume III (1883–1891)*, ed. R.P. Browning, M.B. Frank, and L. Salamo (Berkeley: University of California Press 1979), 78

Smith's (and other critics') mixed conclusions about it. The book appears to be an indeterminable mishmash of modes, styles, genres, and intentions. To borrow Frye's terminology, it has elements of both high and low mimetic. It might be classed in various parts as romantic, tragic, comic, and ironic, and it begs to be read at all four of Frye's levels, the literal, the formal, the mythic, and the anagogic, in its motifs, images, archetypes, and monads! Not content with Frye, we could branch out farther into the genres of utopian and dystopian fiction, children's literature, and homily, and doubtless other modes as well. Of course, in any such analysis we would conclude that *A Connecticut Yankee in King Arthur's Court* is a botch, and we might even go further, with Henry Nash Smith, to see it as a symptom of Twain's defeat by the requirements of form leading to his decline from literature to the frustrations of the unfinished works left behind in the Mark Twain Papers.

One part of the novel helps to make sense of all these disparate and self-contradictory qualities of the work: its basic unifying formal device, the frame. *A Connecticut Yankee in King Arthur's Court* is Twain's only finished work detailing an almost obsessive concern on his part about the relationship between reality and dream and its correspondent analogue in the relationship between real life and fiction. This motif as it appears here and elsewhere in his fictions consists of a person/character living two lives, one apparently in the here-and-now of the fiction, the other in a totally different world: now struggling to survive in a drop of water, now running things in Arthur's England, now as the dream-creator of the entire universe.[10] The dream-character may have fantastic powers, but 'in dreams begin responsibilities,' as Yeats noted, and these powers may cross over uncomfortably to the 'waking state' (assuming the dream and waking states can be distinguished). In this obsessive concern we have the evidence for a variation on Plekhanov's comment on the artist and his society. Although the contradiction between Twain and his society was not 'hopeless,' it was certainly discordant enough to discourage his 'readiness to participate in social struggles' (Plekhanov, 48) when the fruits of capitalism were displayed next to the advantages he had to gain as a successful artist. Torn by this contradiction, Twain as often as not chose to

10 In, respectively, 'Which Was the Dream?', *A Connecticut Yankee in King Arthur's Court*, and *The Mysterious Stranger*

write with that 'readiness to participate in social struggles,' in such late political works as 'To the Person Sitting in Darkness' and 'King Leopold's Soliloquy.' Just as often he chose to escape such matters with romances like *The Prince and the Pauper* and *Joan of Arc*.[11]

Only in *A Connecticut Yankee in King Arthur's Court* did Twain successfully complete a work in which this conflict of *forms* plays the central part, and, as we have seen, his success includes a rupture of the semiotic circuit: that is, critics and readers of the novel in general have not been able to connect with his formal intent. Yet when the text is observed in terms of its topological analogues, its difficulties resolve themselves. If we look at the text as an example of two three-dimensional narratives occupying the same space, it becomes perfectly coherent. One of the texts is a metonymic ironic comedy creating topical satire very successfully. A spatial isomorphism for it would be an unbounded curve because its purpose is direct satire which would lead to specific reforms of contemporary society. The other text is a mythic (hence metaphoric) black comedy (in our terms from chapter 3, in the cusp between Frye's romantic and tragic modes, and therefore in the Plekhanovian hiccup), which is equally successful but which includes a semiotic short-circuit. It could be mapped in the same space as the metonymic satire, but it should be represented in terms of closed curves because its effect is a recursive one concerning the necessary forms of art (see fig. 6.1). Some of the critical difficulties arise simply because of this complex and unusual form, but the most significant problems come from Twain's short-circuiting the more familiar structure – the satire – to force the reader into the insecurities of the approach to Learning II.

Few readers have any problems with the metonymic text. As was the case with *The Confidence-Man*, most of the problems the text raises can be resolved by the kind of foot-work the critic is supposed to perform in the quincuncial garden of aesthetic. It is useful to point out that the anecdote about military appointments under Arthur satirizes the dodges that go with appointments under the spoils system, as criticized by Grover Cleveland, and that the appropriations for Arthur's 'touching' for the King's Evil has its parallels with various pork-barrel

---

11 Both works, of course, also have their social content. See Geismar, *Mark Twain*, 66–71, 112, 140; and V.L. Parrington, *The Beginnings of Critical Realism in America, 1860–1920*, Vol. 3 in *Main Currents in American Thought* (New York: Harcourt Brace 1930), 91, 97, 99.

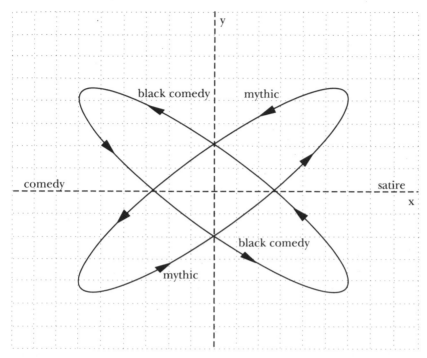

Fig. 6.1   Coding for aesthetic, coding for ideology

laws like the River and Harbor Bill of 1889.[12] Most of these problems of interpretation remain strictly metonymic tasks of combination, and all of them *may* be treated that way. But some few allow the critic to make a dimensional leap, and some others virtually force him to, usually unhappily, like Robert the Ram. The Armageddon/Hiroshima quality of the Battle of the Sand Belt is the best example of the latter, and we shall examine it in some detail. Before we do, however, let us look at several instances where the critical reader is *invited* to free play in the interpretation of a text that has both metonymic and metaphoric qualities.

One of the purest of these is the economic discussion that takes place from chapter 32 to the opening paragraphs of chapter 34. In this section Hank and the king put on a grand feast for the villagers,

---

12 See, among many others who perform this useful function of the critic, Walter
    Blair, *Horse Sense in American Humor* (New York: Russell and Russell 1942), 206–7.

ostensibly in thanks for favours received from Marco, but, upon the introduction of Dowley the blacksmith and his insufferable pretensions, the occasion also proves useful for putting him in his place. The discussion after the feast is about two points of basic economics: money as a relative or absolute determinant of value, and the power of *combination* to determine wealth.[13] The whole discussion is something of a put-up job, since to make it work properly Twain had to use the gimmick of mentioning that The Boss had recently introduced coinage into the society (349).

The metonymic reader may be excused for not seeing very deeply into the implications of these chapters. To begin with, the whole business of coinage seems to be present merely for the effect of the punch-line in chapter 32. After going on and on about the magnificence of the feast, including an itemized bill in five figures, The Boss, 'with an air of indifference amounting almost to weariness, got out [his] money and tossed four dollars onto the table' (364–5). When he then adds that the clerk may keep the change (eight and a half cents, or eight hundred and fifty millrays in The Boss's new coinage, or the cost of one roast of beef and one roast of mutton in the itemized bill [364], it is clear that the effect intended is burlesque, not serious satire. What satire there is seems totally directed at the middle-class pretensions of Dowley the blacksmith. Here is The Boss's summation of the effect he achieved:

Ah, well, it was immense; yes, it was a daisy. I don't know that I ever put a situation together better, or got happier spectacular effects out of the materials available. The blacksmith – well, he was simply mashed. Land! I wouldn't have felt what that man was feeling, for anything in the world. Here he had been blowing and bragging about his grand meat-feast twice a year, and his fresh meat twice a month, and his salt meat twice a

---

13 This point is really confused by Beard's illustrations, which point specifically to the contemporary issue of protectionism as 'natural opportunity' limited to the capitalist, with labour relegated to licking up the profits which have 'trickled down.' The text barely supports that reference (see pages 369 and 373). This is curious because the text would support vigorous illustration of the power of combination in the hands of labour and especially its *revolutionary* possibilities. Beard's illustrations all emphasize the *evolution* of inequality between capital and labour. Perhaps Beard saw the possibility for the reading I am here proposing and held back from its ambivalent implications. It is more likely that as a 'single taxer' he preferred a more gradual approach to socialism.

week, and his white bread every Sunday the year round – all for a family
of three: the entire cost for the year not above 69.2.6 (sixty-nine cents,
two mills and six millrays), and all of a sudden here comes along a man
who slashes out nearly [*sic*] four dollars on a single blow-out; and not
only that, but acts as if it made him tired to handle such small sums. Yes,
Dowley was a good deal wilted, and shrunk-up, and collapsed; he had the
aspect of a bladder-balloon that's been stepped on by a cow. (365)

The ensuing conversation seems to be more of the same, except
that here The Boss's superiority is intellectual rather than economic.
His argument is taken from the opening chapter of Adam Smith's *The
Wealth of Nations*: value is determined by the amount of work involved
in the production of goods. Adam Smith's example finessed the use of
money; if in a primitive society it takes twice as much work to kill a
beaver as it takes to kill a deer, then two deer = one beaver in value.
The Boss, because he allows money to enter into the argument, loses
Dowley in the semiotic maze of the different meanings that may be
applied to words like *high* and *low* when they may stand for absolute
and relative wealth and value. Again and again The Boss *proves* that
'"high wages" and "low wages" are phrases that don't mean anything
in the world until you find out which of them will *buy* the most' (373).
Alas, each time he is defeated by what he comes to feel is the invincible ignorance of his opponent.

Then, without having defined the nature of value, The Boss persists
in continuing the discussion in a most curious way. He introduces the
'unwritten law of wages' as a corollary to the 'law of progress' in an
apparently casual way, but really he is out to 'get even' with Dowley for
'apparently [being] defeated in argument by an ignorant country blacksmith' (374). He then shocks Dowley with the notion that unionized
working men could take over the magistrates' job of setting wages,
provoking him to anger over the thought of 'an age of dogs, an age
barren of reverence for superiors and respect for authority' (377).
Then, after reminding Dowley and the rest of the penalties for even
the most minor violations of the law, he sets up Dowley for his 'smasher'
when he reminds him that he had admitted paying more than the
established wages only moments before.

The result is remarkable. Where the effect of the punch-line of the
earlier deflation of Dowley – the throwing down of the four dollars
with the admonition to keep the change – had been pure comedy, the
effect this time is disastrous. The company cannot 'recover from the
shock, they couldn't seem to pull themselves together. Pale shaky,

dumb, pitiful? Why they weren't any better than so many dead men'
(379). Worse, in the next chapter the villagers retaliate by helping the
slave trader to add the king and The Boss to his collection. The disas-
ter is not limited to the afflicted but is reflected back upon its creator.
What has caused this enormous difference?

When Melville performed almost exactly the same dramatic contrast in *The Confidence-Man*, we saw what he was up to because of the
narrative asides of chapters 33 and 44 that provided a context for
discriminating *formal* paradox from mere paradox of action. Frank's
creation of the 'magic circle' of gold pieces along with his incantation
to Charlie to return with the sign 'My dear Frank' creates its effect
directly upon the reader because of the reader's belief in the reality of
the action of the two characters. Twain lulls us into a sense of splen-
dour by the simple expedient of moving decimal places in the discussion of the feast, only to win us back with the casualness of the gesture
of throwing down four dollars. In both cases the effect is pure comedy
because our expectations were drawn away from the ordinary to the
magical and mythic and then deflated to the ordinary again. In our
terms, these are parallel Learning I experiences.

When Melville does the same sort of thing in the play-within-the play
dialogue between Frank and Egbert (playing Frank and Charlie), the
conclusion is more unsettling because we are momentarily caught unaware of which level of play we are in – exactly the problem Dowley and
the Marcos face with The Boss's cruel manipulation. What has happened
in both cases is that *the consciousness of all concerned has been raised*. The
raising of consciousness is the chief effect of the approach to Learning II, but its effect is radically different on 'teachers' and 'students.'
Robert the Ram, Egbert the disciple, and Dowley the blacksmith all
'learn' metaphoric-metonymic discrimination as an analogue to Learning I. That is, they 'learn' to tell the difference, but they don't understand the nature of the difference. Robert the Ram's 'teachers,' Frank
Goodman, and The Boss have a kind of free play available to them the
others lack, and the results may differ. They may approach Learning II by
achieving awareness of the nature of the discrimination of forms available to them. (Liddell certainly shows awareness of the moral problems
attendant upon his kind of experiment, but I doubt that it caused him to
give up his profession.)[14] Frank goes on to ever more complex encoun-

---

14 That such a result is possible is proved by the well-known case of John Lilly, whose
    dolphin studies raised his consciousness to a level far beyond that of Liddell's
    about Robert the Ram's.

ters aimed at seeing Learning II through a glass, darkly. And The Boss goes on to set the wheels rolling towards the Battle of the Sand Belt and the destruction of chivalry.

The reader has the freest play of all. Most of Liddell's readers presumably add him to their optional reading lists and recommend him to squeamish undergraduates who have problems notching rats' ears. The best of Melville's readers seem to have caught up to him in the last generation and give ontological aid and comfort to their students puzzled over Frank and Charlie's debate. Perhaps some of them even realize that their 'nets and ladders' are primarily useful when they are thrown away. As for the reader of *A Connecticut Yankee in King Arthur's Court*, the freedom of the text is more than subtly subversive, especially since modern readers have had their consciousness raised by the events of the past fifty years about what they tend to think of as particularly 'Yankee' behaviour. The Holocaust, Hiroshima, and especially the Vietnamese and Gulf wars have all changed the *norm* of human understanding about political behaviour. Each of these political events has become a variable which also affects a modern reader's response to the novel. Therefore to understand how the novel works, we must examine how these events have affected us.

The Holocaust stands as a symbol of the excess of horror visited upon the world as a result of the *Führerprinzip*, which is nothing but good old American *Bossism* translated into Old World customs. When the Yankee takes 'The Boss' as his title in the title-conscious world of Arthur's realm, he identifies himself as a political pragmatist outside of the hierarchy of feudalism, but determined to start his own hierarchy from the top down. Twain had shown his interest in the problems of bossism as early as his collaboration with Warner on *The Gilded Age* (1873), and *A Connecticut Yankee in King Arthur's Court* reflects his most mature thoughts on the subject. They are very mature: indeed, they approach Learning II in their awareness of the mixed nature of the formality of leadership.[15] The Boss's political program is quite simple. It consists of *laissez-faire* capitalism softened by paternalistic concern for the working classes. What furthers that program is good; what deters it is bad. He is a complete determinist, apparently, and foresees conflict as the inevitable result of his position in Arthur's realm:

---

15 The period of the writing of *A Connecticut Yankee in King Arthur's Court* was rich in studies of the problems of political leadership or bossism. See chapter 7 of my *The Popular American Novel, 1865–1920* (Boston: G.K. Hall 1980), 96–118.

> Inherited ideas are a curious thing ... I had mine, the king and his
> people had theirs. In both cases they flowed in ruts worn deep by time
> and habit, and the man who should have proposed to divert them by
> reason and argument would have had a long contract on his hands.
> (111)

He is also pragmatic about power and its ability to transform a society.
He cannot help but feel proud about the changes he brings to Arthur's
England with his new program, and he correctly identifies the source
as his transforming imagination and even partly identifies its flaws:

> Unlimited power *is* the ideal thing – when it is in safe hands. The despot-
> ism of heaven is the one absolutely perfect government. An earthly des-
> potism would be the absolutely perfect earthly government, if the condi-
> tions were the same, namely, the despot the perfectest individual of the
> human race ... (127–8)

But he cannot escape the inherent inconsistency in his deterministic
formulation. If man is completely determined, then there is no self;
but if there is a self that is separate from the mechanical quality of
determined behaviour, it must be incalculably more significant than
the rest:

> Training – training is everything; training is all there is *to* a person. We
> speak of nature; it is folly; there is no such thing as nature; what we call
> by that misleading name is merely heredity and training. We have no
> thoughts of our own, no opinions of our own: they are transmitted to us,
> trained into us. All that is original in us, and therefore fairly creditable
> or discreditable to us, can be covered up and hidden by the point of a
> cambric needle, all the rest being atoms, contributed by and inherited
> from, a procession of ancestors that stretches back a billion years to the
> Adam-clam or grasshopper or monkey from whom our race has been so
> tediously and ostentatiously and unprofitably developed. And as for me,
> all that I think about in this plodding sad pilgrimage, this pathetic drift
> between the eternities, is to look out and humbly live a pure and high
> and blameless life, and save that one microscopic atom in me that is truly
> *me*: the rest may land in Sheol and welcome, for all I care. (208)

Here is the heart of the first paradox of Learning II, and it could
hardly be better stated. *Being* has different dimensions, indeed, may
inhabit quite separate worlds, and mastery of the self need have no

connection with mastery of the [other] world. Insofar as The Boss is a mythic creation, a modern parallel to Lancelot or Arthur as the Hero, he takes on the modern quality of the hero, which includes such existential questions as these. This quality is inappropriate to the non-mythic text and begins the process of demolishing the reader's faith in it.

As Der Führer was to the nineteenth-century American political boss, the atomic bomb and the lesson of Hiroshima was to the relatively benign effect of technology in the nineteenth century. Hank Morgan[16] knows that he is taking unfair technological advantage of his opponents when he goes into the tournament with Sir Sagramour and begins the inevitable escalation that ends with the Battle of the Sand Belt. Twain in several of his other works attacks the imperialist use of advanced technology against more primitive cultures, but no writer in the nineteenth century could yet imagine where technological advantage was to lead. The myth of unlimited power used to consist of a sword drawn from a rock and exercised in the name of Righteousness. Hank Morgan discovers that Excalibur can be as destructive to the one who wields it as it is to his victims. Or does he? To the very end of the non-mythic text he remains proud that he has lived up to his boast, 'engraved in brass, posted ... where any priest could read it ... [that he] would take fifty assistants and stand up *against the massed chivalry of the whole earth and destroy it*' (442–3; italics in the original). It takes the reassertion of myth in the form of Merlin giving him the sleep of enchantment to make him resurrect those existential doubts that he had shown earlier.

For, as was the case for the majority of Americans with the Vietnamese War, Hank resists with all his being the superimposition of myth over 'reality.' When his fifty-three boys show some consideration for the people who are marching against them, that they are, as their spokesman says, 'bone of our bone, flesh of or flesh, we love them – do not ask us to destroy our nation!' (475), he resorts to semantic obfuscation. It is not the people of England who are marching against them but its *chivalry*. 'None but nobles and gentry are knights, and *none but these* will remain to dance to our music' (475; italics in the

---

16 The Boss is not given a name until chapter 39, and we have only his disciple Clarence's word for it then. Naming a character who has gone by a badgelike title usually softens his character. 'Hank' certainly countrifies The Boss somewhat, but the associations with the pirate Henry Morgan and that other Morgan, J.P., make the result ambivalent.

original). The dechivalrization of war was well begun by the time
Twain wrote *A Connecticut Yankee in King Arthur's Court*, and Hank's
Gatling guns, glass torpedoes, and electrified fence represent a high
level of impersonality for their time. Almost the last words that Hank
writes in the part of the manuscript that is his text is a foreshadowing
of the Vietnamese War's substitution of a body count for a battle
report: 'Within ten short minutes after we had opened fire, armed
resistance was totally annihilated, the campaign was ended, we fifty-
four were masters of England! Twenty-five thousand men lay dead
around us' (486).[17]

The problem with 'reality,' this novel seems to tell us, is that it gets
confused with ideology[18] and needs myth to straighten it out from
time to time. To a nineteenth-century reader of *A Connecticut Yankee in
King Arthur's Court* Hank Morgan is just a 'typical' Yankee – hence
'realistic' in one sense and symbolic of certain character traits in another. Where these qualities come into conflict with older ideas like
chivalry and *nobility*, that reader is likely to choose sides or ideologies
and 'root' either for progress or for more conservative values, as was
indeed the case in the earliest reviews of the work. The modern reader,
with the experience of the American involvement in Vietnam as part
of her critical apparatus, has had her consciousness raised to the point
that she can read Hank as a *mythic* Yankee for whom the conflict of
ideologies is the issue. For such a reader, Hank recalls the case of
Colonel Corson, as described by Mary McCarthy:

> A graduate of the University of Chicago, studied with Korzybski, taught
> at a college in Florida, worked or served in China. Eleven thousand
> peasants are the material he has been given to work with. He defines the

---

17 Compare Hemingway's well-known opening paragraph to *A Farewell to Arms*, 'The
   cholera was checked and only six thousand died.' Hemingway's ironic intent is
   clear and the satire pronounced and three-dimensional. Hank is still as confused
   about the *quality* of his reality here in the penultimate paragraph of his narrative as
   he was anywhere else in it. Which is the dream?
18 'Ideology is a partial and disconnected world vision; by disregarding the multiple
   interconnections of the semantic universe, it also conceals the pragmatic reasons
   for which certain signs (with all their various interpretations) were produced. This
   oblivion produces a false conscience', (Eco, *A Theory of Semiotics*, 297). Hence
   conflict in ideologies may be described in three-dimensional texts, but criticism of
   aesthetic texts with ideological content requires analysis of *formal* distinctions and
   analogues in hyperdimensional space. For further analysis of this matter, see
   chapters 2 and 9.

method he uses as Empirical Causality. He quotes Lenin: 'Scratch a peasant, and you'll find a bourgeois.' 'Well, I'm scratching. And scratching.' His young officers have made a painted scale model, like a crêche, in papier-maché of an ideal Vietnamese hamlet, which will probably really be built. Colonel Corson is ingenious. He has designed a large pig sty suited to local conditions and he is donating his marine garbage to feed the peasants' pigs, solving two problems with one concise stroke ...

He is a cynic. To him the profit motive is the sole incentive capable of spurring anybody to productive effort. 'You wrote *The Group* to make money, didn't you?' When I answered no, the fact that it had made so much money had surprised me, he looked actually startled. 'What do you write for, then?' In the center of the model hamlet, which his officers, like children at Christmas, had stayed up half the night to finish, was a large dollar sign painted bronze. He gave a crooked smile. He was actually, or so he claimed, planning to erect it as a monument seven feet high, in the hamlet. The young captain and the young lieutenant smiled. He was a man of whom it could be said, 'He was worshipped by his officers.' Partly because he amused them; he was witty and sardonic. And he had a sort of fantasy that did not chime badly with his brass tacks. In one corner of the model hamlet was a thatched apiary, one of the peasants was going to be transformed into a bee-keeper. Bees and pigs ... the colonel's georgic, though, had realism behind it. He was trying to wean the peasants away from the monoculture – rice – the French had saddled them with and which, with the rent system and government taxes, had turned them into paupers.[19]

The post–Vietnamese War reader no longer has the luxury of the kind of innocence with which early readers of *A Connecticut Yankee in King Arthur's Court* greeted the novel. Do we live in myth or in reality? Is Colonel Corson engaged in a pastoral or a war? The colonel's 'georgic' is the more startling for the horror of its surroundings; so Hank's horrendous conclusion to his pastoral fantasy is the more shocking, and therefore the more likely to shift our attention from the probability of the event to the formal pattern which has created our shock. In that respect it has an interesting relationship to the other two works we have examined. Like *Pym* it is so easy to read that the shocking and disturbing part of it has a much more intense effect

---

19 *New York Review of Books*, 18 May 1967, 9; reprinted with minor changes in *The Seventeenth Degree* (New York: Harcourt, Brace 1974), 137–8

than the equivalent in *The Confidence-Man*. Unlike *Pym* its hyper-dimensional shift is not to the world of aesthetic forms but from aesthetic to *political* forms. And, as we saw in chapter 2 was the case with Eco and de Man, this path to the threshold of Learning II is particularly disturbing. Since Twain, like Poe and unlike Melville, has only recently been given much credit for his intellectual capabilities, the academic and critical community has been more resistant to accepting his works when they challenge the norms of either metonymic or metaphoric interpretation. Let us hope that the exercise we have just undertaken will prove to more critics that he is worth the imaginative effort.

PART THREE

Three Postmodern Texts

7

The Lemniscate Topology of
Pale Fire

Vladimir Nabokov's *Pale Fire* (1962) is the *archetext* of postmodernism. Although *Lolita* (1955) represents Nabokov's earliest best-known fully postmodern fiction, and *Ada* (1969) is arguably his most fully developed exercise in the mode, *Pale Fire* remains the most striking example of the essential postmodern ever written. As such, of course, it has been thoroughly examined by critical specialists of the postmodern mode to such an extent that it is hard to imagine anything new could be discovered in it.[1] Nevertheless, a survey of the novel's readings turns up the same kinds of evidence for multiple variables that we found for our nineteenth-century texts. As was the case with *Pym* and *A Connecticut Yankee in King Arthur's Court* there is a basic division of interpretive stances: the novel may be either 'Shade-based' or 'Kinbote-based.' Second, like *The Confidence-Man*, the novel has had a reputation for *difficulty* since it appeared, but there has been some question all along as to whether its content is of ontological interest or merely

---

1 There is even some criticism of *Pale Fire* that attempts various kinds of analogical readings. These include Carol T. Williams, ' "Web of Sense": *Pale Fire* in the Nabokov Canon,' *Critique* 6 (1963), 29–45; J. L. Lee, 'Vladimir Nabokov's Great Spiral of Being,' *Western Humanities Review* 18 (1964), 25–36; David Walker, ' "The Viewer and the View": Chance and Choice in *Pale Fire*,' *Studies in American Fiction* 4 (1976), 203–21 [analogy to three-dimensional chess]; June Perry Levine, 'Vladimir Nabokov's *Pale Fire*: The Method of Composition as Hero,' *International Fiction Review* 5 (1978), 103–8; D. Barton Johnson, 'The Index of Refraction in Nabokov's *Pale Fire*,' *Russian Literature TriQuarterly* 16 (1979), 33–49. The last two are not, strictly speaking, analogical in their method, but they work from respectively structuralist and physical analogues.

Nabokovian game-playing. Therefore *Pale Fire* seems to be the ideal text to begin our examination of the possibility that a search for hyperdimensional analogues may contribute to the novel's interpretation ... the more so in this case because there is good evidence that *Nabokov himself directly suggested that the novel be read as a hyperdimensional narration.*

As anyone can imagine, the first reviews of a novel in the form of a poem with annotations, a foreword, and an index are likely to be confused and even aggressively negative.[2] But Nabokov was fortunate that one of the earliest reviews of *Pale Fire* was also one of the best critical insights into the text and is still cited in many critical essays on *Pale Fire.* Mary McCarthy reviewed the novel for the *New Republic* the week after it was published and correctly identified the lines of interpretation that are still the principal concerns of critical investigation.[3] She pointed out that the writing of the poem and the narrative element of the annotations are linked and that this relationship between parts is the central issue of interpretation. She also, along with many other early commentators, pointed out how important verbal play was to the novel and explicated a number of telling examples. She was only among the first in a long line of annotators who have helped pick out the path in this novel's aesthetic garden. Indeed, it is probably fair (albeit unkind) to say that most criticism of *Pale Fire* consists of bravura displays of interpretive insight on the part of the critic at explaining Nabokov's verbal pyrotechnics.

Formal criticism of *Pale Fire* has largely bogged down on the problem of determining the relative importance of the two main characters. Since Mary McCarthy, critics have begun with the assumption that the critical 'key' to the novel is the interpretation of the relationship between John Shade, poet, and Charles Kinbote, editor-annotator, with '*Gradus, Jakob* ... alias Jack Degree,'[4] the principal intermediary be-

---

2 Some, of course, were. See 'Another Fancy Failure by the Author of "Lolita,"' *People's World* [San Fransisco], 13 Oct. 1962, 7; and Kenneth Allsop, 'After *Lolita* Is This Nabokov Just Pulling Our Legs?' *London Daily Mail*, 8 Nov. 1962, 12.

3 'A Bolt from the Blue,' *New Republic* 146 (4 June 1962), 21–7; modified slightly in *Encounter* 19 (Oct. 1962), 71–2, 74, 76–8, 80–2, 84

4 *S.v.* Gradus. Reference to *Pale Fire* is complicated by the fact that the original Putnam printing (1962) was small and most academics, like me, own one or another of the many printings by Berkeley Medalion Books. Mine is the eleventh printing (1975; bought at Cedarn, Utana, in a most grubby used bookstore), and it is so heavily annotated that I would be lost without it. So I have decided to refer to line numbers for the poem, annotation numbers for the annotations, and *sub verbo*

tween them. Among less insightful critics, this has led to a controversy somewhat like the one among *Pym* critics. Those who find the novel to be 'Shade-based' have problems with what they feel are the artistic inadequacies of the poem,[5] while those who believe it to be 'Kinbote-based' must struggle with 'the fact that the poem is completely self-contained and self-explanatory, while the commentary, as it stands, does not make sense without the poem.'[6]

Thwarted in their efforts to discover the formal *potaynik*,[7] some of the best critics have turned to the hardly less valuable exercise of pointing out the richness of the tradition in English and Russian literature that Nabokov draws upon for *Pale Fire*. Thus John O. Lyons points out that much of the comedy proceeds from Nabokov's own experience translating (and annotating) Pushkin's *Eugene Onegin*;[8] Bader emphasizes the influence of the Romantics, especially Wordsworth, but also footnotes Matthew Arnold and Andrew Marvell (39, 53); Lucy Madox emphasizes the Boswell-Johnson relationship;[9] G.M. Hyde ranges through Pope and the Augustans, Boswell and Johnson, 'history as taught in the school of Sir Walter Scott,' Robert Frost, the Romantics again, Johnson's *Rasselas* and concludes with emphasis on Pushkin and *Eugene Onegin* again.[10] All of these efforts are useful guides to the pathway through the garden of the text, but dependence upon traditional and conventional techniques of logical and phenomenological analysis may not work at all on postmodernist fiction. If our esemplastic scalpels do not allow for greater dimensional possibilities than are available to common sense, we may end up critically disembowelling

references to the Index. The Foreword in my text runs from page page 7 to 19, so that I will cite page numbers for it which the reader can prorate for her text. OK?

5 Andrew Field, in his *Nabokov: His Life in Art* (Boston: Little, Brown 1967), takes delight in making this point to the pro-Shaders.

6 Julia Bader, *Crystal Land: Artifice in Nabokov's English Novels* (Berkely: University of California Press 1972), 55

7 *S.v.* see also *taynik, hiding place*, and *Crown Jewels*.

8 John O. Lyons, '*Pale Fire* and the Fine Art of Annotation,' in *Nabokov: The Man and His Work*, ed. L.S. Dembo (Milwaukee: University of Wisconsin Press 1967), 157–64; reprinted from *Wisconsin Studies in Contemporary Literature* (Spring 1967)

9 Lucy Maddox, *Nabokov's Novels in English* (Athens: University of Georgia Press 1983), 31–3.

10 G.M. Hyde, *Vladimir Nabokov: America's Russian Novelist* (London: Marion Boyars 1977), 171–87. The chapter title also alludes to Pirandello: 'One Character in Search of an Author.' Yet Hyde is aware of the deceptiveness of his approach. He remarks that '*Pale Fire* is ... a gift to the explicator (actually a fatal poison wrapped up like a chocolate cream)' (176).

ourselves. *Pale Fire* is a perfect example. *Only* through the recognition that the structure of the fiction is hyperdimensional can we begin to discover that 'locus of meaning' when it approaches Learning II. Keeping these ideas in mind, let us proceed this time by examining the process that the reader must go through when he encounters this most unusual work.

Nabokov wastes no time. The first three paragraphs of the Foreword introduce us to the multiple dimensions of the work.[11] The first introduces the nine hundred and ninety-nine lines of the manuscript poem on the eighty index cards: its physical form; the second the near-perfect triptych form of the text; the third the act of creation of the work by John Shade, and, with its apparently irrelevant last sentence, the character of its annotator, Kinbote. From that point on, the Foreword continues its triple function of introducing the physical form of the poem, its formal structure, and the characters who shape it and are it, including, of course, Kinbote. The reflections upon the editor himself serve chiefly to clarify for the reader the very great differences between this introduction and the normal, functional introduction that the Foreword impersonates. It is impossible to estimate the ironic content of the Foreword accurately. Kinbote's self-revelation is inadvertent, a circumstance which of course serves to make the reader even more suspicious of all the information he imparts. That the Foreword pretends to be a serious introduction by a serious scholar, when it ludicrously fails to be so, tends to make even the most naïve reader suspicious and to at least raise the possibility that the poem which follows is also pretending to be something it is not.

That suspicion is not easy to maintain. The only element of the Foreword which is authoritative and subject to verification by the reader is its description of the formal structure of the poem. Kinbote informs us that the poem consists of four cantos of 166, 334, 334, and 165 lines. Furthermore, the last line of Canto 4 rhymes with the first line of Canto 1, which leads Kinbote to what I shall call the 'Kinbotean Conjecture': that Shade intended to reprint line 1 as the concluding line, thereby fulfilling the symmetry. Kinbote bolsters our belief in the Kinbotean Conjecture with further documentation from Sybil Shade that her husband 'never intended to go beyond four parts' (8), and

---

11 Foreword-skippers still exist in this imperfect world, but I doubt many could negotiate a work which begins its text with a long poem and then proceeds to tell its 'story' with prose annotations without returning to the Foreword for aid and comfort.

his recollection that he heard his 'poor friend's own voice proclaim on the evening of July 21' that he was at or near 'the end of his labors' (9). All this protesting of the obvious might warn us that the obvious is not always the necessary, but when we verify what we can of Kinbote's comments on the poem, we find it very hard not to accept the Kinbotean Conjecture, willy-nilly.

The Foreword seems only less authoritative on the physical form of the poem because we do not have the eighty index cards in evidence as we do the text of the finished poem. But the accuracy of Kinbote's commentary on the shape of the text lends credence to his description of the physical form of the original manuscript almost as much as it convinces us of the correctness of the Kinbotean Conjecture.[12] The same is true of the apparent normality and naturalness of John and Sybil Shade as they appear in contrast to Kinbote. The more outrageous his behaviour towards them, the more the reader sympathizes with their responses to Kinbote and *sees through* the narrator in both senses: he is our window into their characters, but he is a distorting window. He is a sham, but the reader is in on the joke. Thus the reader is led through the Foreword in a delicate state of suspended disbelief in Kinbote's 'evidence' – the poem as manuscript, as text, as creation of John Shade of the Shade family – while at the same time she recognizes that the narrator she depends upon seems engaged in setting some sort of world record for unreliability.

This equipoise is possible through the text of the Foreword, but at its conclusion the reader arrives at the first of many discontinuities, which we shall call the 'Kinbotean Injunction.' Kinbote suggests that the reader read the notes to the poem first and then study the poem

---

12 Perhaps I belabour this point, but I have discovered in teaching *Pale Fire* to undergraduate students that they are as unwilling to accept the straightforwardness of Kinbote's description of his copytext as Edmund Wilson was eager to ridicule the principles of the CEAA. That nature – or in this case scholarship – was once again outdoing art I could only convince my classes by reading from my own analysis of Washington Irving's treatment of his manuscript of *Bracebridge Hall.* Kinbote may not be a good critic, but he gives the appearance of careful scholarship on this matter, thereby increasing the credibility of the Kinbotean Conjecture. As for his competence as an editor, this sample leads the reader to the inevitable conclusion: 'Frank has acknowledged the safe return of the galleys I had been sent here and has asked me to mention in my Preface – and this I willingly do – that I alone am responsible for any mistakes in my commentary. Insert before a professional. A professional proofreader has carefully rechecked the printed text of the poem against the phototype of the manuscript ...' (11). We need *authority* for the text of the poem, of course, but not for the text of the Foreword.

with their help (buying two copies of the text to make the comparative reading easier). This injunction immediately follows a suggestive
paragraph describing Kinbote's intense admiration for Shade as a
poet. The description is clothed in a metaphor of Kinbote's feelings
for a magician whom he had observed in his childhood:

> I am looking at him. I am witnessing a unique physiological phenom-
> enon: John Shade perceiving and transforming the world, taking it in
> and taking it apart, recombining its elements in the very process of
> storing them up so as to produce at some unspecified date an organic
> miracle, a fusion of image and music, a line of verse. And I experienced
> the same thrill as when in my early boyhood I once watched across the
> tea table in my uncle's castle a conjurer who had just given a fantastic
> performance and was now quietly consuming a vanilla ice. I stared at his
> powdered cheeks, at the magical flower in his buttonhole where it had
> passed through a succession of different colors and had now become
> fixed as a white carnation, and especially at his marvelous fluid-looking
> fingers which could if he chose make his spoon dissolve into a sunbeam
> by twiddling it, or turn his plate into a dove by tossing it up in the air.
> (18)

Shade the 'powdered' conjurer; Kinbote the 'naïve' admirer; the
'magic' of performance the subject matter! The reader is split exactly
in two. He must make a decision at this point. Should he accept the
artful Kinbote as editor and annotator of the pale Shade, he must
then follow Kinbote's advice:

> Let me state that without my notes Shade's text simply has no human
> reality at all since the human reality of such a poem as his (being too
> skittish and reticent for an autobiographical work), with the omission of
> many pithy lines carelessly rejected by him, has to depend entirely on the
> *reality of its author* and his surroundings, attachments, and so forth, a
> reality that only my notes can provide. (18–19; italics added)

The reader who follows this advice and reads the notes first, the poem
as a supplement – let us call her the novelistic reader – by accepting
the primacy of prose and the authority of the Kinbotean voice has
accepted Kinbote as manipulator of meaning. Alternatively, the reader
who takes the irony of Kinbote's metaphor for disingenuousness and
therefore determines to reject the advice and read the poem first, the
notes as a supplement where necessary, is thereby accepting Kinbote's

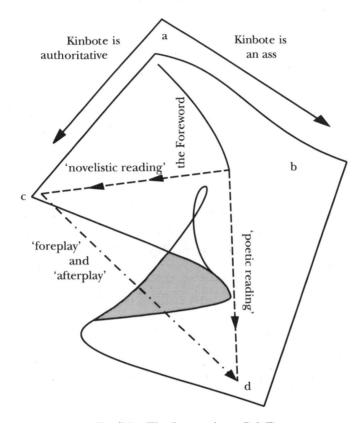

Kinbote is
authoritative

a

Kinbote is
an ass

the Foreword

'novelistic reading'

b

c

'foreplay'
and
'afterplay'

'poetic reading'

d

Fig. 7.1   The four paths to *Pale Fire*

only barely hidden metonymy of magic for performance. Such a reader
– whom we shall call the poetic reader – will be reading *a completely
different novel*: a Shade-based novel in which Kinbote is the interloper,
the intruder, upon the formality of the Shadean construct. These two
different kinds of readings going on in the same space, as it were, are
as mutually exclusive as the two readings of *A Connecticut Yankee in
King Arthur's Court* and will lead to a breakdown into confusion and
incoherence unless the reader recognizes that they are an invitation
to a hyperdimensional reading. Figure 7.1 shows what they look like
when graphed onto a conventional catastrophe theory surface.

Let us examine first the route *b–c*, the novelistic reading. From the
very beginning, the note to lines 1–4, the novelistic reader is faced
with a further choice concerning procedure. He may read systemati-
cally through the notes as though they constituted a continuous text,

or he may follow the many cross-references to the poem, the later notes, some even to the Index and the Foreword. Alas, this apparent option is no choice at all. While some cross-referencing is deliberately neglected (the note to line 12 might have been cross-referenced to the note to line 550, for example), any reader who attempts to follow up all cross-references will soon find herself irretrievably lost in an infinite and self-referential maze: a rhizome maze of the type Eco described in *Reflections on 'The Name of the Rose.'* On the one hand, references expand exponentially outward to ever more references; on the other (and often at the same time), the expanse of cross-references recursively returns upon itself. The reader is lost between incrementation and recursiveness. Eventually he gives up and settles down into a rather straightforward reading of the text of Kinbote's notes.

Rather straightforward reading is the best we can do, because even here, in the simplest possible construct of the novel, the text is far from simple proairesis. The complexity, however, is more of a traditional kind. The novelistic *Pale Fire* is essentially a main plot with three sub-plots. The main plot, of course, is the life, the reign, imprisonment, and escape of Charles Xavier, King of Zembla. But in spite of multiple discontinuities, the inevitable result of using a poem's notes as a vehicle for fiction, this plot moves along straightforwardly and carries along its three sub-plots. The first, and, paradoxically, most disruptive, is the progress of the poem. How odd it is that the reader is delayed in his perusal of Charles's pimpernel plot by those annoying distractions of Hazel's extrasensory experiences, Shade's birthday, and the other munutiae of *la vie domestique de chez Shade.* Here form and content are totally at odds, and the reader unwilling to pursue the *lusus naturae* in its various forms of the Shade family human tragicomedy inevitably skips back to the saga of Charles x.

Less disruptive, because it serves as a flash-forward epilogue of the Charles saga, is the social novel of New Wye. Kinbote is the protagonist narrator. Our concerns are with his sexual predilections, his efforts to achieve intimacy with John Shade (for which Sybil is the Enemy), and in the larger sense his problems of adaptation to the life of exile. A part of this sub-plot is the role Kinbote assumes as Boswell to Shade's Johnson. In this sub-sub-plot both men are allowed to reflect freely on some of the most interesting ideas of the novel about art, philosophy, teaching, etc. More about that later.

Finally there is the Gradus plot. The creation of the fateful assassin in pursuit of the exiled king who inadvertently kills the innocent bystander poet is the essence of melodrama. It is the natural *reductio ad absurdum* of the ultra-romantic quality of Charles's narration. Yet Gradus is somehow tied by Kinbote to the creation of the poem, as he remarks in his note to line 17:

> We shall accompany Gradus in constant thought, as he makes his way from distant dim Zembla to Green Appalachia, through the entire length of the poem, following the road of its rhythm, riding past in a rhyme, skidding around the corner of a run-on, breathing with the caesura, swinging down to the foot of the page from line to line as from branch to branch, hiding between two words (see note to line 596), reappearing on the horizon of a new canto, steadily marching nearer in iambic motion, crossing streets, moving up with his valise on the escalator of the pentameter, stepping off, boarding a new train of thought, entering the hall of a hotel, putting out the bedlight, while Shade blots out a word, and falling asleep as the poet lays down his pen for the night.

The wildness of the conceit has its charm, but no reader can swallow that metaphor for the length of the novel. All of the Gradus references are far-fetched, obvious products of the Kinbotean imagination at its most vagrant extreme.[13] It is the very *extravagance* of the Gradus who makes his entrance into the lives of Shade and Kinbote at the very end of the novelistic reading that provides the necessary discontinuity to propel the reader from the conclusion of the notes back to the beginning of the poem. For the reader must be terribly unsatisfied with the conclusion of the notes, terribly uncertain even as to what 'happened,' if anything can be said to happen in a melodramatic narrative. The otherwise and otherplace self-assertive Kinbote at the end of the notes seems to pale away into a wishy-washy dissolution. He humbly asserts that his commentary is merely 'an attempt to sort out those echoes and wavelets of fire, and pale phosphorescent hints, and all the many subliminal debts to me' (n.l.1000). He asserts and then denies the assertion that his interpretation of the events might be corroborated by the possible material witnesses, the three students, Gerald Emerald, and the girl at the desk of the library. He is unsure even if he had one or two interviews with Gradus in prison and concludes with a project that must shake the faith of even the most believing of readers (n.l.1000):

---

13 As with most of the extravagances of this novel, Nabokov drops hints for the explicator to explain away Gradus. One of these (n.11.47–8) suggests that he was a homicidal maniac sentenced by Judge Goldsworth. Another (n.l. 80) ties him palindromically to the mirror-artist Sudarg of Bokay. *Caveat explicator!*

> I may pander to the simple tastes of theatrical critics and cook up a stage play, an old-fashioned melodrama with three principles: a lunatic who intends to kill an imaginary king, another lunatic who imagines himself to be that king, and a distinguished old poet who stumbles by chance into the line of fire, and perishes in the clash between the two figments.

Surely when she reads this comment, the reader who willingly suspended disbelief in Kinbote's authority and took the road *b–c* on our imaginary surface is here forced by the discontinuity of the conclusion to return to point *b* to see where she went wrong.

Let us now accompany this chastened reader and return to the discontinuous reading we posited on our catastrophe theory surface for the line *b–d*. The reader who concludes that the Foreword is ironic and that the Kinbotean Injunction is not to be trusted has a somewhat easier time than the more ingenuous reader – but not much. As the novelistic reader has problems with the wildness and extravagance of the Zemblan plot, so the poetic reader has problems with the symmetrical structure of the poem. As I remarked in the discussion of the Foreword, the poetic reader has almost no choice but to accept the Kinbotean Conjecture: line 999 was to be followed by a repetition of line 1, concluding a very two-dimensional and remarkably symmetrical poem of exactly 1,000 lines. The structure is a poetic analogy of the triptych:[14] Cantos 2 and 3 are to be viewed as the central subjects, with Cantos 1 and 4 providing the 'wings' or supports for them. It may also be argued by the nature of the form of the poem that Cantos 1 and 4 ought to *reflect* each other as should Cantos 2 and 3.

The verse provides a second formal problem. It is basically heroic couplets – or is it? Enjambment is so frequent that from time to time the reader might almost think the poem was written in blank verse – might also think it was prose. The reader is at a minor discontinuity. A choice must be made about end-stopping lines which are not punctuated, thereby choosing to read the poem as a formal structure, or letting the lines run on, creating a more informal, colloquial work. Whichever choice is made, the reader will sit on it uneasily as he encounters a series of further choices. The style is mock-heroic, but the content may be comic one moment and mystical and meditative the next. What response from the reader is appropriate to a poem which announces in one couplet, 'A curio: *Red Sox Beat Yanks 5–4 / On Chapman's Homer*, thumbtacked to the door' (11.97–8), followed a few lines later with: 'There was a

---

14 See line 381.

sudden sunburst in my head. / And then black night. That blackness was sublime. / I felt distributed through space and time' (11.146–8)?

As the poem continues, the dichotomizing of the reader becomes ever more painful. Shade has written a book on Pope, but as a poet he is 'just behind / (One oozy footstep) Frost' (11. 424–5). Canto 2 is elegiac in content, matter-of-fact in tone; Canto 3 is satirical about the I.P.H. and the investigation of supernatural evidence for the possibility of the afterlife, but ends ambiguously with some 'faint hope' (1.834). Throughout the poem the reader has semantic problems and, of course, is tempted to turn to the notes for help. Kinbote is only too pleased to oblige, but the results only contribute to the dichotomy. Probably one of the first words the ordinary reader will need help for is *stillicide* (1.35). The note *is* helpful, apparently, giving as the definition from Kinbote's dictionary 'a succession of drops falling from the eaves, eavesdrop, cavesdrop.' That seems close enough to the definition in the *OED* to be reliable: 'A falling of water, etc., in drops; a succession of drops.' An incautious reader might conclude there is nothing 'funny' about Kinbote's dictionary if she does not fix on the last three words of the definition – 'eaves, eavesdrop, cavesdrop' – and notice how the definition itself is an onomatopoeic reproduction of word being defined.[15] The reader is also likely to want to help with the word *preterist*, which appears first in line 79 with its 'definition' attached: 'A preterist: one who collects cold nests.' Kinbote, instead of defining the word, prints a 'marginal' line which he says is Shade's attempt to reproduce this bit of Zemblan wisdom:

> The wise at nightfall praise the day,
> The wife when she has passed away,
> The ice when it is crossed, the bride
> When tumbled, and the horse when tried. (n.1.79)

All of this is probably preparation for the second appearance of the word at line 518, where it refers to the I.P.H.; and its accepted historical meaning, referring to the problem of election and grace, is appropriate, but only if the reader has absorbed the tonal modifications of the word presented by Shade's flippant definition and Kinbote's *Volkisch* addendum.

---

15 The note also plays upon Kinbote's predilection for eavesdropping, which also represents a 'feedback' to the lines of the poem in which the word appears. It is very difficult writing notes to a work which is recursive in virtually every aspect.

But these are only interesting preparations for the definitional problem presented by the word *lemniscate* in line 137. The word appears in a description of Shade's dreams as a child immediately before the appearance of his mysterious illness. It needs discussion in its full context.

> I was the shadow of the waxwing slain
> By feigned remoteness in the windowpane.
> I had a brain, five senses (one unique),
> But otherwise I was a cloutish freak.
> In sleeping dreams I played with other chaps
> But really envied nothing – save perhaps
> The miracle of a lemniscate left
> Upon wet sand by nonchalantly deft
> Bicycle tires. (11.131–9)

The wise reader of any poem assumes that there are no irrelevancies. In this poem and this novel that strategy is severely tested frequently, as we perhaps can recognize from the simpler cases of *stillicide* and *preterist*. This emphasis on the image of a pattern left by a bicycle tire in the sand as seen in the dream of a poet about to tell us about his mysterious losses of consciousness cries out for explanation just because it is such an eccentric detail. In this case the word undergoes Kinbotean obfuscation in the notes, increasing our interest:

Line 137: lemniscate
'A unicursal bicircular quartic,' says my weary old dictionary. I cannot understand what this has to do with bicycling and suspect that Shade's phrase has no real meaning. As other poets before him, he seems to have fallen here under the spell of misleading euphony.

To take a striking example: what can be more resounding, more resplendent, more suggestive of choral and sculptured beauty, than the word *coramen*? In reality, however, it merely denotes the rude strap with which a Zemblan herdsman attaches his humble provisions and ragged blanket to the meekest of his cows when driving them up to the vebodar (upland pastures).

Ah, that crafty old Nabokov! Kinbote's 'weary old dictionary' that defined *stillicide* onomatopoeically without regard to the connotative qualities of the English language, here plunges into deepest mathematese to define *lemniscate*. Then the purveyor of folk wisdom of Zembla

Fig. 7.2

coincidentally describes another 'euphonic' word which just happens to correspond with the actual definition of *lemniscate*. The word derives from *lemnis*, a ribbon, and describes the shape of the infinity symbol in a continuous two-dimensional form: in other words, what is better known as a Möbius strip – a continuous *one*-sided infinite surface (fig. 7.2). Here is what seems to be a delightful bit of textual evidence for the Kinbotean Conjecture, that line 999 was to be followed by a repetition of line 1 to create a seamless Möbius-strip poem of infinite reference.

All of this is subordinate to the central problem for the reader of any poem, but especially this one: 'the contrapuntal theme; / Just this: not text, but texture' (11.807–8). It is the problem of form and meaning and their relationship to each other that is deconstructed in the poem, as it is in the novel, as an act of faith. Shade's faith, as he describes it, is based on his sensual love for the '*consonne / D'appui*' (11.967–8), which leads him to conclude that life, like his poem, is 'richly rhymed' (1.970), which any reader might grant, but also 'fantastically planned' (1.969), which is perhaps more relevant to the novel as a whole than the poem. He is then led to a triumphal statement of this faith-based-on-poetry:

> And if my private universe scans right.
> So does the verse of galaxies divine
> Which I suspect is an iambic line.
> I'm reasonably sure that we survive.
> And that my darling somewhere is alive (11.974–8)

Alas, this climax of faith is undercut immediately by his prediction that he will be alive the following day and, at the very end of the poem, his reference to the gardener with the wheelbarrow, which is a perfect reflection of the 'tin wheelbarrow pushed by a tin boy' that led to the mysterious and unresolved conclusion of Canto 1.

What is the reader to make of all this: a perfect symmetry of form, on the one hand, and a perfect irresolution of content, on the other? For Canto 4, though it begins with the rich (but undercut) assurance – 'Now I shall spy ... Now I shall cry ... Now I shall try ...' (11.835–7) – and ends with a triumphant (but undercut) statement of faith, wanders erratically elsewhere. Irrelevancies follow each other repeatedly: Shade's method of composition, his favourite time for writing, his technique for *shaving*, for heaven's sake, his likes and dislikes – especially his dislikes – his razor's passage through the growth of his whiskers like the plow through 'old Zembla's fields,' which prompts him to jot down a note for 'further use,' but, because of the mood of the moment, composed in an heroic couplet,

> *Man's life as commentary to abstruse*
> *Unfinished poem.* Note for further use. (11.939–40)

And suddenly Charles Xavier Kinbote is born. Here is the Kinbotean Conjecture in reverse, and the most violent discontinuity of them all. It is not the repetition of line 1 that 'concludes' the poem, but the creation of Kinbote *ex nihilo* from the mind of John Shade. The 'poem' continues, not with the repetition of 'I was the shadow of the waxwing slain,' but with the tale of Zembla, Charles, his reign, his attempted assassination, all. Shade the poet has created Kinbote the commentator, the editor, the critic, the prosaic mirror of his poetic 'Pale Fire.' The alternative to line 1,000 is the totality of the construct of the Notes, the Foreword, and the Index (which also, it is worth noting, form a triptych, with the poem and notes being mirror versions of each other, one in verse, the other in prose). Kinbote is Shade's imagined critic-editor. We can observe the word being made flesh. The poet's usual view of the critic – a royal pain in the ass – literally takes the shape of Charles Xavier's royal purple fading to the lavender of the sodomite Kinbote! With delight, the reader makes the return leap on our catastrophe theory surface over the discontinuity from *c* to *d* and back, revelling in the mirror imagery, the Zemblan reflections of the Shades' garden, Gradus as the reflection of the bowels and the body (and 'time's winged chariot,' no less, at the same time). Oh, the richness of the joke, the delight in the creation!

But, of course, it is not all a joke. There are many serious reflections of the ideas of the poem in the vagaries of the prose, and vice versa. While Kinbote is a rather wicked creation out of Shade's mind, he is also a mirror image of his (imagined) creator. There are wonderful coincidences of agreement – *points d'appui* which are also *consonant* on many matters concerning criticism, literature 'engazhay' (1.378), the teaching of literature, and the like. Even where they do not agree, as in matters of religion, Kinbote's orthodoxy is but a reflection of Shade's own 'faint hope' based upon the misprint of 'fountain' for 'mountain.' Kinbote has his own vision of a universe that 'scans right' in his prose, but perceptive, version of the relationship between 'text and texture': 'I can do what only a true artist can do – pounce upon the forgotten butterfly of revelation, wean myself abruptly from the habit of things, see the web of the world and the warp and the weft of that web' (n.l.991).

Thus has Nabokov succeeded in creating the world's first lemniscate novel. Just as the Index will lead you from *Lass* to *Male* and back, the reading of *Pale Fire* is a Möbius trip along a path of infinite discontinuities between Shade and Zembla, Kinbote and botkin, and yet is a *gradus ad Parnassum* from verse to prose and back again. As the searchers for the Crown Jewels are led a merry chase through the Index to the secret receptacle behind Eystein's *trompe-l'oeil* painting, there to find nothing but some 'broken bits of a nutshell' (n.l.130), so is the reader deceived in any effort she may make to pull out any plump 'meanings' from the 'warp and the weft' of the web Nabokov has woven. It is all a perfect single surface, yet multidimensional, reflecting and refracting text and texture through its continuous series of discontinuities. The 'warp and weft of the web' turn out to be like the 'nets and ladders' and the quincunxes we have found over and over again in these hyperdimensional fictions: 'the only truths that are useful are instruments to be thrown away.'[16] The reader who has taken the trip from Newton's universe to Einstein's treats them like the 'broken bits of a nutshell' they are.

Perhaps the best metaphor to explain this quality of *Pale Fire* is one we shall encounter in the next chapter. Scheherazade and the genie describe the act of fiction as an act of intercourse between writer and reader:

Narrative ... was a love relation, not a rape: its success depended upon the reader's consent and cooperation, which she could withhold or at

---

16 Eco, *The Name of the Rose*, 600; see also *Reflections*, 58.

any moment withdraw; also upon her own combination of experience
and talent for the enterprise, and the author's ability to arouse, sustain,
and satisfy her interest.[17]

The metaphor is supremely apposite to *Pale Fire*. The reader who
hurries to any of the several 'climaxes' of the poem or the notes is
letting down the relationship. In *Pale Fire* there are no conclusions,
only discontinuities as the nature of the play changes. The Foreword
is a kind of *foreplay*, urging the reader to assume a poetic or a novelistic position, to be changed to another position as another discontinuity arises. The Index, of course, is a kind of *afterplay*, which can also
turn into narrative arousal at any moment. Because of this reversibility
and possibly infinite variation, the reading of *Pale Fire* is limited only
by the reader's willingness to pursue these possibilities beyond the
three dimensions of pre-Einsteinian physics and the rigidities of pre-
post-structuralist criticism. That is why *Pale Fire* is the archetext of
postmodern fiction. As we shall see, however, it is not the only work
with these qualities.

---

17 John Barth, *Chimera* (New York: Random House 1972), 26

8

$\emptyset^n$/Chaos = *Chimera*, the Novel

If Nabokov's *Pale Fire* is the archetext of postmodernism, John Barth is
the archetype of the postmodernist writer. Barth began his career as a
novelist with a pair[1] of neo-realist fictions, *The Floating Opera* (1956)
and *End of the Road* (1958), both of which explored that peculiarly
American manifestation of existentialism, 'cheerful nihilism.'[2] In that
respect he was like dozens of other young American novelists of the
1950s, different perhaps only for the interesting narratological metaphors he couched his fictions in: the novel as opera floating past the
reader, who can only glimpse occasional scenes and must make up
those which took place when he was not watching; narrative as *road*
with only an artificial or conventional *end* or, as that novel had it, an
ambiguous 'terminal.'[3] This concern for the *vehicle* of fiction then led
him to experiment with the form of the genre in a most curious and
typically postmodernist way. His next novel, *The Sot-Weed Factor* (1960),
played with a series of apparently incompatible dichotomies: the *form*
of the historical novel in the mold of the mythic quest; a neo-authen-

---

1 It is standard critical practice to divide Barth's *oeuvre* into pairs, perhaps because of
his own recursive Alexandrine about it: 'My books tend to come in pairs, my sentences in twin members' (*The Friday Book* [New York: G.P. Putman 1984], 3).
Probably the recursiveness of the statement ought to warn the critic away, but it
doesn't. As we shall see, there are good reasons to assume that these first novels are
the only 'pair.'

2 See above, chapter 5, note 5.

3 The problem of *closure* appears over and over again in these hyperdimensional
works. Notice the many techniques used to conclude the text yet not to end the
writer-text-reader connection in *Pym*, *The Confidence-Man*, *A Connecticut Yankee in*

tic parody of historical language being used as a vehicle for contemporary concerns (with hints of parody there as well); 'real' characters
and texts mixed inextricably with parodies of themselves to defeat the
reader seeking data-validation. When commentators on *The Sot-Weed
Factor* suggested that Barth had patterned the novel on Otto Rank's
Myth of the Birth of the Hero and/or Joseph Campbell's *The Hero with a
Thousand Faces*, Barth (who hadn't) *did* read those works and quite
self-consciously incorporated self-conscious myth-making in the character of the hero of his next novel, *Giles Goat-Boy* (1966).[4] By this point
the pattern of Barth's career-as-novelist had been set: it was to be a
constantly intensifying involution, but one that was to be *interactive*,
incorporating, as it increased its gravitational pull, all the text and
context adjacent to it, but always metamorphosing that material, using
it self-consciously, *transmuting* it into new forms of energy in mysterious ways, like a cosmic whirlpool, a textual 'event horizon,' a literary
black hole.

Barth then *seemed* to embark on a new strategy, marked by two
works. 'The Literature of Exhaustion' is undoubtedly his best known
non-fiction and, as he has noted, has been 'frequently misread as one
more Death of a Novel or Swan Song of Literature piece' (*Friday Book*,
64). It is, of course, anything but. It is, however, a *theoretical* work and
marks Barth's first straightforward[5] move into literary theory. Its main
thrust is that through formal experimentation, the writer may achieve

---

    King Arthur's Court, and *Pale Fire* (not to mention *The Name of the Rose* and *The
Pleasure of the Text*; and, of course, see especially *Gödel, Escher, Bach*, 403). Here the
metaphor of 'nets and ladders' is especially apt, particularly in its quincuncial form,
which 'pleasingly confounds, / Surprises, varies, and conceals the Bounds.' If one
were to seek a single 'genetic marker' to define hyperdimensionality in fiction, I
would choose this defeat of closure.

4 *The Friday Book*, 41–4. Many of his readers concluded somewhat prematurely that
Barth had 'painted himself into a corner' by this process of involution, including
my doctoral student, Campbell Tatham, whose dissertation on Barth (Wisconsin
1968) implies (over my strong objections, I must add) that Barth would soon lapse
into silence. This case illustrates the perils of restricting abductive thinking to two
dimensions.

5 I think. But that's always a dangerous assumption. See, as examples of the possible
pitfalls, Borges's 'The Analytical Language of John Wilkins' and 'The Mirror of the
Enigmas' in his *Other Inquisitions* (Austin: University of Texas Press 1964), 101–5
and 125–8. Who can say that 'The Literature of Exhaustion' and/or *The Friday Book*
are/is not another fiction of Barth's incorporating in such minutiae as the footnote on page 71 the kind of essential text and context by which he and Borges
impart Delphic wisdom about the nature of art?

new conceptual freedom; its hero is Borges and, through his use of the *regressus in infinitum*, Scheherazade. But he cites the example of many other writers, including Nabokov, to forward the thesis that the novel may exist in many non-novelistic forms.[6] At the same time he was engaged in exactly that: *Lost in the Funhouse* (1968) is a novel in the form of a collection of short stories that began as an experimental work for performance by live voice and tapes. The reader is warned of the work's general hyperdimensionality in the 'Author's Note' and the 'Frame Tale' that begins the text: a cut-out Möbius strip with the text 'ONCE UPON A TIME THERE WAS A STORY THAT BEGAN^n.' The 'Author's Note' comments that the tale may be considered 'one-, two-, or three-dimensional.' I think there can be no doubt that Barth, like Nabokov in *Pale Fire*, was consciously engaged in the writing of hyperdimensional fiction. I think also that his arrival at that technique was an inevitable result of his development as a writer.

Chimera (1972) followed and has had a curious history. It tied for the National Book Award and was selected as an 'alternate' by three book clubs in the demi-monde of that particular index of popular culture; two excerpts from it, amounting to almost one-half of the volume of the book text and two-thirds of that chimera, the novel, were printed in semi-popular magazines before publication.[7] Both the reviewers and the early critical responses were very favourable, but one can't avoid the feeling that all this generous approbation has a void at the core. Why had Barth not received the National Book Award long before this novel? Why only half of it now? The serial excerpts and book club selections seemed to suggest a rather specialized audience: soft porn readers not yet lured away to *GQ* by their Louis Vuitton underwear or to *Penthouse* by their baser urges; eastern intellectuals keeping up with what they knew they *ought* to be reading. And mixed with all the critical praise was a leavening of sympathy for what virtually every critic seemed to assume was an almost terminal case of 'writer's block'[8] integral to the design and the writing of the novel.

---

6 He remarks that 'Nabokov's recentest [novel] was his multivolume annotated translation of Pushkin' (*Friday Book*, 69).

7 The book clubs were the Saturday Review Book Club, the Time Inc. Book Club, and the American Journal Book Club; the magazines were *Esquire* (June 1972) and *Harper's* (Sept. 1972). Oh, reader, can you read demographics? Can you imagine a whole reading public with a mass guilty conscience?

8 Or, as Jac Tharpe has it (*John Barth, the Comic Sublimity of Paradox* [Carbondale: Southern Illinois University Press 1974], 106), 'writer's cramp.' This universal critical assumption that Barth suffered from a horrendous case of writer's block

Now, although our concern in this chapter will be *Chimera* exclusively, we must continue briefly to consider the works that followed it, because Barth's career-as-text is important to the discussion of that work. *Chimera* was followed by *Letters* in 1979, *Sabbatical* (1982), *The Friday Book* (1984), and *Tidewater Tales* (1988). The connection with *Letters* is especially relevant because parts of the text of *Chimera* refer to certain characters and situations in *Letters* as though *that text already existed.*[9] That caused some problems for reviewers and critics of the novel whose essays appeared before *Letters* did, and even goes unobserved in some later critical essays where it should be remarked upon.[10] *The Friday Book* gives some very important details of Barth's thinking about the mathematical properties of *Chimera*, and *Tidewater Tales* carries on (in the context of the CIA/FBI confusion of *authority* developed in *Sabbatical*) the synchronic importance of Scheherazade and the motif of TKTTTITT, albeit as a T-shirt motto. In short, *Chimera* is a very central work in Barth's career, even though his involution as a novelist appears to be as quincuncially seamless as the spiral pattern in the sunflower (see the motif on each part-title page of this book). If *Chimera* does not represent the *phi*-point of Barth's own career-as-text,[11]

---

seems to be based upon some comments by the genie who appears to Scheherazade and Dunyazade in part 1 of *Chimera* (New York: Random House 1972), 9–10, and is 'documented' in a reference to a case of writer's block Barth apparently suffered in 1969 in David Morell, *John Barth: An Introduction* (University Park: Pennsylvania State University Press 1976), 149. I wish my writer's blocks could be limited to one year. Barth's publishing chronology is very uneven, but then so is the comparative size and difficulty of the works that constitutes his *oeuvre*. Why otherwise sophisticated critics are so eager to accept the 'word' of a character pretending to be the author in this case only is beyond me ...

9 See note 14.

10 This caused no little trouble to the earliest critics of *Chimera* and remains a problem to many of the later ones, who either ignore or fail to see the point of an *extra*textual reference, while weaving extensive critical hypotheses on *inter*textual byplay. Jerry Powell's 'John Barth's *Chimera*: A Creative Response to the Literature of Exhaustion,' *Critique* 18 (1976), 59–72, reprinted in *Critical Essays on John Barth*, ed. Joseph J. Waldmeir (Boston: G.K. Hall 1980), 228–40, suffers from the first problem particularly because it is such a good summary of how Barth used patterns from his earlier fictions in *Chimera* and could have been much better if Powell had been able to observe how the references to Jerome Bray, for example, stretched ahead extratextually to *Letters* as well as back intertextually to *Giles Goat-Boy*. E.P. Walkiewicz, in *John Barth* (Boston: G.K. Hall 1986), seems completely unaware of the matter. Heide Zeigler, in *John Barth* (London: Methuen 1987), notices that 'the reader will learn more of Jerome Bray in Barth's next novel' (56) but makes no special point of it.

11 To do so is to require his untimely decease from publishing fiction – unless, of

it certainly does represent a very self-conscious use of *phi* as an order-ing principle.[12] *Phi* is omnipresent in *Chimera*, from references to snail shells and navels in the 'Dunyazadiad' to Calyxa's logarithmic spiral shape of Perseus's mural, to the dimensions of three *nouvelles* that form the text of *Chimera* itself and the proportions of that mythical beast, the chimera, that Bellerophon may or may not have slain.[13] Barth worked with *phi* as he worked with myth-making in *Giles Goat-Boy*; that is, his self-conscious use recapitulates the self-conscious use of the concept by his character (and vice versa, of course). In one sense, this use merely marks the generic case for the *involuting* quality of his writing that I have already remarked. That is, the paradigm for *phi* –

$$\text{When } A + B = C, \text{ } A{:}B{:}{:}B{:}C = \emptyset$$
$$\text{When } B + C = D, \text{ } B{:}C{:}{:}C{:}D = \emptyset$$

– is already remarkably present in the *oeuvre* of Barth. Think of myth-making in *The Sot-Weed Factor* as A; in *Giles Goat-Boy* as B; in *Lost in the Funhouse* as C; in *Chimera* as D. You can easily perform the same kind of *ratio/escalatio* from complex narration, texts-within-texts, and many, if not all, of the other hallmarks of postmodernist writing.[14] Barth

---

course, he were to publish 2.3 more novels, in which case *Chimera* would represent a *phi*-point reciprocal. But that way lies madness. See H.E. Huntley, *The Divine Proportion: A Study in Mathematical Beauty* (New York: Dover 1970), 62.

12 See *Friday Book*, 166–71; Walkiewicz (*John Barth*, 110–11) *attempts* something of an explanation of Barth's use of the Fibonacci sequence and the 'golden ratio,' Ø, but the wise reader will look elsewhere after she reads that 'the overall form of *Chimera* is roughly suggestive of both a spiral and the *first three numbers* in the series (1, 1, 2, 3, 5, 8 ...)' [my italics]. As far as I know, no critics noticed how important *phi* is to *Chimera* until Barth pointed it out in *The Friday Book*, and explanations since have not been as intelligent as Barth's. I believe Barth used Huntley as his source for the exotica of *phi*, but creatively. For example, he accepts the bit of numerology about Caucasian women's navels (169) that Huntley cites (62) as an example of how 'the golden section has attracted the enthusiastic attention of cranks.' Who would give up the connection between the golden ratio and the belly button, even if the numerical relationship were chimerical?

13 ... and the proportions of that mythical beast, the *Chimera*, that 'Bellerophoniad' may or may not have slain.

14 Including, of course, Ø itself, which appears modestly in 'Lost in the Funhouse' as part of the parody of do-it-yourself 'creative writing.' Then, according to Barth in *The Friday Book*, it came up again in his plans to include both the 'Perseid' and the 'Bellerophoniad' at a point six-sevenths of the way through *Letters* (under the *R*, as they say in the bingo parlours), but far from the Ø-point of that novel (pages 168–9). Funhouse: *Letters*-in-progress::*L*-i-p:*Chimera* = Ø.

seems to be a living, breathing *phi*genitor of fiction! Why, we could easily make a Fibonacci sequence of his canon (and get rid once and for all of that notion that his books, after the first two, come in pairs):

u_1	1	*The Floating Opera*
u_2	1	*End of the Road*
u_3	2	*The Sot-Weed Factor*
u_4	3	*Giles Goat-Boy*
u_5	5	*Lost in the Funhouse*
u_6	8	*Chimera*
u_7	13	*Letters*
u_8	21	*Sabbatical*
u_9	34	*The Friday Book*
u_{10}	55	*Tidewater Tales*

I modestly submit that, not allowing for incidentals like 'The Literature of Exhaustion' and the few uncollected short pieces not listed, this is a fair qualitative summary of Barth's career.[15]

If we grant hypothetical validity to that last (I admit) rather whimsical generalization, there is nothing to stop our fancy from pushing on to one more perhaps even less self-evident conclusion. *The career-as-text of John Barth also recapitulates ontogenically the phylogenic generation of modes and styles as described in chapter 3 of this text.* The two first novels are in a generally realistic mode, corresponding to *metonymy* in Lodge's dichotomy, *ironic* on Frye's continuum, iconically winter; *The Sot-Weed Factor* is metaphoric, romantic, spring; and we leave the two-dimensional world of Jakobson-Lodge and Frye with *Giles*, as Barth left the Plekhanovian *doxa*, spiralling outward with the extraordinary 'freedom' of the 1960s to break the semiotic circuit. But a curious thing happened with Barth; instead of breaking the circuit, the logarithmic regularity of his Fibonacci spiral guided some of his readers with him and makes him singularly accessible to a fairly large readership, even though he makes no concessions whatsoever to popular taste.

Needless to say, *Chimera* is a continuation of that spiral, as any member in a Fibonacci[16] sequence includes implicitly in itself the 'golden

---

15 I am tempted to exclude *Sabbatical* from the series, for obvious reasons, not excluding its very title. But the Fibonacci sequence resteth not, neither on its sabbath nor its eighth member.

16 Or other sequence based on the rule $u_{n-1} + u_n = u_{n+1}$, all of which will produce the ratio of Ø, approximately 1.618, as soon as the numbers generated become large enough.

ratio' of its proportionate relationship with its predecessor and its follower. But *Chimera* is a special case, nonetheless, because it alone among Barth's novels plays upon the concept of *phi* self-consciously, as we have seen *End of the Road* plays upon narrativity, *The Sot-Weed Factor* plays upon historicity, *Giles Goat-Boy* plays upon mythicness, etc., *usw. Chimera* is thus the only novel in the sequence that is 'about' the sequence, and the sequence, as we noted in the last paragraph, not entirely facetiously, is 'about' the artist freeing himself from the Plekhanovian orthodoxy and approaching an aesthetic of *forms* themselves, in other words, Learning II. If this delicate spiral of suppositions is at all accurate, we may then claim for *Chimera* a unique status: as a work entirely concerned with the process of aesthetic creation (as manifested by the self-conscious manipulation of *phi* in its various forms), *Chimera* approaches what Bateson imagines is Learning III.[17]

Now, Learning III is an order of magnitude greater than Learning II, but if we can recall what Learning II was to Learning I (especially the part about Robert the Ram and the reader engaged in free play compared to the one who has to publish or perish), we can begin to imagine it. Bateson does not gloss over the difficulties the concept of Learning III presents. He surmises that scientists will find it difficult 'to imagine or describe this process,' and that 'Zen Buddhists, Occidental mystics, and some psychiatrists assert that these matters are totally beyond the reach of language' (301–2). The evidence he invokes suggests strongly that the approach to Learning III is far more likely to produce Robert the Ram than enlightenment, but Bateson concludes nevertheless that

> for others, more creative, the resolution of contraries reveals a world in which personal identity merges into all the processes of relationship in some vast ecology *or aesthetics* [italics added] of cosmic interaction. That any of these can survive seems almost miraculous, but some are perhaps saved from being swept away on oceanic feeling by their ability to focus in on the minutiae of life. Every detail of the universe is seen as proposing a view of the whole. These are the people for whom Blake wrote the famous advice in the 'Auguries of Innocence':
>
> > *To see the World in a Grain of Sand,*
> > *And a Heaven in Wild Flower,*

---

17 Bateson, *Steps to an Ecology of Mind*, 301–8

Hold Infinity in the palm of your hand
And Eternity in an hour. (306)

Let us assume that *Chimera* is 'about' the 'processes of relationship in some vast ... aesthetics of cosmic interaction' which is that most popular of modern written texts, the novel. That may seem like a considerable assumption, but it is not far from our *conclusion* about *The Confidence-Man*: that it was concerned with the 'cosmic interaction' involved in any epistemological or ontological system. *Chimera*'s concern only for a minor subset of that much larger set might almost seem unduly limited, but of course if Barth really does take the 'processes' to the level of Learning III, he (and his reader) will have travelled farther than *The Confidence-Man* and his 'victim,' who, we will recall, arrived only at *conception* – the zygote. *Chimera* promises to take us to birth. Moreover, our intentions are further limited in *Chimera* by its concern with aesthetics only,[18] in which it is more like *Pym* than *The Confidence-Man*. In any case, we may certainly assume that *Chimera* will test our capacity for Learning III severely, and that if we do not approach it playfully, we risk recapitulating the awful fate of Robert the Ram.

The 'cosmic interaction' begins about as simply as is humanly possible. 'Dunyazadiad' introduces us to *story* in all of its dimensions, but relatively straightforwardly (for Barth). It barely hints at the paradoxes to come – but the hints are telling. Intertextuality and extratextuality are neatly introduced in the 'strange loop' of the genie passing on to Scheherazade the stories which he reads from the book drawn from her telling of them; the talismanic quality of the semiotic circuit is prominent in the magic words 'the key to the treasure is the treasure'; most important of all, the mutually dependent relationship of teller to hearer, writer to reader, is fully examined, in the abstract discussions about sex and story between Scheherazade and the genie and the much less abstract – indeed, tactilely painful – position taken between

---

18 This point is debatable since the politics of feminism is clearly a topic in *Chimera*, as Charles B. Harris argues most convincingly in the best critical study of Barth to date, *Passionate Virtuosity: The Fiction of John Barth* (Urbana and Chicago: University of Illinois Press 1983), 127–58. I would only shift Harris's emphasis somewhat. Fiction has to be about something, and to my mind the topic of the relationship between the sexes is used here primarily for the same metaphoric purpose that Barthes used the sex act in *The Pleasure of the Text*. Otherwise the emphasis on the magic words 'the key to the treasure is the treasure' makes little sense.

Dunyazade and Shah Zaman for the telling of her tale. Other important aspects of story are also introduced: multiple narrative voices as purposeful confusions and diminutions of authority; the 'final word' to the 'Destroyer of Delights and Desolator of Dwelling-places'; the usefulness of beginning *in medias res*, Ø, if only in occasional references to snail shells and belly buttons; the 'tragic view' of storytelling as justification for art.[19]

There has been some critical controversy over Barth's intentions for the location of the 'Dunyazadiad.' Zeigler (90–1n. 9) argues that Barth originally intended it as the concluding tale and that his first choice would have been an improvement over the text as we have it. Walkiewicz agrees that his 'original intention ... would precipitate the successful consummation of all seven sections of *Chimera* as a whole' (122). Harris, however, agrees with Barth (in *Friday Book*) that the central ordering pattern of *Chimera* is the 'golden ratio,' in which case 'Dunyazadiad' must come first (150).[20] If the primary purpose of an introductory section is to introduce, there should be little doubt that Harris and Barth are correct and the others wrong. *Story* is an important part of the novel, but it, and the paradoxes arising from it, are barely listed in 'Dunyazadiad.'

'Dunyazadiad' is in the romantic mode. 'Perseid' is written in the equivalent of Frye's next mode, the heroic. The 'content' remains the same – story – but the relational mode changes in the same way that summer turns into fall. Both parts begin *in medias res*, but the rich inter- and extratextuality of 'Dunyazadiad' is tempered to a more classical pattern in 'Perseid.' Perseus's story is triply told by Perseus to Calyxa as it is sculpted in relief by Calyxa for Perseus and 'constellated' by Perseus and Medusa as the 'silent, visible signs' for 'those with eyes to see and understanding to interpret' (133–4). That is an Ovidian metamorphosis of the 'strange loop' of the genie's telling of

---

19 This last point is most important. It is best (most completely) considered in *The Friday Book*, 51–2, where Barth reduces it to the simplicity of a syllogism. Because the world is morally ambiguous and brutally compensatory, and the self, as far as we can know, is not transcendable, there are no victories, only different ways to lose. Therefore the human condition is essentially ironic and technically absurd. More about this important article of faith later.

20 Barth, for all his emphasis on *phi*, is no numerologist. The comparative lengths of the three sections of *Chimera* are not even good approximations of *phi*; note that it is only Jerome Bray (surely a self-caricature of John Barth, at work on his word-counting word-processor program, grinding out fiction RESET) whose concern is *only* for the mechanics of the aesthetics of Ø.

Scheherazade's tales that corresponds to the second paragraph of 'Perseid': 'Stories last longer than men, stones than stories, stars than stones' (59).[21] Such a metamorphic spiralling outward must make the modern storyteller, dependent upon his retelling of the old stories in however interesting a 'strange loop' of narrative interdependence, green with envy.

Similarly, the writer-text-reader/teller-tale-hearer relationship is moved from the romantic to the classical mode. Surely the mutual jeopardy between Dunyazade and Shah Zaman, freely given, freely accepted by each partner, is intended to represent the ideal semiotic relationship of Barth(es)ian writer to reader for 'the pleasure of the text.' The ideal is 'passionate virtuosity' for both; the tactile metaphor of sharpened blade to tender flesh could hardly be improved upon. When we pass on from the romantic mode to the classical, it is the restraints upon the classical mode compared to the sensuous freedom of romantic storytelling that are the most striking. Perseus's status as mythic hero is a mixed blessing when it's showtime. First he has to deal with the necessities of the heroic style grafted onto a modern semiotic sensibility. The result is truly baroque, with its epithetic neologisms ('I saw depicted *alabasterly* the several chapters of my youth, most pleasing to a *couched* eye' [italics added]) and hip epic metaphor ('behind them Zeus in *golden-showerhood* rained in upon their frockless daughter, *jackpotting* her with me' [61; more italics added]). Fun, and oddly effective, especially in comparison with Bellerophon's efforts in the same direction, but surely a reminder of Frye's point that the heroic is a decadent form of the romantic.

Then there is the parallel problem of the relationships among herohood, authorship, and virility. In 'Dunyazadiad' coitus is a metaphor for the semiotic circuit, but the two halves of the metaphor are also interconnected, each serving as foreplay or afterplay for the other. Moreover, while the sexes are far from equal at the beginning of the *One Thousand and One Nights*, they are very delicately balanced in the telling of the 'Dunyazadiad.' Not so in 'Perseid.' There the three separate tellings are most unequally present. Calyxa's logarithmic spiral bas-relief provides a *fixed* text, hence traditional, but one provided

---

21 This relationship is remarkably thematic to 'Perseid,' especially in the final erotic choice of the hero as he refaces Medusa to be either petrified or estellated. 'Petrification' is how most classical art is passed to us, by sculptors; Calyxa's bas-reliefs are *compromises,* as their subject is compromised by the situation he finds himself in.

by a groupie of mythic herohood, hence suspect. Perseus's linguistic interpretation of it, we have seen, is baroque in style. The lovemaking that accompanies these two semioses also presents problems. Herohood becomes associated with *performance*, and one doesn't have to be Masters and Johnson to know where that leads.

Fortunately, because both tale-telling and lovemaking take place in an open-ended, logarithmic *Nautilus pompilius* chamber, they open out into what becomes the infinity of the constellated Perseus and Medusa. There, at the conclusion of 'Perseid,' the spatial/temporal problems created by the multiple telling of the tale are resolved according to the story/stone/star progression.[22] But, as Perseus remarks, · he and Medusa 'have become, like the noted music of our tongue [i.e., classical Greek], these silent, visible signs; to *be* the tale I tell to those with eyes to see and understanding to interpret' (133–4). In other words, they have become *story* itself, or the process of semiosis. But, unlike the lovers of the 'Dunyazadiad,' they are fixed in place and must say 'good night,' terminally, where the romantic lovers conclude by saying 'good morning,' suggesting that they are at the beginning of a genre rather than at its end.

The process of analysis consists of breaking down wholes into parts arbitrarily and artificially. Critical analysis of *Chimera* has concentrated on the 'Bellerophoniad' as the longest, most problematic, and most central (to the slaying/interpreting of the title) segment of the novel. Many critics conclude that it is a botch, and, indeed, Barth seems to support that reading in several comments in *The Friday Book* (98, 138–9). I agree on almost every point made by Charles B. Harris (146–55) that it is a deliberate botch by Barth, used as a metaphor at 'considerable esthetic risk' (148). If *Chimera* is truly a Learning III confrontation with the novel as an 'aesthetics of cosmic interaction,' then just such risks must be taken. My comments on the 'Bellerophoniad' are intended as a supplement to Harris's excellent scouting of the pathway in this rather unkempt garden, and an effort to explain its function in the larger purpose of the novel.

The first thing to notice about the 'Bellerophoniad' is that it is to 'Perseid' as 'Perseid' is to 'Dunyazadiad' in all relevant structural terms, not just length. In Frye's series (as modified dimensionally in chapter 3) it represents the hiccup of the parodic, 'making strange,' black

---

22 Surely the reader does not have to be reminded that such choosing sequences are endless, like Möbius strips, when stories are also about stars.

comedy. Thus it is necessarily a 'botch' in the smooth cycle of ortho-doxy, but at the same time a leap into a new dimensionality of forms, like all the fictions we have considered in this book. This quality becomes clear if we consider it in relation to those aspects of storytell-ing which were introduced in 'Dunyazadiad' and mutated to their classical or heroic forms in 'Perseid.'

The first of these is inter- and extratextuality. Whereas the genie is talismanically summoned by the magic words and functions creatively with barely a hitch, and Perseus moves in a classical spiral of Ovidian metamorphosis from story through stone to stars, 'Bellerophoniad' is a textual fuck-up from its opening 'good night.' The genie is present, this time unbidden and unexplained, in a lecture perhaps given at the 'University of Lycia's newly established Department of Classical Mythology' (197, 198–203) along with an entry *s.v. Bellerophon* from Graves's *The Greek Myths*. The genie is also present, this time evoked accidentally by Polyeidus, in the form of an alter ego named Jerome B. Bray, confusing the issue extratextually with references to *Bellerophontic letters* as they might appear in the not-yet-written *Letters*.[23] Polyeidus also functions as a genie but is constantly committing the primary semiotic sin of confusing the signifier for the signified, the map for the territory. It is no accident that he gives the final count (five) of the last words of the novella à la Jerome Bray's concern for the numerical values of NUMBERS and NOTES.

The same quality (or lack of it) obtains in the theme of the semiotic circuit and the issue of narrative complexity. 'Bellerophoniad' may be narrated to Queen Philonoë (or lectured to her or to the faculty of the University of Lycia) or read to second wife and/or Oedipal daugh-ter/wife Melanippe or humped on an IBM PS/2 by Jerome RESET or shape-shifted by Polyeidus and washed up along with the jellyfish on a marsh of the eastern shore of Maryland. Compare this with the care Barth lavished on the logic and consistency of narrative voice[24] and textual pleasure in 'Dunyazadiad.' Compare it with the spiralling out-ward of the narration in 'Perseid.' Can there be any doubt that Barth

---

23 Barth's next novel, *Tidewater Tales*, may be alluded to in the fourth paragraph of 'Bellerophoniad' (148). This kind of synchronicity makes explicators go grey very young. Notice also that inter- and extratextuality is very central to *Letters* in a Fibonacci ratio to its use in *Chimera*.

24 Or, if our concern is merely with technical mastery of the logic of narration, compare it with the ultimate *tour de force* of this skill, the 'Menelaiad' in *Lost in the Funhouse*.

deliberately confused the logic of the narration and intentionally implied the rape of the reader of 'Bellerophoniad'? As for Ø, it is mechanically present only in Jerome Bray's explanation of his plans for NUMBERS and NOTES (esp. 251) and perhaps in Bellerophon's Mendelian lecture on the possibilities for 'semidemigodhood' (182–3), since genetic inheritance also creates a Fibonacci sequence.[25]

Need I go on? The principal reason for these apparent infelicities of 'Bellerophoniad' is succinctly given by Harris (148):

> The result is a botched life and a botched book – but that botched book
> is Bellerophon's, not Barth's. The 'longeurs, lumps, lacunae' that
> Bellerophon complains of in his 'beastly ..., ill-proportioned' fiction (308)
> are as functional in their way as the verbal stratagems in 'Perseid' are in
> theirs. Throughout *Chimera* Barth employs *'The Principle of Metaphoric
> Means: the investiture by the writer of as many of the elements and aspects of his
> fiction as possible with emblematic as well as dramatic value: not only the "form"
> of the story, the narrative viewpoint, the tone and such, but, where manageable,
> the particular genre, the mode and medium, the very process of narration – even
> the fact of the artifact itself'* (203).

Harris then argues that Barth took this 'considerable esthetic risk, for failed art as metaphor may be mistaken for *actual* failed art,' because he wanted to dramatize the contrast between Bellerophon's failure as a hero and as teller of his myth and the 'propitious consequences, at the artistic and personal levels, of successful anima integration' in the first two novellas (148). It is an interesting argument, but I think it misses the main point of the relationship between the three novellas.

To begin with, Barth is on record (*Friday Book*, 91–3) as being resistant to using his writing to further causes of any sort, no matter how sympathetic. He also commented that he personally considers *Chimera* 'to be ... a story about story-writing' (ibid., 98). If one part of the explanation for the apparent failure of 'Bellerophoniad' is the 'Principle of Metaphoric Means,' another is Barth's often-used paradigm of the 'tragic view' of practically anything (see above, note 19). Such an existentialist view of all kinds of human activities (and Barth has invoked it for purposes ranging from motherhood to the granting of literary prizes), when applied to the aesthetics of the novel, almost *requires* the production of something like a 'Bellerophoniad.'

---

25 See Huntley, *The Divine Proportion*, 157–61.

'Dunyazadiad' is perfect semiosis in the romantic mode: sender and receiver united in 'passionate virtuosity' ensured by equal parts of a metaphor of coitus (warm flesh to warm flesh) and the metaphor of castration and/or sudden death (cold steel to warm flesh). In place of passionate virtuosity, 'Perseid' is a Ø-based version of storytelling, reflecting the classical nature of the 'golden ratio' in forms familiar since Ovid, albeit in a more modern and hip diction. The semiotic circuit is still complete, but is now distributed over a spiralling series of senders and receivers: a groupie bas-reliefist to an off-and-on potent mythic hero[26] to a sometime petrifying, finally estellating receiver surrogate.

Phi is the perfect symbol for classical semiosis. It was at the centre of the Pythagorean brotherhood with its pentagram symbol; it provides the connection for the five Plantonic solids. Perhaps it is best represented in the Golden Rectangle of the Parthenon.[27] If there is a classical solution to the problem of an 'aesthetics of cosmic interaction,' it would have to be Ø. But classical heroes are long since extinct. The novel until *Chimera*, has never been associated with anything like a 'golden ratio.' Yet the 'tragic view' would insist that if Bellerophon, for example, imagines himself fated to be a mythic hero, he has almost no alternative but to oblige, even though he may be aware that the results will be at best doubtful and most likely absurd.

But they need not to be ugly. Indeed, for all of the negative criticism that 'Bellerophoniad' has provoked, few readers do not prefer it to the rather arch 'Dunyazadiad' and the baroque 'Perseid.' It is indisputably funny, and it is funny in hundreds of ways, from the lowliest of puns to the most delicate psychological humour of character. Moreover, it is *thematically* and *modally* correct in its position in this work. The theme of storytelling (not the same, of course, as novel-writing) needs an incompetent Bellerophon to balance the 'passionate virtuosity' of Scheherazade and Dunyazade. The 'golden' quality of Perseus and his myth, their very *phi*-ness, needs some baser metal – lead, as in the pencil-like spear that may have done in the Chimera – for contrast. And perhaps 'Bellerophoniad' proves, for the paradoxical purposes of Learning III, that the classical way is not the only way, and that even 'passionate virtuosity,' for all its quality, is but one of the ways to the Tao of art.

Can there be beauty in chaos when it is deliberately created as such?[28] Can there be beauty in chaos under any circumstances? Only a

---

26 Who has to proclaim that 'virtuoso performance is my line of work' (70)!
27 See Huntley, 23–34, 62–3.
28 One passage (238) is particularly appropriate to this question. Melanippe raises the

few years ago the answer to that question would have to be an un-equivocal 'no'. But in the last few decades scientists in various disci-plines have begun the study of a new branch of science and math-ematics called *chaos theory,* and some of the results suggest that in apparent randomness and disorder there may be a kind of universality that is strangely reminiscent of the persistence of Ø in nature and art.[29] The illustrations of the Mandelbrot set recall the possibilities of proto-experiments in quincunx and arabesque that Poe may have had in mind when he wrote *Pym.* If Ø is beautiful because it is found so commonly in nature and because it somehow reassures us that rela-tionship can be restful and ultimately satisfying in its persistence, chaos theory reminds us that blind seeking, restless pursuit, *the apparently mindless disorder of chaos itself,* can also create beauty, and that its beauty may be more breathtaking than the ordered regularity of Ø. True, Bellerophon is a failure and an absurd hero, blindly seeking to follow, as Barth describes it,

> the ritual pattern of mythic heroism – by getting all A's and four letters of recommendation, as it were – [to] become a bona fide mythic hero like his cousin Perseus. What he learns, and it is an expensive lesson, is that by perfectly imitating the pattern of mythic heroism, one becomes a perfect imitation of a mythic hero, which is not quite the same thing as being Perseus the Golden Destroyer. (*Friday Book,* 138)

question of confusion of the self with the literary abstraction of the self (map with territory again) and compares our two heros, '... as Perseus, she believes, confused himself with his mythical persona *Perseus,* Bellerophon *Bellerophon.*' Bellerophon then 'acknowledges this wise, well-taken point, kisses its taker,' but then announces that 'his identification with "Bellerophon" is clear and systematic policy, not confusion – even as is, was or imaginably could be the apparent chaos of this tale.' In one sense he is referring to the final turn on self-revelation, when it becomes clear that he is Deliades (perhaps a surprise only to those who have not adequately considered the insertion from Graves's *The Greek Myths* [200]); in another, he is showing his semiotic mythopoeia to be more self-aware than Perseus's, and suggesting that a deliberately created chaos can be as much a work of art as any Ø-based classical structure.

29 The best introductory text is James Gleick, *Chaos: Making a New Science* (New York: Penguin 1987), but see also N. Katherine Hayles, *Chaos Bound: Orderly Disorder in Contemporary Literature and Science* (Ithaca, NY: Cornell University Press 1990), and *Chaos and Order: Complex Dynamics in Literature and Science* (Chicago: University of Chicago Press 1991).
  Chaos theory differs radically from catastrophe theory in the number of allowable variables and in structure and purpose. Catastrophe theory is purely

And 'Bellerophoniad' fails every known test of aesthetic regularity and proportion – in spades. Readers and critics dislike it equally – but only if they have to publish or perish on it or pass in their 'themes' by Friday. 'Baaa,' they cry. But the 'free-playing' reader or critic, let loose in its pastures to gambol or browse where she will, has a different response. She finds 'Bellerophoniad' a delight from its misplaced beginning ('good night') to its implied lemniscate avoidance of closure (the substitution of the title for final word being very like the Kinbotean Conjecture). The final delight of 'Bellerophoniad' is perhaps in the impossibility of explaining the 'Eternity in an hour' that free play can discover in it. Perhaps only the unspoken analogue of the one-million-to-one difference in the scale of the top and bottom of the Mandelbrot set speaks clearly at all. The ultimate solution to paradox can never be more than silence.

The fourth part of *Chimera* is much easier to understand than the third. A novel, of course, consists of the sum of its parts, although, as we have seen in the case of *Pale Fire*, these parts may have very paradoxical relationships to each other and to the whole. But a Fibonacci sequence requires that Parts B and C – in this case, 'Perseid' and 'Bellerophoniad' – have as the sum of their parts in the ratio of Ø a new creation. 'Dunyazadiad' is about story-telling; the sum of 'Perseid' and 'Bellerophoniad' is the novel. But 'Perseid' is based on Ø, the 'golden ratio,' and 'Bellerophoniad' is based on chaos, infinite regress leading to an unpredictable but predictably beautiful formal series. Hence, the novel is a chimera, unattainable, infinite. Yet here is that *Chimera* in all its beauty and chaos.

QED

---

mathematical and topological; chaos theory has a universality that is almost teleological and a descriptive potential that rivals the great Mother Artist, nature herself. Chaos theory is also so complex that I doubt any single person can understand even most of it – certainly not I. But it seems to depend upon the qualities of certain attractive relationships that become apparent only through the kind of number-crunching repetition that modern computers have made possible. As the illustrations of the Mandelbrot set suggest, these relationships are concealed from normal view by their *scale* and by their apparent functional irregularity.

I am not arguing here that Barth is deliberately using chaos theory in 'Bellerophoniad,' only that it provides an aesthetic validity for the kind of structure he creates. For an example of the self-conscious, deliberate use of chaos theory for fictional intent with no postmodernist values at all, see John Updike, *Roger's Version* (New York: Knopf 1986), in which Dale Kohler, a young computer theorist suspiciously resembling Arthur Dimmesdale in many respects, attempts to prove the existence of God by the application of chaos theory.

Integrating Chaos: *The Crying of Lot 49*

Our *tour d'horizon* of the possibilities for hyperdimensional abductions in fiction (including some rather lengthy stopovers) is rounding us off (like most good postmodernist art) right where we began: in the paradoxical impossibility of the creation before our very eyes. Theory can only speak the locus of that meaning; it cannot name it. Now, by juxtaposing *The Crying of Lot 49* with Barth's *Chimera*, we raise again the theoretical problem posed at the end of chapter 2. Are aesthetic coding and ideological coding different operations, as Eco characterizes them in sections 3.8 and 3.9 of his 'Theory of Sign Production' in *A Theory of Semiotics*? Or are they, as my posing this question in chapter 2 and here implies, more complexly related? The problem is anything but trivial, although, as the inconclusive ending to chapter 2 suggests, its solution may depend upon a choice based on metaphoric/ metonymic preference. In any case, before we attempt a resolution of that problem, we must first take a long look at the hyperdimensional qualities of *The Crying of Lot 49*.

Even more than was the case with Barth, Thomas Pynchon's *oeuvre* is delicately interconnected. It consists of a series of short stories, most of which Pynchon himself dismisses as juvenilia,[1] followed by his ma-

---

1 See Thomas Pynchon, *Slow Learner* (Boston: Little, Brown 1984), 'It is only fair to warn even the most kindly disposed of readers that there are some mighty tiresome passages here, juvenile and delinquent too.' How much of this dismissal is appropriate is considered further on in this chapter. Many critics find these early works interesting harbingers of Pynchon's later work.

ture production of two mammoth novels, *V* (1963) and *Gravity's Rainbow* (1973), with, nestled between them, like a diamond pendant in a deep *décolletage, The Crying of Lot 49* (1966).² But where Barth's fictional concerns developed over a rather long period of years in an outward spiral (or a Fibonacci sequence), Pynchon's seem to have remained constant. They are three, but they all tend to blend together because they are really structural oppositions:

Language

Freedom vs Authority

Class

Freedom vs Authority

Entropy

Life vs Death

Pynchon's hip style and comic strip characterizations are probably the key to his popularity, but they are also deeply rooted in his fictional values. As he wrote in the introduction to *Slow Learner*, the freeing up of fictional style by 'Kerouac and the Beat writers, the diction of Saul Bellow in *The Adventures of Augie March*, emerging voices like those of Herbert Gold and Philip Roth ... was exciting, liberating, strongly positive' (6–7). Pynchon associates this new freedom of language with the problem of 'where to put ... loyalties' (6) in matters of class. His own loyalties, of course, are as anti-authoritarian as his style. Of all the American postmodernists, he is probably the most consistently outrageous to the delicate political and stylistic sensibilities of the orthodox.³ His style and his politics undoubtedly account for the Robert the Ram response of the Pulitzer advisory board,

---

2 *V* and *The Crying of Lot 49* were both published by Lippincott (Philadelphia); *Gravity's Rainbow*, by Viking (New York). My citations in the text will be to the Bantam edition of *The Crying of Lot 49* (1966).

3 And he manages to provoke varied responses among even quite sympathetic readers. See Scott Sanders, 'Pynchon's Paranoid History' in *Mindful Pleasures*, ed. George Levine and David Leverenz (Boston: Little, Brown 1976), 139–59, especially his four objections (157–9), and David Leverenz, 'On Trying to Read *Gravity's Rainbow*,' in ibid., 222–49, especially page 248: 'To the Pynchon who throws shit in my white male established American face and then calls it mine, I respond first with confused intimidation, even guilt, and then with annoyed dismissal, both to what he preaches and to the fact that he preaches ... But to the Pynchon who creates the most powerfully aching language for natural descriptions in our literature, who can make me feel so keenly the moments of loss, separation, impingement, and simple sheltering human gestures, I respond with astonished

who found *Gravity's Rainbow* 'unreadable,' 'turgid,' 'overwritten,' and 'obscene,' despite the unanimous recommendation of the judges for fiction.

But critics and analysts of Pynchon have been most concerned with the third structural opposition that occupies so much of his work. Because of his flippant style and apparently adolescent posturing over various abuses of authority, he would probably not be taken seriously as a writer were it not for his obvious concern for matters pertaining to life and death and his familiar use of entropy as the most appropriate physical metaphor for such matters. From his earliest fiction to his latest comment on it and his other fictions, Pynchon asserts that 'when we speak of "seriousness" in fiction ultimately we are talking about an attitude toward death – how characters may act in its presence, for example, or how they handle it when it isn't so immediate' (*Slow Learner*, 5). Pynchon does not hesitate to look into that 'blackness ten times black' that has marked serious American literature since Melville. More than any other contemporary writer, Pynchon chooses to examine this existential issue through metaphors from physics and engineering, especially the metaphor of entropy.

Pynchon has denied that he has 'some sort of proprietary handle' on entropy in fiction (*Slow Learner*, 12), but the data contained in his fictions speak for themselves.[4] From the short story 'Entropy' through *Gravity's Rainbow* the metaphor is universal. The mechanical universe is inevitably moving towards the coldness of death; only the archipelagos of organic warmth and life defeat this tendency (and that only temporarily, of course). In that form, the metaphor is nothing more than a cliché. Nathanael West could transform it into something more by putting it into the surrealist imagination of Miss Lonelyhearts, and F. Scott Fitzgerald suggested his opinion of it by having Tom Buchanan

---

praise, again and again, for all the singular exactitudes of seeing. True, my participation in this language intricates me into the vision I so roundly disapprove of, though on the level of Lost rather than Found. But he hooks me nevertheless.'

4 One of Pynchon's most admirable qualities as a writer is his reticence about his work. Indeed, of all contemporary writers, he comes closest to Eco's ideal that 'the author should die once he has finished writing. So as not to trouble the path of the text' (*Reflections*, 7). Pynchon's critical reclusion was perfect until the 'Introduction' to the short stories collected in *Slow Learner*, and there he has generally avoided any interpretive hints except this one, which is used mainly to admit the connection that many critics had made (notably Thomas Schaub, *Pynchon: The Voice of Ambiguity* [Urbana: University of Illinois Press 1981]) about his dependence upon Norbert Weiner, *The Human Use of Human Beings* and, through him, Henry Adams and Willard Gibbs, for his use of the metaphor of entropy.

give voice to it along with his fears of the Yellow Peril. Little wonder
Pynchon wanted to deny a 'proprietary handle.' But Pynchon does
have something almost approaching a copyright on fictively connect-
ing physical entropy to the entropy metaphor in information theory,
a squaring of the metaphor that makes *The Crying of Lot 49* a
hyperdimensional problematic fiction.[5] It is also a returning of the
metaphor to the first of those three structural oppositions –

Language
Freedom vs Authority

– thereby closing the recursive cycle. The closed cycle implies that the
values of language, ideology, and life are *all* entropic, at least in the
opinion of Thomas Pynchon, and they all consist of conflict between
freedom, which is life-seeking, and authority, which is death-seeking.

Wow. Here is Learning III with a vengeance. Here is a truly revolutionary theory of 'cosmic interaction' which includes aesthetic *and*
ideology in a new 'vast ecology.' And we need not stop with Bateson
and Learning III: Pynchon also here fulfils the requirements that Kuhn
proposes for the 'paradigm shift' of a scientific revolution.[6] And, although these ideas are introduced in *V* and elaborated extensively in
Gravity's Rainbow, it is more than fair to say they are crystalized in *The
Crying of Lot 49*. Thus *The Crying of Lot 49* not only sits jewel-like
between the bosomy masses of the two longer novels, it is also the
jeweled bearing supporting their enormous weight.[7]

---

5 The earliest work to explore this connection is Anne Mangel, 'Maxwell's Demon,
  Entropy, Information: *The Crying of Lot 49*,' *TriQuarterly* 20 (Winter 1971), 194–208;
  reprinted in Levine and Leverenz, eds., *Mindful Pleasures*, 87–100. Many critics have
  used Mangel's gathering of materials from physics and communications theory to
  generate conclusions quite different from hers.
6 Bateson, *Steps to an Ecology of Mind*, 306; Thomas S. Kuhn, *The Structure of Scientific
  Revolutions* (Chicago: University of Chicago Press 1962), 95. Let me call to the
  reader's attention two other comments by Bateson and Kuhn in this context that
  are particularly appropriate to *The Crying of Lot 49*. Bateson: '... the resolution of
  contraries reveals a world in which personal identity merges into all the processes
  of relationship ... That any ... can survive seems almost miraculous, but some are
  perhaps saved from being swept away on oceanic feeling by their ability to focus in
  on the minutiae of life. Every detail of the universe is seen as proposing a view of
  the whole' (306). Kuhn: 'When paradigms enter, as they must, into a debate about
  paradigm choice, their role is necessarily circular. Each group uses its own paradigm to argue in that paradigm's defense' (94).
7 Sorry about that. There's something about Pynchon that brings on these attacks of
  metaphor.

At the centre of *The Crying of Lot 49* is the metaphor of the Nefastis machine, Maxwell's Demon, and the possibility that the second law of thermodynamics and some 'laws' of a new science, somewhat confusingly named 'information theory,' are not merely paradigmatically isomorphic but *interrelated*.[8] Since *The Crying of Lot 49* is a novel and not a textbook of physics or transformational grammar, we might expect that the details of the putative interrelationship are not precisely given – are, in short, fictional. That is not entirely the case, but, as we shall see, they are a bit tricky. Oedipa Maas first encounters the Nefastis machine in a sketch shown her by Stanley Koteks. It is described as 'a box with a sketch of a bearded Victorian on its outside, and coming out of the top *two pistons attached to a crankshaft and flywheel*' (61–2; italics added; explanation to follow). Koteks goes on to introduce Oedipa to the paradox of a 'Maxwell's Demon,' who might sit in the box and sort fast-moving molecules from slow-moving ones. 'Since the demon only sat and sorted,' he concludes, 'you wouldn't have put any real work into the system. So you would be violating the Second Law of Thermodynamics, getting something for nothing, causing perpetual motion.' Oedipa instantly seizes on the flaw in the argument: 'Sorting isn't work?' Oedipa said. 'Tell them down at the post office, you'll find yourself in a mailbag headed for Fairbanks, Alaska, without even a fragile sticker going for you.' 'It's mental work,' Koteks said, 'but not work in the thermodynamic sense' (62).

Oedipa goes on to meet John Nefastis and test the machine herself. We are told 'it looked about the way the patent had described it' (77). Nefastis gives her a thumbnail sketch of the interrelationship between

---

8 This is far from an original observation. Virtually all of the perceptive critics of Pynchon accept the premise that was first proposed by Anne Mangel, as cited above. There is very little agreement about what to make of it, however. Mangel limits herself to some general observations about distortion by transformation of language, redundancy, and imprecision. All true and all helpful guides to the reader. Thomas Schaub (*Pynchon*, 21–42) goes much further, to examine the use of Mangel's observation by Edward Mendelson, who concludes from it that *The Crying of Lot 49* is a pre-Pentecostal revelation (Edward Mendelson, 'The Sacred, the Profane, and *The Crying of Lot 49*,' in *Pynchon: A Collection of Critical Essays*, ed. Edward Mendelson [Englewood Cliffs, NJ: Prentice-Hall 1978], 112–46). Schaub finds that Mendelson's interpretation is more transcendent than he would wish.

There are many other suggestions, but most are variations on these themes. Pynchon has been extremely fortunate in the ingenuity and intellectual prowess of the critics he has attracted. I agree with the possibility of all of their interpretations. My remarks are intended only to supplement these well-marked paths through Pynchon's garden and perhaps to suggest a few relatively unexamined *dimensions* that previous critics have neglected.

the second law of thermodynamics and information theory that is 'too technical for her':

> 'Help,' said Oedipa, 'you're not reaching me.'
>
> 'Entropy is a figure of speech, then,' sighed Nefastis, 'a metaphor. It connects the world of thermodynamics to the world of information flow. The Machine uses both. The Demon makes the metaphor not only verbally graceful, but also objectively true.'
>
> 'But what,' she felt like some kind of a heretic, 'if the Demon exists only because the two equations look alike? Because of the metaphor?'
>
> Nefastis smiled; impenetrable, calm, a believer. 'He existed for Clerk Maxwell, long before the days of the metaphor.' (77–8)

Now, the second law of thermodynamics, for all the difficulties it presents in its philosophical implications,[9] is rather easy to understand extensionally. I recall two classical examples from my grade-twelve physics class. (1) A cigarette burning in a completely enclosed room will send its smoke straight upward only for a relatively short time because the molecules in the air have 'Brownian' movement, which will inevitably tend to disperse the smoke. The form the column of smoke takes when it begins to break up is unpredictable, but that it will break up is certain. (2) Divide a tank into two parts and fill one part with ink and one with water. Remove the barrier between the two fluids; they begin to mingle and eventually they will mingle completely; yet the mixing is entirely a probability process and there is nothing except the concept of entropy to prevent all the ink molecules from gathering on one side and all the water molecules gathering on the other.

Information theory is somewhat harder to understand, not because it is implicitly more difficult, but because, in spite of its familiar name, it applies to somewhat less familiar systems.[10] It is 'hardware based' in

---

9 These are considerable, and none of them very pleasant to contemplate. They include the inexorable tendency of the universe and any coherent part of it (which, as we know from Gödel's Theorem, we can't know everything about anyway) to move into greater and greater disorder, thereby making time as we know it irreversible and all projections into the future irredeemably bleak.

10 The usual text to cite is Claude E. Shannon and Warren Weaver, *The Mathematical Theory of Communication* (Urbana: University of Illinois Press 1963). This is a quite readable text. An even better introduction, plus a discussion of the literary significance of the chaos theory elements of Shannon's work, is in Hayles's *Chaos Bound*, or in more concentrated form, her article 'Chaos as Orderly Disorder: Shifting Ground in Contemporary Literature and Science,' *New Literary History* 20 (1988–9),

that it depends upon binary on-off switches and has little to do with 'information' and 'communication' as they appear to us in their everyday uses. It reduces 'information' to 'bits.' A 'bit' is the amount of information delivered in one operation of an on-off switch. All 'language' – which is to say all organized systems of any kind – consists of coded bits. *Error* interferes with communication within the system, but less than one would think because of *redundancy*, which allows you 2 ndrstnd wt ths sntnce is abt evm tho it hs lts uv errs.

To understand information theory, let us look at that old chestnut about the monkey and the typewriter and Shakespeare. For the moment put aside *King Lear* and look at how long it would take a monkey at a typewriter to duplicate Hamlet's line 'Methinks it is like a weasel.' A computer set to generate random phrases is very like a monkey at a typewriter. The sentence has twenty-eight spaces or characters, so that we set the computer to generate a 'string' of twenty-eight characters or spaces and let it run until it comes up with METHINKS IT IS LIKE A WEASEL. [Pause while the machine is working.] Had enough? When you have, press control/reset to stop the screen from filling up with lines like WDLMNLT DTJBKWIRZREZLMQCO P. Let's do a little calculating. Since the odds are twenty-seven to one that our monkey will get the first letter correct and twenty-seven to one that it will get the second, and so on, we can see that the chances of getting the entire phrase correct is one over twenty-seven to the twenty-eighth power, that's about a one with forty zeroes after it. Not a good bet.

But if we program the monkey to reproduce a random string of twenty-eight letters and spaces but to make one error each time, and then to choose to reproduce the string with an 'error' in it whenever the 'error' is closer in any way to the 'target' string, METHINKS IT IS LIKE A WEASEL, then our monkey will come up with the phrase in no time flat. Here's a sample (first generation is the line above):

10th generation: MDLDMNLS ITJISWHRZREZ MECS P
20th generation: MELDINLS IT ISWPRKE Z WECSEL (Aha, you say.)
30th generation: METHINGS IT ISWLIKE B WECSEL
40th generation: METHINKS IT IS LIKE I WEASEL

305–22. However, the example I cite is from Richard Dawkins, *The Blind Watchmaker* (Burnt Mill, England: Longmans 1986), 46–9. Dawkins's example, of course, suits his purpose; he wants to show how apparently 'random' mutation of genes can produce apparently 'designed' change. But, as we shall see, Pynchon has his purpose too.

And success at generation 43. Time for a program written in BASIC: under thirty minutes; rewritten in Pascal: eleven seconds (Dawkins, 47–8).

The molecules in the stream of smoke and the ink and water tanks are very like the *bits* of letters and spaces in the monkey's typewriter. At first both are only minimally constrained. The smoke molecules move upward because they are lighter than the surrounding air, but because of their interior motion, they eventually disperse and mingle inextricably with the surrounding air molecules. The fluid molecules in the two tanks do the same. Their only organization is being limited to the confines of the two now-joined tanks, as the dimensions of the room define the only organization of the smoke. These constraints are isomorphic to the monkey-computer's limit of twenty-seven characters plus a space. As long as the monkey keeps banging away, its results will obey the second law of thermodynamics. But as soon as we program the monkey even in the most minimal way, as little as the heat of the cigarette determines the upward motion of the smoke, patterns will soon develop that will look like something, even if not Shakespeare. A computer programmed for as little as three-letter sequences common to English will produce nonsense, but recognizably English nonsense (Gleick, 256).

Curiously, the same kind of thing happens with the two-fluid tank if the barrier between the two is punctured by a tiny pinhole, let us say only slightly larger than a water molecule. The mingling of fluids will take much longer, of course, but it will also take a different form, much more like the form the smoke takes as it is dispersed by Brownian motion. There will be a considerable variety of patterns of swirls of the coloured liquid, as there is a wide range of patterns of the swirls of rising smoke (and two- or three-letter patterns of letter and space bits on the typewriter), but they will be recognizable *patterns*, more like the Mandelbrot set we saw as analogue to Barth's 'Bellerophoniad' than the homogeneous blob they become when their entropy is complete. 'Maxwell's Demon' is best seen as the phenomenon of *reductionism* applied to a massive event when it can be reduced to unidemensional form. 'To seek eternity in a grain of sand' is to discover that the most complex of relationships can be examined as single-bit comparisons with astonishing results. 'Language' consists of bits which are transmitted unidimensionally. That can be across a printed page, into the memory bank of a computer, by pulses on a telephone line, or even along a string of DNA: perhaps even at the end of a stream of cigarette smoke or at the pinhole opening between two fluids. As Thoreau said when he discovered that the thawing fecal matter along the railroad bed at Walden Pond took the same shape as the new buds of spring, 'The Maker of this earth but patented a leaf.'[11]

Of course Oedipa is correct when she says that sorting is work. And there is a recognizable distinction between organic and inorganic substances. Chaos theory suggests that these statements may be true on *macroscales* but are less true and perhaps not even true at all on *microscales*. When systems are reduced in scale to the level of those last Mandelbrot graphics, about one million to one, chaos theory accounts for the apparent paradox that 'the total energy living in the microscales could outweigh the energy in the macroscales, but in classical systems this thermal motion was irrelevant – isolated and unusable ... however ... chaotic and near-chaotic systems bridged the gap between macroscales and microscales. Chaos was the creation of information.'[12]

Oedipa cannot move a piston of the Nefastis machine because it is a macrosystem.[13] Her interaction with it does create information, however, but in a microsystem way, and perhaps is understood only by her subconscious. Recall the original description of the machine. It is a box that has 'coming out of the top two pistons attached to a crankshaft and a flywheel.' If we reduce these parts to 'bits' that the information system I am using can produce, we might describe them as << (two pistons), — (a crankshaft) and o (a flywheel). And we could then put them together as –o–<<, a shape which Oedipa and the reader are not altogether unfamiliar with: the muted posthorn of Tristero.

Oedipa's problem is partly that she is looking for macro answers from micro information. Blake needs that one grain of sand; Thoreau *that* robin, *that* twig. The zen of information theory requires that deliberate seeking never finds, that information arrives in patterns unbidden and unannounced through the side door. It is no accident that Oedipa's closest approaches to awareness happen when she is least aware of them and when they are most meaningless. The first of these is her encounter with the sailor (93–5), with whom she re-enacts

---

11 But he also wrote, 'O the evening robin, at the end of a New England summer day! If I could ever find the twig he sits upon! I mean *he*; I mean *the twig*. This at least is not the *turdus migratorius*.' Thoreau is perhaps a bit more scatalogical than Blake, but he insists no less upon the single object, not the generic.

12 Gleick, *Chaos*, 260, citing Robert Shaw, 'Strange Attractors, Chaotic Behavior, and Information Flow'

13 And, of course, for other, funnier reasons as well; Nefastis asks her for an act of faith, when his own motives definitely include the prospect of screwing her while watching the news about the teeming Chinese. Perhaps the best gloss on this scene is in chapter 32 of *The Confidence-Man*.

the encounter of the Ancient Mariner with the watersnakes, as she blesses him 'unaware.'[14] The second happens just one evening and two pages (97) later, at the conclusion of her 'dark night of the soul.'[15] She is swept up in a gathering of drunken

> deaf-mute delegates in party hats ... into [a] ballroom, where she was seized about the waist by a handsome young man in a Harris tweed coat and waltzed round and round, through the rustling, shuffling hush, un-der a great unlit chandelier. Each couple on the floor danced whatever was in the fellow's head: tango, two-step, bossa nova, slop. But how long, Oedipa thought, could it go on before collisions became a serious hin-drance? There would have to be collisions. The only alternative was some unthinkable order of music, many rhythms, all keys at once, a choreogra-phy in which each couple meshed easy, predestined. Something they all heard with an extra sense atrophied in herself. She followed her partner's lead, limp in the young mute's clasp, waiting for the collisions to begin. But none came. She was danced for half an hour before, by mysterious consensus, everybody took a break, without having felt any touch but the touch of her partner. (97)

These two inadvertent moments of discovery give the reader two important clues which pass unnoticed by Oedipa. The first is the pun-ning connection between DT's as delirium tremens affecting the drunken sailor and dt's as the sign of differentiation in calculus. She senses that

> behind the initials was a metaphor, a delirium tremens, a trembling unfurrowing of the mind's plowshare. The saint whose water can light lamps, the clairvoyant whose lapse in recall is the breath of God, the true

---

14 Cf. Gregory Bateson and Mary Catherine Bateson, *Angels Fear: Towards an Epistemol-ogy of the Sacred* (New York: Bantam 1987), especially 89–90, where this archetype of the sacred is described as the 'integration' of a 'disintegrate' personality only when the search is random and the 'blessing unaware.'

15 The importance of these scenes has been remarked by most of Pynchon's commen-tators. This one is particularly well examined by George Levine in 'Risking the Moment: Anarchy and Possibility in Pynchon's Fiction,' in Levine and Leverenz, eds., *Mindful Pleasures*, 113–36, who in his turn cites another interesting examina-tion, Lance Ozier, 'The Calculus of Transformation: More Mathematical Imagery in *Gravity's Rainbow*,' *Twentieth Century Literature* 21 (1975), 193–210. The deeper we plunge into the microscales of Pynchon's Mandelbrot-like creation, the lovelier the patterns become.

paranoid for whom all is organized in spheres joyful or threatening about the central pulse of himself, the dreamer whose puns probe ancient fetid shafts and tunnels of truth all act in the same special relevance to the word, or whatever it is the word is there, buffering, to protect us from. The act of metaphor then was a thrust at truth and a lie, depending where you were: inside, safe, or outside, lost. (95)

Oedipa is able to recall that *dt* is the sign for differentiation in calculus, but the significance of the recollection is lost in the generalization of her comment that metaphor was both a 'thrust at truth and a lie.' She recalls that *dt* 'meant also a time differential, a vanishingly small instant in which change had to be confronted at last for what it was, where it could no longer disguise itself as something innocuous like an average rate' (95). The point is to concentrate on *that* robin and *that* twig, and to ignore the *turdus migratorius*. But is Oedipa 'inside, safe, or outside, lost'? And, ignoring the argument from parallel structure for the moment, which state yields the thrust at truth, which the lie?

Oedipa 'did not know where she was,' inside or outside the metaphor, but the reader does. Oedipa is mightily engaged in *differentiating* the events taking place around her as part of a vast and vaguely evil conspiracy, or paranoid projection of her own mind.[16] Indeed, *The Crying of Lot 49* is an exercise in differentiation, or 'sorting it all out' (1), from the very first paragraph. That puts it in unusually direct contrast with the short story by Pynchon which immediately precedes it, 'The Secret Integration.' Integration and differentiation are opposite operations in calculus and opposite metaphors for life. Differentiation seizes upon the single moment – the grain of sand, *that* robin, *that* twig – and discovers all that is to be found in its uniqueness. Integration is explained to Tim by his scientific genius friend Grover Snodd in 'The Secret Integration':

'What's integration mean?' Tim asked Grover.

'The opposite of differentiation, 'Grover said, drawing an x-axis, y-axis and curve on his greenboard. 'Call this function of x. Consider values of the curve at tiny little increments of x' – drawing straight vertical lines from the curve down to the x-axis, like the bars of a jail cell – 'you can have as many of these as you want, see, as close together as you want.'

---

16 Or, worst of all, the 'bad shit' of an excluded middle: plotlessness, pointlessness (136).

'Till it's all solid,' Tim said.

'No, it never gets solid. If this was a jail cell, and these lines were bars, and whoever was behind it could make himself any size he wanted to be, he could always make himself skinny enough to get free. No matter how close together the bars were.'[17]

'This is integration,' said Tim.

'The only kind I ever heard of,' said Grover. (*Slow Learner*, 186–7)

Integration is to be 'inside, safe,' yet always able to become 'skinny enough to get free.' It supplies the central metaphor for this story of childish imagination and rebellion, creativity and growth within the secure but always penetrable 'bars' of childhood. But then the boys discover the other kind of integration and the bad shit that goes with it – racial hatred, the failure of their parents to live up to their ideals for them, even the impossibility to transcend race themselves, when they find they must give up their imaginary friend Carl Barrington because they cannot make up for the racist vandalism by their parents. 'Are we still integrated?' asks one of the boys at the end of the story, and their 'brain,' Grover, can only reply, 'Ask your father' (*Slow Learner*, 192).

'The Secret Integration' and *The Crying of Lot 49* are paired opposites.[18] Tim and the other boys (who may be the products of Tim's imagination as easily as they are products of Pynchon's) plot the violent overthrow of authority casually and pleasurably, safe within the flexible bars of the security of childhood; it is not their tragedy but the tragic racism of their parents that 'frees' them from their integrated lives. Oedipa, by contrast, is disintegrated personally from beginning to end of *The Crying of Lot 49* by the inexplicability of it all. The concentration on the moment that is differentiation 'where velocity dwelled in the projectile though the projectile be frozen in midflight, where death dwelled in the cell though the cell be looked in on at its

---

17 Pynchon here broaches one of the basic concepts of chaos theory. *Fractals* are self-reproducing at ever-shrinking scales, so that no matter how large a magnification is used in, for example, the Mandelbrot set, someone behind them could 'make himself skinny enough to get free.'

18 This is Pynchon's opinion, and, for what it is worth, he prefers the earlier story to 'the next story I wrote ... "The Crying of Lot 49," which was marketed as a "novel," and in which I seem to have forgotten most of what I thought I'd learned up till then' (*Slow Learner*, 22). Perhaps it would be a good idea to recall at this time Eco's comments quoted above (note 4) on the desirability of the premature death of the author.

most quick' (96), is a discipline for saints and mystics. She is trying to straddle the two states: safety behind the protection that Pierce Inverarity hath wrought; and risk of the unknown and the revolutionary that the more integrated boys of the other story plan almost casually, though they 'knew ... that the reality would turn out to be considerably less than the plot, that something inert and invisible, something they could not be cruel to or betray (though who would have gone so far as to call it love?) would always be between them and any clear or irreversible step' (*Slow Learner*, 188).

The boys are ideological Bakunins in Tom Sawyer bodies; that is integration and the way things ought to be. Pierce Inverarity is their more terrifying opposite: a Tom Sawyer grown up into the real power of adulthood but still tripping on the power games of youth. Like the 'imaginary playmate(s)' of the earlier story, Pierce has become a fictional, a noumenal character. Jesus Arrabal calls him a 'miracle':

> 'You know what a miracle is. Not what Bakunin said. But another world's intrusion into this one. Most of the time we coexist peacefully, but when we do touch there's cataclysm. Like the church we hate, anarchists also believe in another world. Where revolutions break out spontaneous and leaderless, and the soul's talent for consensus allows the masses to work together without effort, automatic as the body itself. And yet, séña, if any of it should ever really happen that perfectly, I would also have to cry miracle. An anarchist miracle. Like your friend. He is too exactly and without flaw the thing we fight. In Mexico the privilegiado is always to a finite percentage redeemed – one of the people. Unmiraculous. But your friend, unless he's joking, is as terrifying to me as a Virgin appearing to an Indian.' (88–9)

Miraculously and unmiraculously, Pierce's influence extends beyond the grave. That is, he persists in memory to Oedipa and others, and he seems also to persist noumenally as *the* oligarchist (88), like Thoreau's robin and Blake's grain of sand. His persistence in memory is curiously bland: a night of telephone voices, recalled trips to Mexico, one cryptic recommendation for a 'way to wealth' curiously unlike Ben Franklin and like a boy with a yoyo: 'Keep it bouncing ... that's all the secret, keep it bouncing' (134).[19] But his testament that is *The*

---

19 Although I fear that my bringing it out into the open may make some readers doubt my seriousness, the yoyo is the only important central metaphor of this novel that no critic has seriously considered. 'Yoyodyne,' the air-space conglomerate that

Crying of Lot 49 is baffling, miraculous ... fictional and ideological in miraculous (and terrifying) conjunction. Intrusion of the *ideal*, especially if that ideal is comic-book noumenalism, represents an ultimate Learning III paradox. To have the Virgin appear to us ignorant Indians and say, 'Keep it bouncing,' is to puncture all of those 'customary social reflex[es]' (Eco, *Theory of Semiotics*, 132) we have come to expect from our standard fare of metonymic or metaphoric texts. It is also to make us doubt our too easy, reflexive association of 'serious' art with liberal humanism.

In section 3.9.2 of *A Theory of Semiotics* Umberto Eco gives us what he calls a 'laboratory model' to discuss ideological overcoding which very closely resembles the Nefastis machine. He imagines a container divided into two parts with a small hole in the dividing membrane guarded by a 'Maxwell's Demon.' The demon does his Maxwell's demon's thing: that is, he lets only slow molecules into one chamber and only fast molecules into the other. But he is also a 'smarter' demon than Maxwell's in that he sends a signal to an outside observer when the number of exchanged molecules has become 'pertinent' to the observer (for instance, a given calculation of the pressure and heat tolerable in a given situation). Thus it is the purpose that determines '*the criteria of pertinence*' (290; italics Eco's). So far we have a fair approximation of Nefastis's experiment with Oedipa. If she observes the piston moving, a message has been passed. Eco specifically states that the receiver of the message is a machine, 'it registers «minimum» or «maximum» values and reacts according to instructions received. The signal, in this case, is not a "sign," nor does the machine "understand" its "meaning." If on the contrary the receiver is a human being, his reaction transforms the signal into a *sign* that is the correlation between an expression and a content. *But at the same time the human addressee will add certain connotative markers to the denotative ones*' (292; italics added). There can be no doubt what those 'connotative markets' are in Oedipa's case: either an integration into 'miracle' (violation of the second law, hence *belief*, however erroneous); or continua-

---

is at the centre of Pierce's fortune, is a curious manifestation of boyhood intruding upon the seriousness of the adult world. The yoyo is a reverse analogue to the ballistic missile, so central to the action and meaning of *Gravity's Rainbow*, since it is a pendulum-based 'missile' absolutely useless for any kind of aggressive act. Moreover, it is a verbal/figurative pun on the muted posthorn, consisting of its two flywheel cylinders on a crankshaft and flexible pendulum, the only purpose of which is to 'keep it bouncing.'

tion of her futile effort to differentiate, like Robert the Ram, between the macro effects of distinctions too subtle to record. Her failure with the Nefastis machine is isomorphic to her understanding of Pierce's other side. She knew his oligarchic activities 'to be a fraction of him that couldn't come out even, would carry forever beyond any decimal place she might name; her love, such as it had been, remaining incommensurate with his need to possess, to alter the land, to bring new skylines, personal antagonisms, growth rates into being' (134). That is to say that Pierce as noumenal oligarch creates endlessly on a finer and finer scale, like a Mandelbrot set, which has no limit to its magnification, while Oedipa's love remains 'incommensurate' because it is necessarily limited to what she can observe on the larger scale.

Eco goes on to criticize the ideological distinctions that may grow out of the 'connotative markers' human addresses add to the results of unidimensional information flow, as I have shown at the end of chapter 2. When he dismisses them as 'fuzzy concepts,' he seems to have the weight of powerful analogues on his side.[20] It is likely that at the very simplest level – the level of propaganda – conditioned response – Robert the Ram *before* he is subjected to smaller and smaller discriminations – Eco is correct when he concludes that 'ideology is a partial and disconnected world vision' (297).[21] But there is no reason why this kind of coding cannot coexist – cannot be graphed directly onto – an aesthetic text. One need only examine the three texts we have been looking at in this section of this text to discover how complex the relationship between aesthetic and ideological coding can be. *Pale Fire* is ideologically conservative, but because its form is recursive, both of its reactionary narrative voices are undercut. Ideology becomes secondary to the generation of aesthetic pleasure. *Chimera* is virtually ideologically negative, almost totally concerned with aesthetic coding. Yet, as we have seen, the largest single part of it, the 'Bellerophoniad,' paradoxically violates aesthetic coding to show how chaos

---

20 See his tables 58 to 60 reproduced in figure 2.6 above. He has four other tables leading up to the ones reproduced in my text, illustrating how linear information flow (one-dimensional) becomes subject to 'connotative markers' as it increases in dimensionality (see 290–3). In no instance does he consider the possibility of *micro effects* as they might function in such aesthetic representations as Oedipa's unnameable 'decimal places' for Pierce's oligarchic needs, or the boys' shrinking through their 'integrated' prison bars.

21 In some ways the best part of this argument takes place in the footnotes. See also 311–13, notes 51 to 55.

can be integrated into its opposite, what the Greeks called *kosmos*. Finally, *The Crying of Lot 49*, especially when considered jointly with the *yang* to its *yin*, 'The Secret Integration,' is wholly ideological. All of the characters are attempting to decode by differentiation the *bits* of information flooding them (always unidimensionally, like rioters being dispersed by a firehose, unlike bathers being crushed by a tidal wave). They always fail. Differentiation is value-free and valueless. The 'inside, safe' observer must eventually, like the Manichaean Scurvhamite, fall victim to the appeal of the 'gaudy clockwork of the doomed with a certain sick and fascinated horror' (116) and move 'outside, lost.' Pynchon's nihilism is perfect. Even the boys of 'The Secret Integration' can remain integrated in their/Tim's/Pynchon's imagination only until social 'integration' brings them into contact with the destructive power of racism. That reality deprives them of their power of imagination, driving 'each finally to his own house, hot shower, dry towel, before-bed television, good night kiss, *and dreams that could never again be entirely safe*' (193; italics added).

Non in commotione, Dominus.

Epilogue

The preceding chapters were written before the Ayatollah Khomeini gave a new meaning to the concept of negative criticism by putting a price on the head of Salman Rushdie for publishing *The Satanic Verses*. The events that followed have forcefully turned the attention of the Western world to the problems inherent in ideological coding. Several times, in vain, Rushdie has insisted that his novel is not ideological. 'The book isn't actually about Islam,' he wrote in an open letter to Rajiv Ghandi, 'but about migration, metamorphosis, divided selves, love, death, London and Bombay.' The part of the novel that was called blasphemous and that provoked the notorious *fatwa* by Khomeini 'deals with a prophet who is not called Muhammad living in a highly fantasticated city – made of sand, it dissolves when water falls upon it – in which he is surrounded by fictional followers, one of whom happens to bear my own first name. Moreover, this entire sequence happens in a dream, the fictional dream of a fictional character, an Indian movie star, and one who is losing his mind, at that. How much further from history could one get?'[1]

His argument seems unassailable, and, indeed, it has provoked a heart-warming response in his defence from writers, critics, and intellectuals of all sorts from all over the Western world. It has not removed, however, the threat of death hanging over his head as I write

---

1 *The Rushdie File*, ed. Lisa Appignanesi and Sara Maitland (London: Fourth Estate 1989), 44. The original letter appeared in various newspaper in England and India and throughout the English-speaking world.

this. Indeed, in spite of recanting, Rushdie seems doomed now to the status of a perpetual fugitive from the world of Islam, albeit with the conveniences and comforts of a considerable support group from the West to ease the pain.

Rushdie is the example *par excellence* of Plekhanov's case of a writer suffering from a 'hopeless contradiction' between him and his 'social environment,' though I doubt that Plekhanov even considered Islam as such an environment. Even more than a declining capitalist culture, Islam has the power to punish those artists who produce 'art for art's sake' instead of art for the sake of the continuation of the culture. That a theology is involved is almost entirely irrelevant. As we have seen in the case of Melville's *The Confidence-Man*, theology is just another ontology, just another 'consistent axiomatic formulation' in which 'undecidable propositions' will occur. But Rushdie's decision, conscious or not, to risk non-comprehension on the part of his Muslim readers because of his dissociation from their culture was bolstered by his transition from one culture to another – from Islam to the world of postmodern, post-structural literary creation and theory. In that world he is so much at home that he gladly 'risks' non-comprehension because he knows that artful obscurantism is far preferable to an obvious 'readiness to participate in social struggles,' to quote Plekhanov again. In this postmodern, post-structural world 'literature is transactional,' as Gayatri Spivak remarks. 'The point is not the correct description of a book, but the construction of readerships.'[2] In many ways, exactly those parts of the novel cited as evidence of Rushdie's blasphemy of Islamic culture and religion were the same ones that marked his happy adoption of postmodernism and post-structuralism. For example, one of the earmarks of the postmodern is the incorporation of some form of the author into the narrative, as Barth injects himself as the genie and a Jerome Bray in *Chimera*, hyperdimensionally confusing the action of the novel with the world it is set in. Thus, late in *The Satanic Verses*, the betrayed prophet Mahound threatens his disciple 'Salman' at knife-point, saying, '... your blasphemy, Salman, can't be forgiven. Did you think I wouldn't work it out?'[3] In the sad irony of what has happened to 'Salman' as a result of the publication of the novel, one is inclined to forget the brilliance of this scene as a bridge between the real world and the fiction which here replaces it.

---

2 G.C. Spivak, 'Reading *The Satanic Verses*,' *Public Culture* 2 (Fall 1989), 87
3 Salman Rushdie, *The Satanic Verses* (London: Penguin 1988), 374

But, as Malise Ruthven has pointed out,[4] the problem is complicated by the fact that Islamic culture is essentially *oral*, while fiction
decidedly is not:

> The oral-typographic distance is particularly apposite in discussing the
> forms of literature. Whereas most types of poetry, or for that matter
> 'divine recitation' such as the Qur'an, belong firmly at the oral end of
> the literary spectrum, the novel is 'clearly a print genre, deeply interior,
> de-heroicised and tending strongly to irony.' This applies particularly to
> the post-modernist novel, where stories are de-plotted and characters
> 'hollowed out' to represent extreme states of consciousness, as in Kafka,
> Beckett, Pynchon – and of course Salman Rushdie.[5]

Melville could write a blasphemous fiction about middle American
culture because he knew he could write it so obscurely that the only
consequences he would suffer would be a failure of his readers to
comprehend. Twain wrote a blasphemy about American political power
that could not be understood by his readers because his reputation as
a humorist made it impossible for them to judge the implications of
his writing, at least at the time he wrote it. But Rushdie was understood only too well by both the culture he was rejecting and the
culture which he had adopted. *The Satanic Verses* is unmistakably coded
aesthetically for any hip postmodernist reader or post-structuralist critic.
No reader sophisticated enough to finish the novel could possibly see
it as any sort of blueprint for action, any manual for the building of a
bicycle. But its Islamic audience *does not even have to read it to know that
it is blasphemous.* In Islam, words ARE deeds; the signifier and the signified are not separate entities as they are in the post-Saussurian Western world. As a result, Salman Rushdie's goose is, I am afraid, cooked.

But there is one historical precedent for Rushdie's case that offers
some hope for him. In 1702 Daniel Defoe published *The Shortest Way
with Dissenters* and immediately put himself in greater jeopardy than
even Rushdie finds himself. For, while Rushdie has the whole literate
world willing to help preserve him from those who would kill him,
Defoe managed to alienate both the Church of England, to the point
that he risked death for sedition, and at the same time *the very dissenters*

---

4 Malise Ruthven, *A Satanic Affair: Salman Rushdie and the Rage of Islam* (London:
   Chatto and Windus 1990), 147–9
5 Ruthven, 148. The quotations in the passage are from Walter J. Ong, *Orality and
   Literacy* (London 1982), 159, 154.

he believed he was supporting! When the warrants went out for his arrest, many of Defoe's dissenter friends were unwilling to hide him, believing that he had turned against them and was proposing seriously, with no irony intended, that they be mercifully hanged instead of slowly starved through failure to find employment as a result of the Test Acts. When he was captured and sentenced to stand upon a pillory for an hour on two separate occasions, Defoe legitimately feared for his life. In those days, a pilloried prisoner was likely to be stoned to death if he had any enemies (and Defoe had plenty), or even if he did not, since his very helplessness could be a goad to the sadistic impulses of a mob.

But Defoe transformed his punishment into a triumph by publishing his *A Hymn to the Pillory* just before his public display on 31 July 1703. Instead of a mob of enemies supplied with rocks, he was surrounded by a cordon of friends, dissenters all, presumably, who supported him through the hour and then accompanied him back to Newgate prison, 'expressing their affections, by loud shouts and acclamations when he was taken down.'[6]

Rushdie is unlikely ever to escape the condemnation of Islam. Therefore the other society to which he belongs – the world of postmodern fiction and post-structuralist criticism – must continue to provide a life-saving cordon of support. This will not be easy, because Rushdie has also alienated a *third* culture with *The Satanic Verses*. Even before the book and its author achieved notoriety through the ayatollah's *fatwa*, Rushdie and Penguin did what any modern (or postmodern) author and publisher would do for any novel – they publicized its controversial aspects. Since Rushdie's life has been threatened, the controversial nature of the novel has kept it before the public *unnaturally*. It is still being bought because people are curious about it, but the market for readers who are able to read it and digest anything of it has long since been saturated. Its celebrity as a cause for commercial censorship in the United States was quickly over, once the first reflexive fear of fire-bombing of bookstores ended. In the United Kingdom it still provokes skinheads to bash Pakis and will probably remain a staple of the BBC for decades, at about the level of interest for programs on the cruelties of fox-hunting. But it will be forgotten eventually. Then, perhaps, Rushdie might appear publicly at a signing of

---

6 John Robert Moore, *Daniel Defoe, Citizen of the Modern World* (Chicago: University of Chicago Press 1958), 142

another book (as he did recently), but this time with a cordon of postmodernist supporters ranged about him, like dissenters around a pilloried Defoe. When that happens, the ideological coding will have disappeared and *The Satanic Verses* will be pure aesthetic.

Bibliographical Notes

I have divided this note into two parts. First is an annotated bibliography of works useful for leading the reader towards an appreciation of speaking the locus of meaning in literature with a full awareness of the value of paradigms from other ways of speaking the locus of meaning (like linguistics, anthropology, mathematics, neurology, etc.). This list is very selective and personal; these are the works that have helped *me* most. Second is a list of all the works cited in the text.

1. The Locus of Meaning: An Annotated Bibliography

Barth, John. *The Friday Book.* New York: G.P. Putnam 1984

Barthes, Roland. *The Pleasure of the Text.* Trans. Richard Miller. New York: Hill and Wang 1975. The ultimate isomorphism for the locus of meaning. Better not read linearly.

– *S/Z.* Trans. Richard Miller. New York: Hill and Wang 1974. Why do so many North American critics not understand that this work is a *parody* of the old New Criticism as well as a brilliant application of hyperdimensional forms of narration?

Bateson, Gregory. *Mind and Nature.* New York: Bantam 1979. Bateson trying to popularize himself.

– *Steps to an Ecology of Mind.* New York: Ballantine Books 1972. The essential Bateson, especially the Introduction, Metalogues, 'The Logical Categories of Learning and Communication,' and the first three chapters of part 5.

– and Mary Catherine Bateson. *Angels Fear: Toward an Epistemology of the Sacred.* New York: Bantam 1987. Compare these new metalogues with the originals.

178   Bibliographical Notes

Borges, Jorge Luis. *Other Inquisitions.* Trans. Ruth L.C. Simms. Austin:
   University of Texas Press 1964. The ultimate hyperdimensional thinker in
   fiction or critical prose, if there is a difference.
Bunn, James. *The Dimensionality of Signs, Tools, and Models.* Bloomington:
   Indiana University Press 1981
DeGeorge, Richard and Fernand. *The Structuralists: From Marx to Lévi-Strauss.*
   Garden City, NY: Doubleday, Anchor 1972. A very useful anthology.
Eco, Umberto. *The Name of the Rose.* Trans. William Weaver. New York:
   Warner Books 1983
– *Reflections on 'The Name of the Rose.'* Trans. William Weaver. London: Secker
   and Warburg 1985
– *A Theory of Semiotics.* Bloomington: Indiana University Press 1979. The ideal
   is to read all three books concurrently; failing that, read in the order given
   but *in a cycle,* around twice.
Federman, Raymond. *The Twofold Vibration.* Bloomington: Indiana University
   Press 1982
Gleick, James. *Chaos: Making a New Science.* New York: Penguin 1987. A
   revelation for the literary critic, and not only in the section dealing with
   'information theory' (255–68).
Henn, T.R. *The Apple and the Spectroscope: Lectures on Poetry Designed (in the
   Main) for Science Students.* New York: Norton 1966. Rather old-fashioned,
   but sound; I used it as a textbook for a 'poetry for chemists' course and
   learned a lot.
Hofstadter, Douglas R. *Gödel, Escher, Bach: An Eternal Golden Braid.* New York:
   Vintage 1980. The one essential interdisciplinary text on paradox.
Huntley, H.E. *The Divine Proportion: A Study in Mathematical Beauty.* New York:
   Dover 1970. See chapter 8.
Jakobson, Roman. *Selected Writings.* The Hague: Mouton 1962–. The Darwin
   of the neurological basis for literary criticism.
Klinkowitz, Jerry. *Structuring the Void: The Struggle for Subject in Contemporary
   American Fiction.* Durham, NC: Duke University Press 1992
Kuhn, Thomas S. *The Structure of Scientific Revolutions.* Chicago: University of
   Chicago Press 1962. You can't see anything until you have a metaphor to
   see it through.
MacCannell, Dean. *The Tourist.* New York: Schocken 1976
Pirsig, Robert. *Zen and the Art of Motorcycle Maintenance.* New York: Bantam
   1964. Much more than building Japanese bicycles in this.
Plekhanov, George V. *Art and Society.* New York: Critics Group 1937. The best
   treatment of the exiled artist.
Shklovsky, Victor. 'Art as Technique.' In *Russian Formalist Criticism: Four
   Essays.* Ed. and trans. Lee T. Lemon and Marion J. Reis. Lincoln: University

of Nebraska Press 1965. The *pons asinorum* of modern criticism is the final
statement of this essay: 'Tristram Shandy is the most typical novel in world
literature.'

Spariosu, Mihai I. *Dionysus Reborn: Play and Aesthetic Dimension in Modern
    Philosophical and Scientific Discourse*. Ithaca, NY: Cornell University Press 1989
Thompson, Michael. *Rubbish Theory: The Creation and Destruction of Value*.
    Oxford: Oxford University Press 1979
Wilson, R. Rawdon. *In Palamedes' Shadow: Explorations in Play, Game, and
    Narrative Theory*. Boston: Northeastern University Press 1990
Woodcock, Alexander, and Monte Davis. *Catastrophe Theory*. New York: E.P.
    Dutton 1978

2. Works Cited in This Text

Allsop, Kenneth. 'After *Lolita* Is This Nabokov Just Pulling Our Legs?' *London
    Daily Mail*, 8 Nov. 1962, 12
'Another Fancy Failure by the Author of "Lolita."' *People's World* [San
    Francisco], 13 Oct. 1962, 7
Bader, Julia. *Crystal Land: Artifice in Nabokov's English Novels*. Berkeley:
    University of California Press 1972
Barth, John. *Chimera*. New York: Random House 1972
– *The Friday Book*. New York: G.P. Putnam 1984
Barthes, Roland. *The Pleasure of the Text*. Trans. Richard Miller. New York: Hill
    and Wang 1975
– *S/Z*. Trans. Richard Miller. New York: Hill and Wang 1974
Bateson, Gregory. *Mind and Nature*. New York: Bantam 1979
– *Steps to an Ecology of Mind*. New York: Ballantine Books 1972
– and Mary Catherine Bateson. *Angels Fear: Towards an Epistemology of the
    Sacred*. New York: Bantam 1987
Blair, Walter. *Horse Sense in American Humor*. New York: Russell and Russell 1942
Bloom, Harold. 'Freud and the Sublime: A Catastrophe Theory of Creativity.'
    In his *Agon: Towards a Theory of Revisionism*. Oxford: Oxford University
    Press 1982
Borges, Jorge Luis. *Other Inquisitions*. Austin: University of Texas Press 1964
Brassens, Georges. *Poèmes et chansons*. Paris: Editions musicales 1974
Bryant, John. '*The Confidence-Man*: Melville's Problem Novel.' In his *A
    Companion to Melville Studies*. Westport, CT: Greenwood Press 1986
Buell, Lawrence. 'The Last Word on *The Confidence-Man*?' *Illinois Quarterly* 35
    (1972), 15–29
Bürger, Peter. *Theory of the Avant-Garde*. Trans. Michael Shaw. Minneapolis:
    University of Minnesota Press 1984

Calinescu, Matei. *Faces of Modernity: Avant-Garde, Decadence, Kitsch.* Bloomington: Indiana University Press 1977

Campbell, Joseph. *The Hero with a Thousand Faces.* Princeton: Princeton University Press 1968

Chase, Richard. 'Melville's Confidence Man.' *Kenyon Review* 11 (1949), 122–40

Cobley, Evelyn. 'Catastrophe Theory in Tom Stoppard's *Professional Foul.*' *Contemporary Literature* 25, no. 1 (Spring 1984), 53–65

Croce, Benedetto. *Breviario di estetica.* Bari: Laterza 1913

Culler, Jonathan. *On Deconstruction.* Ithaca, NY: Cornell University Press 1982

Dawkins, Richard. *The Blind Watchmaker.* Burnt Mill, England: Longmans 1986

Deleuze, Gilles, and Alan Guattari. *On the Line.* Trans. John Johnstone. New York: Semiotext(e) 1983

Dryden, Edgar A. *Melville's Thematics of Form: The Great Art of Telling the Truth.* Baltimore: Johns Hopkins University Press 1968

Eco, Umberto. *The Name of the Rose.* Trans. William Weaver. New York: Warner Books 1983

– *Reflections on 'The Name of the Rose.'* Trans. William Weaver. London: Secker and Warburg 1985

– *Semiotics and the Philosophy of Language.* Bloomington: Indiana University Press 1984

– *A Theory of Semiotics.* Bloomington: Indiana University Press 1976

Field, Andrew. *Nabokov: His Life in Art.* Boston: Little, Brown, 1967

Foster, Elizabeth S. Introduction. *The Confidence-Man.* By Herman Melville. New York: Hendricks House 1954

Francis, Robert. *The Orb Weaver.* Middletown, CT: Wesleyan University Press 1950

Frank, Frederick S. 'Polarized Gothic: An Annotated Bibliography of Poe's *Narrative of Arthur Gordon Pym.*' *Bulletin of Bibliography* 38 (1981), 117–27

Franklin, H. Bruce. *The Wake of the Gods: Melville's Mythology.* Stanford: Stanford University Press 1963

Frye, Northrop. *Anatomy of Criticism: Four Essays.* New York: Athenaeum 1967

Fussell, Edwin. *Frontier: American Literature and the American West.* Princeton: Princeton University Press 1965

Geismar, Maxwell. *Mark Twain: An American Prophet.* New York: McGraw-Hill 1970

Gleick, James. *Chaos: Making a New Science.* New York: Penguin 1987

Gosse, Edmund. *Father and Son.* New York 1907

Gosse, P.H. *Omphalos.* London 1857

Harris, Charles B. *Passionate Virtuosity: The Fiction of John Barth.* Urbana and Chicago: University of Illinois Press 1983

Hauck, Richard Boyd. *A Cheerful Nihilism: Confidence and 'The Absurd' in American Humorous Fiction.* Bloomington: Indiana University Press 1971

Hayles, N. Katherine. *Chaos and Order: Complex Dynamics in Literature and Science.* Chicago: University of Chicago Press 1991

– 'Chaos as Orderly Disorder: Shifting Ground in Contemporary Literature and Science.' *New Literary History* 20 (1988–9), 305–22

– *Chaos Bound: Orderly Disorder in Contemporary Literature and Science.* Ithaca, NY: Cornell University Press 1990

– *The Cosmic Web: Scientific Field Models and Literary Strategies in the Twentieth Century.* Ithaca, NY: Cornell University Press 1984

Henn, T.R. *The Apple and the Spectroscope: Lectures on Poetry Designed (in the Main) for Science Students.* New York: Norton 1966

Hoagland, Clayton. 'The Universe of Eureka: A Comparison of the Theories of Eddington and Poe.' *Southern Literary Messenger* 1 (1939), 307–13

Hofstadter, Douglas R. *Gödel, Escher, Bach: An Eternal Golden Braid.* New York: Vintage 1980

– *Metamagical Themas.* New York: Bantam 1985

Huntley, H.E. *The Divine Proportion: A Study in Mathematical Beauty.* New York: Dover 1970

Hyde, G.M. *Vladimir Nabokov: America's Russian Novelist.* London: Marion Boyars 1977

Irwin, John T. *American Hieroglyphics: The Symbol of the Egyptian Hieroglyphics in the American Renaissance.* New Haven: Yale University Press 1980

Jakobson, Roman. *Selected Writings.* The Hague: Mouton 1962–

Johnson, D. Barton. 'The Index of Refraction in Nabokov's *Pale Fire*.' *Russian Literature TriQuarterly* 16 (1979), 33–49

Kaplan, Justin. *Mister Clemens and Mark Twain.* New York: Simon and Schuster 1966

Kempton, Daniel. 'The Gold/Goole/Ghoul Bug.' *ESQ* 33 (1987), 1–19

Keyser, Elizabeth. '"Quite an Original": The Cosmopolitan in *The Confidence-Man*.' *Texas Studies in Literature and Language* 15 (1973), 279–300

Kuhn, Thomas S. *The Structure of Scientific Revolutions.* Chicago: University of Chicago Press 1962

Lakoff, George, and Mark Johnson. *Metaphors We Live By.* Chicago: University of Chicago Press 1981

Lee, J.L. 'Vladimir Nabokov's Great Spiral of Being.' *Western Humanities Review* 18 (1964), 25–36

Leverenz, David. 'On Trying to Read *Gravity's Rainbow*.' In *Mindful Pleasures.*

Ed. George Levine and David Leverenz. (Boston: Little, Brown 1976), 229–49

Levine, George. 'Risking the Moment: Anarchy and Possibility in Pynchon's Fiction.' In *Mindful Pleasures.* Ed. George Levine and David Leverenz. Boston: Little, Brown 1976, 11–36

Levine, June Perry. 'Vladimir Nabokov's *Pale Fire:* The Method of Composition as Hero.' *International Fiction Review* 5 (1978), 103–8

Liddell, Howard S. *Emotional Hazards in Animals and Man.* Springfield, IL: Thomas 1956

Lodge, David. *The Modes of Modern Writing.* London: Edward Arnold 1977
– *Working with Structuralism.* Boston: Routledge and Kegan Paul 1981

Luria, A.R. *The Man with a Shattered World.* New York: Basic Books 1972

Lyons, John O. '*Pale Fire* and the Fine Art of Annotation.' In *Nabokov: The Man and His Work.* Ed. L.S. Dembo. Milwaukee: University of Wisconsin Press 1967, 157–64. Reprinted from *Wisconsin Studies in Contemporary Literature* (Spring 1967)

MacCannell, Dean. *The Tourist.* New York: Schocken 1976

McCarthy, Mary. 'A Bolt from the Blue.' *New Republic* 146 (4 June 1962), 21–7. Modified slightly in *Encounter* 19 (Oct. 1962), 71–2, 74, 76–8, 80–2, 84
– *The Seventeenth Degree.* New York: Harcourt, Brace 1974

MacDonald, Dwight, ed. *Parodies.* New York: Random House 1960

Maddox, Lucy. *Nabokov's Novels in English.* Athens: University of Georgia Press 1983

Mallet, Robert, ed. *Self-Portraits: The Gide-Valéry Letters.* Chicago: University of Chicago Press 1955

Mangel, Anne. 'Maxwell's Demon, Entropy, Information: *The Crying of Lot 49.*' *TriQuarterly* 20 (Winter 1971), 194–208. Reprinted in *Mindful Pleasures.* Ed. George Levine and David Leverenz. Boston: Little, Brown 1976, 87–100

Melville, Herman. *The Confidence-Man.* Evanston and Chicago: Northwestern-Newberry Library 1984
– *The Confidence-Man.* Afterword by R.W.B. Levis. New York: NAL 1964
– *The Confidence-Man.* Ed. H. Bruce Franklin. New York: Bobbs-Merrill 1967

Mendelson, Edward. 'The Sacred, the Profane, and *The Crying of Lot 49.*' In *Pynchon: A Collection of Critical Essays.* Englewood Cliffs, NJ: Prentice-Hall 1978 112–46.

Mitchell, Edward. 'From Action to Essence: Some Notes on the Structure of Melville's *The Confidence-Man.*' *American Literature* 40 (1968), 27–37

Morell, David. *John Barth: An Introduction.* University Park: Pennsylvania State University Press 1976

Nabokov, Vladimir. *Pale Fire.* Berkeley: Medalion 1975

Ozier, Lance. 'The Calculus of Transformation: More Mathematical Imagery in *Gravity's Rainbow*.' *Twentieth Century Literature* 21 (1975), 193–210

Parker, Hershel. 'The Metaphysics of Indian-Hating.' In *The Confidence-Man*. By Herman Melville. Norton Critical Edition. New York: W.W. Norton 1971, 323–31

Parrington, V.L. *The Beginnings of Critical Realism in America, 1860–1920*. Vol. 3 of *Main Currents in American Thought*. New York: Harcourt, Brace 1930

Pearce, Roy Harvey. 'Melville's Indian-Hater: A Note on the Meaning of *The Confidence-Man*.' *PMLA* 67 (1952), 942–8

Peirce, Charles Sanders. *Collected Papers*. Cambridge: Harvard University Press 1938–51

Pierce, J.R. *Symbols, Signals and Noise: The Nature and Process of Communication*. New York: Harper and Row 1961

Pirsig, Robert. *Zen and the Art of Motorcycle Maintenance*. New York: Bantam 1964

Plekhanov, George V. *Art and Society*. New York: Critics' Group 1937

Plutarch. *Moralia*. Loeb Classical Library

Poe, Edgar Allan. *The Narrative of Arthur Gordon Pym*. Ed. Burton R. Pollin. Boston: Twayne 1981

Poggioli, Renato. *The Theory of the Avant-Garde*. Trans. Gerald Fitzgerald. Cambridge: Harvard University Press 1968

Powell, Jerry. 'John Barth's *Chimera*: A Creative Response to the Literature of Exhaustion.' *Critique* 18 (1976), 59–72. Reprinted in *Critical Essays on John Barth*. Ed. Joseph J. Waldmeir. Boston: G.K. Hall 1980 228–40

Pynchon, Thomas. *The Crying of Lot 49*. New York: Bantam 1966
– *Slow Learner*. Boston: Little, Brown 1984

Rank, Otto. *Myth of the Birth of the Hero and Other Writings*. Ed. Philip Freud. New York: Vintage 1959

Richards, I.A. T*he Philosophy of Rhetoric*. New York: Oxford University Press 1936

Robinson, Douglas. *American Apocalypses*. Baltimore: Johns Hopkins University Press 1985

Sacks, Oliver. *The Man Who Mistook His Wife for a Hat and Other Clinical Tales*. New York: Harper 1987

Sanders, Scott. 'Pynchon's Paranoid History.' In *Mindful Pleasures*. Ed. George Levine and David Leverenz. Boston: Little, Brown 1976, 139–59

Schaub, Thomas. *Pynchon: The Voice of Ambiguity*. Urbana: University of Illinois Press 1981

Seltzer, Leon F. *The Vision of Melville and Conrad*. Athens: Ohio University Press 1970

Shannon, Claude E., and Warren Weaver. *The Mathematical Theory of Commu-
    nication.* Urbana: University of Illinois Press 1963
Shroeder, John W. 'Sources and Symbols for Melville's *The Confidence-Man.*'
    In *The Confidence-Man.* By Herman Melville. Norton Critical Edition. New
    York: W.W. Norton 1971, 298–316
Smith, Henry Nash. *Mark Twain: The Development of a Writer.* Cambridge:
    Harvard University Press 1962
– *Mark Twain's Fable of Progress: Political and Economic Ideas in 'A Connecticut
    Yankee.'* New Brunswick, NJ: Rutgers University Press 1964
Smith, Herbert F. *The Popular American Novel, 1865–1920.* Boston: G.K. Hall
    1980
– 'Usher's Madness and Poe's Organicism: A Source.' *American Literature* 29
    (1967), 379–89
Sussman, Henry. 'The Deconstructor as Politician: Melville's *Confidence-Man.*'
    Glyph 4 (1978), 32–56
Tharpe, Jac. *John Barth, the Comic Sublimity of Paradox.* Carbondale: Southern
    Illinois University Press 1974
Thomas, Lewis. *The Lives of a Cell.* New York: Bantam 1979
Thompson, Craig, and Allen Raymond. *Gang Rule in New York.* New York:
    Dial Press 1940
Thompson, Lawrance. *Melville's Quarrel with God.* Princeton: Princeton
    University Press 1952
Thompson, Michael. *Rubbish Theory: The Creation and Destruction of Value.*
    Oxford: Oxford University Press 1979
Trachtenberg, Stanley. '"A Sensible Way to Play the Fool": Melville's *The
    Confidence-Man.*' *Georgia Review* 26 (1972), 38–52
Turner, Arlin. *Mark Twain and George W. Cable: The Record of a Literary
    Friendship.* East Lansing: Michigan State University Press 1960
Twain, Mark. *A Connecticut Yankee in King Arthur's Court.* Ed. Bernard L. Stein.
    In *The Works of Mark Twain.* Berkeley: University of California Press 1979
– *Mark Twain's Notebooks and Journals, Volume III (1883–1891).* Ed. R.P.
    Browning, M.B. Frank, and L. Salamo. Berkeley: University of California
    Press 1979
Waddington, Warwick. *The Confidence Game in American Literature.* Princeton:
    Princeton University Press 1975
Walker, David. '"The Viewer and the View": Chance and Choice in *Pale Fire.*'
    Studies in American Fiction 4 (1976), 203–21
Walkiewicz, E.P. *John Barth.* Boston: G.K. Hall 1986
Watson, William. *Chemical Essays.* 5 vols. London 1787
Weaver, Herman. *Herman Melville, Mariner and Mystic.* New York: Doran 1921

Weiner, Norbert. *The Human Use of Human Beings: Cybernetics and Society.*
  Garden City. NY: Doubleday 1954
Williams, Carol T. '"Web of Sense": *Pale Fire* in the Nabokov Canon.' *Critique*
  6 (1963), 29–45
Woodcock, Alexander, and Monte Davis. *Catastrophe Theory.* New York: E.P.
  Dutton 1978
Ziegler, Heide. *John Barth.* London: Methuen 1987

Index